Transforming
LATIN AMERICA

Pitt Latin American Series

George Reid Andrews, General Editor

Catherine M. Conaghan and

Jorge I. Domínguez, Associate Editors

Transforming
LATIN AMERICA

The International and Domestic Origins
of Change

Craig Arceneaux and David Pion-Berlin

University of Pittsburgh Press

Published by the University of Pittsburgh Press, Pittsburgh, Pa., 15260

Manufactured in the United States of America
Printed on acid-free paper
10 9 8 7 6 5 4 3 2 1

LIBRARY OF CONGRESS CATALOGING-IN-PUBLICATION DATA

Arceneaux, Craig L., 1965–
    Transforming Latin America : the international and domestic origins
of change / Craig Arceneaux and David Pion-Berlin.
        p. cm. – (Pitt Latin American series)
    Includes bibliographical references and index.
    ISBN 0-8229-5882-1 (pbk. : alk. paper)
    1. Latin America–Politics and government. 2. Democratization–Latin
America. 3. Latin America–Foreign relations. 4. Social change–Latin
America. I. Pion-Berlin, David. II. Title. III. Series.
JL960.A73 2005
320.98–dc22
                                                        2005001762

To Jeremy, Emma, Danielle, Anthony, Chloe, Donald,
and their generation: may they live in a society of freedom,
not fear, of reason, not rage.

Contents

Acknowledgments

This was a collaborative project in more ways than one. As a coauthored book, it certainly took imaginative, intense, and persistent collaboration between the two of us to bring the research and writing to fruition. Over the course of some four years, we engaged in a constant give-and-take, exchanging ideas, questions, outlines, notes, texts, and critiques. We prodded and pushed each other along, sometimes to the point of annoyance but always in good spirit and with final objectives in mind. In a broader sense, this was a collaborative exercise as well, since we involved others in our undertaking. Chapter revisions were done only after receiving feedback from numerous friends and colleagues. Our gratitude goes out to Felipe Agüero, Michael Desch, Rita Giacolone, Cynthia McClintock, Deborah Norden, Paulo Roberto de Almeida, Mark Ruhl, and Kurt Weyland, whose detailed and insightful comments contributed to making this a better book. Two anonymous reviewers for the University of Pittsburgh Press provided important comments on the entire manuscript, and for those we are grateful. Others helped stimulate our thinking through conversation and e-mail exchanges. Among those, we'd like to mention Andrew F. Cooper, Javier Couso, Hugo Frühling, Thomas Legler, David Mares, and José Zalaquett. In addition, portions of this book were presented at a poster session at an International Studies Association Conference, as well as panels at a Latin American Studies Association Conference, and a Western Political Science Association Conference. Thanks to those who provided valuable feedback on those occasions.

Craig Arceneaux's fieldwork in Washington, DC, was made possible by a Professional Development Grant from California Polytechnic State University, San Luis Obispo. A California State Faculty Support Grant provided further funding as well as some relief from coursework which was implemented with great understanding by Dianne Long and Phil Fetzer, in their respective rotations as Chair of the Department of Political Science at Cal Poly, San Luis Obispo. Dean

Harry Hellenbrand of the College of Liberal Arts also made life more comfortable as Arceneaux juggled research on this book with his adaptation to Cal Poly. He would also like to recognize the research assistance received from Cara Mae Wooledge, Daniel LeTendre, and Beau Rizzo, and Dan O'Leary's work on the book's tables and diagrams. David Pion-Berlin's fieldwork in Chile and Washington, DC, was financed by Academic Senate grants from the University of California, Riverside, as well as funds from the Department of Political Science. He would like to acknowledge the research assistance received from the library staff at the Organization of American States and from Amber Lee Smith, head librarian for the Foreign and International Law section of the Los Angeles County Law Library.

We express our deep gratitude to all those in Chile and Washington, DC, who graciously gave of their time in agreeing to be interviewed for this project. Those encounters would not have taken place without the assistance of others. A special thanks to Ingrid Wittebroodt, of the Centro de Derechos Humanos, Universidad de Chile, who arranged interviews with Chilean appellate and Supreme Court judges, and lawyers and human rights leaders, and also assembled data on high court appointments. In Washington, DC, interviews with diplomats and military officers were made possible with the help of Jay Cope from the National Defense University, Lt. Col. Alex Crowther from the Department of Defense, and Luis Aparicio from the Embassy of El Salvador.

Finally, Nathan MacBrien took a keen interest in our project from the beginning, keeping us, the book proposal, and the manuscript on track through the review and revision process. We are grateful to him and the rest of the staff at the University of Pittsburgh Press. As always, any errors of commission or omission are ours alone.

Transforming
LATIN AMERICA

1. Explaining Political Change in Latin America

Analysts probing the impact of international influence in Latin American politics cannot ignore U.S. hegemony in the Western Hemisphere. The gripping nature of this hegemony is reflected in the titles of survey studies such as *The Hovering Giant* (Blasier 1976) and *Talons of the Eagle* (Smith 2000). Packaged with studies that foretell the demise of the nation-state in the face of globalization, one wonders if domestic actors in Latin America hold any real relevance to processes of political change in their own countries. Proponents of this view would point to democratic crises that bespeak the frailty of government capabilities, and endemic economic crises that force Latin American states to seek outside aid, which routinely arrives with burdensome conditionality. If governments are so vulnerable to the designs of the hegemon or the dictates of the global economic system, then they have lost the ability to chart their own course.

But the brash conclusions of these perspectives must contend with one indisputable fact—the region of Latin America continues to exhibit noticeable variations. Economic progress in Chile stands in contrast to Caribbean countries mired in backwardness. Militaries wield substantial influence in Guatemala and Ecuador, face advancing civilian control in Argentina, and have been dismantled in Costa Rica and Panama. Brazil secures more lenient IMF loans while the heavy hand of conditionality is levied upon Argentina. Insurgencies are effectively crushed in Peru, addressed politically in Mexico, and continue unabated in Colombia. Brazil and Mexico attract the lion's share of foreign direct investment in the region, as Central America is overlooked. Allegiances to U.S. policy run from dependable adherents in Chile and Central America, standoffish criticism from Brazil, rumblings of defection in Venezuela, and the renegade position of Cuba. Clearly, the domestic does matter, for in its absence, we would expect to see greater convergence in Latin America, as states fall under the sway of a common external force, be it the Pentagon, the IMF, or global capitalism.

If both international and domestic forces hold relevance to political change in Latin America, what are the conditions under which either comes into play? This is the central question guiding the research in this book. It is easy enough to assert that external and internal forces matter to the conduct of politics in Latin America. It is more difficult to identify the general conditions that explain why the balance of influence tips toward the internal in one context and the external in another. From here, other questions arise. Are there opportunities for domestic forces to have input in cases dominated by international forces, and vice versa? And what of those situations that are caught between the two? Why do the motivations and abilities of foreign and domestic actors to immerse themselves in politics vary from topic to topic? Why does power express itself differently from issue to issue? How do coordination problems manifest themselves in the domestic and international arenas? And what weights should we assign to ideas, interests, and institutions? A few scholars have suggested some answers to these questions, but too often they apply them only to single cases, compile their answers in disparate edited works, or tailor them to descriptive commentaries on contemporary events.[1]

These questions guide the case studies in this book, which together illustrate a range of possibilities surrounding political change in Latin America. Our principal studies examine neoliberal reform in the Southern Cone, democracy in the Andean countries, human rights policy in Chile, and regional security institutions in Central America. Those are followed by additional capsulelike studies on environmental degradation in Brazil, drug trafficking in Colombia, and immigration from Mexico. The studies reveal their respective sets of significant characters, particular balances between foreign and domestic factors, and distinct parameters, processes, and opportunities for political change. Each is a story unto itself, illuminating a portion of the Latin American landscape. Combined, they offer a more complete view of how foreign and domestic influences enter the mix to shape political transformations regionwide. But weaving such disparate stories together into a compelling and coherent narrative demands a strong analytical thread.

Without this thread, political change appears as an incalculable force, one in which everything and anything holds significance. Indeed, we must begin by recognizing that political change is absolutely amorphous as a topic of investigation. Actors ranging from the Pentagon to Latin American politicians to European courts crowd the stage. Influence flows both from the financial ropes of the IMF at one end to the moral suasion of human rights activists at the other. Institutions such as the Organization of American States (OAS) or Conference of Central American Armed Forces stand firm at one time, only to be trampled underfoot by U.S. hegemony at another. Self-interested actors, ideas, and institutions stand shoulder to shoulder as compelling, often competing explanations for unfolding political developments in Latin America.

So what is our excuse for such a sweeping investigation? Only by placing disparate forms of change alongside one another can we begin to see larger patterns emerge—ones that reveal whether influences are bound to come from the domestic or the international. Only by standing a few paces back and looking at the broader picture can we impose some regularity on what is otherwise a dizzying array of influences—whether those take the form of ideas or self-interest—and a long parade of actors, be they states, nongovernmental organizations (NGOs), intergovernmental organizations (IGOs), informal networks, or individuals.

The study of political change need not be an exercise in the affirmation that anything and everything matters. There is a thread that weaves its way through seemingly discordant but equally compelling works that verify the power of multinational corporations (MNCs), document the successes of the Madres de Plaza de Mayo in Argentina, and chronicle U.S. hegemony. This thread is issues, and it tells us not only what actors, institutions, or ideas matter, but when, where, and how they do. Through issue-based comparison, we bring order to the postulate that there are as many sources as subjects of political change.

Why do issues matter? Take Argentina, for example, a nation that seemed well heeled by the imposing presence of the International Monetary Fund (IMF) and U.S. Treasury during the 1990s. When it came to devising internal economic policies, Argentina always adhered closely to the fund's guidelines and took Washington's admonishments seriously. Understanding their subordinate relation to the United States and the international financial institutions (IFIs) that it dominates, Argentine leaders developed the notion that if you can't beat them, join them. Under President Carlos Menem, the country seemed more slavishly devoted to following Washington's economic lead than did practically any other nation on earth.

But that was not the case when it came to matters of military and internal security policy. Argentine leaders resisted Washington's call to redeploy its troops to fight the drug syndicates, terrorists, and other unconventional foes. In fact, in 1995, at a time when Argentina was at the pinnacle of its compliance with the IMF-U.S. economic agenda, its representative stood up at the hemisphere-wide inaugural meeting of the Defense Ministerial of the Americas to assert that there could be no discussion of the struggle against narco-terrorism as a matter of regional security cooperation. That must not have pleased U.S. defense secretary William Perry who earlier that day had noted how the scourge of narco-trafficking and terror "threatened the very existence of our democracies" and urged all the militaries of the region to "support joint counter-drug efforts"(U.S. Department of Defense 1995). But Argentina has stood firm. To date, the country's military observes legal restrictions on its internal missions; nothing that the United States has said or done has appreciably altered that fact, even under the weight of military hegemony and looming financial bankruptcy.

No sweeping characterization of Argentina will work: it is neither the structurally weak and dependent nation that its economic subservience suggests, nor is it the tall and proud independent nation that defends its turf, as its security policy suggests. It is both. We must ask how it is that a nation can be so vulnerable to foreign influence on one subject, and so invulnerable on another? After all, should not relations of power between these two states dictate who the weaker and stronger parties will be across the board? Why should power have any regard for the boundaries between one issue and another? Answers begin to emerge once we identify how issues influence the motivations and capabilities of states.

The United States is the perennial hegemon on security affairs and should be able to dictate to nations in the hemisphere what their defense priorities shall be. But in the post–Cold War era, when threats to U.S. security have subsided, and danger lurks in other corners of the globe, Washington perceives that there is less at stake in this region. Consequently, it is insufficiently motivated to contest the independent security choices of Latin American states (like Argentina) despite its misgivings about those choices.

But what happens when motivation is suddenly unleashed? Do power relations then run roughshod over issue classifications? Can the United States get its way by hanging prized issues over the heads of Latin American states like the sword of Damocles? Not necessarily, for issues not only shape motivation—they also circumscribe capabilities. One need look no further back into history than 2003, in the United Nations Security Council, where Mexico and Chile defied U.S. aspirations to legitimate military action against Iraq. With a Chilean free

trade agreement winding its way through the U.S. Congress, and Mexico's singular status in NAFTA threatened by hemispheric trade negotiations, the scene
seemed ready-made for triumph by the United States. But the United States' ea-
gerness to validate its goals was met headlong by Mexican and Chilean political
leaders driven by memories of U.S. intervention into their own affairs and overwhelming popular opposition to the war. For these countries, the prospective
resolution was just as much a domestic as it was an international issue. And
while the United States had military might and economic threats at its disposal,
what Joseph Nye terms "hard power," this was an issue of international law,
where "soft power," or the ability to influence through reputation and persuasion, played a greater role (2002). Overt, coercive measures to secure passage by
linking the war vote to Chile's and Mexico's economic needs would have undermined the very sense of righteousness and legal rectitude offered by a Security
Council resolution. Issue arenas defined by international law and soft power dis-
credit issue linkage and allow weak states with strong wills to have a chance, regardless of how motivated the hegemon may be.

In the end, the United States invaded anyway, which represented a new issue,
the use of force, where hard power obviously does matter. Nonetheless, the invasion stands as testimony to the fact that muscle, even when backed by motivation and action, still remains only an incomplete determinant of international relations. After all, the denial of a widely recognized legal mandate eventually
deprived the Unites States of international manpower and monetary contributions to support its occupation.

By classifying the pursuit of legitimacy and the act of invasion as two distinct
issue areas, we reveal dynamics unique to each, which is the purpose of issue-
guided analysis—to employ issues as signposts that identify important actors
and viable modes of influence. Each subject represents a distinct constellation of
opportunities and barriers for every prospective participant, including nonstate
agents. Actors find that they are more highly motivated to pursue their goals in
one arena than another. They also realize that they hold particular skills or resources tailor-made to advance their interests in one domain while they are distinctly ill equipped elsewhere. Hence, to explain the U.S. invasion of Iraq, U.S.
might and motivation in light of U.S.-Iraqi tensions is sufficient. But to explain
the quest for international legitimacy, new actors and mechanisms of persuasion
suddenly enter the picture—UN Security Council voting procedures, soft power,
political leaders in Mexico and Chile, and popular opposition movements in

these same countries. To underscore and complete this example, we note that France could veto the pursuit for legitimacy, but it could not veto the invasion.

Issues then determine the cast of characters drawn to a particular case of political change based on motivations and capabilities. As we move from issue to issue, the principal protagonists change in tandem. For instance, outside states may be much more motivated to engage on the economic or security-related front than they are on the human rights or environmental front. Given the power differential in the Western Hemisphere, the former issues typically fall under the sway of the United States, which can easily dampen the aspirations of would-be rivals from outside the region. While human rights and the environment unfold primarily in the domestic arena, they routinely draw the attention of international organizations and social activists from afar. Those nonstate actors may discover that wider avenues of influence open up for themselves precisely because foreign states are ill prepared to deal with these topics or are simply uninterested. And yet those nonstate actors are resource poor and appreciably less powerful than states and cannot easily effect change from afar unless they leverage foreign states to lend a hand, however briefly they may do so.

But what determines why actors will be lured into one set of issues but not another, or why external players seem more influential on certain matters and domestic players on others? To answer this question, we categorize issues into the realms of "high politics" and "low politics" (Keohane and Nye 1977). This division is a time-honored distinction used to describe areas of state policy making within the international arena. It is adapted here to understand where states, when driven by the fundamental logic of self-interest, are most likely and least likely to intervene in or otherwise exert decisive influence over the affairs of foreign countries. High politics means high stakes; governments believe their vital interests hang in the balance. They will be strongly inclined to intrude on the domestic affairs of other nations if doing so is perceived as necessary to protect or enhance national security, economic well-being, or prominent goals on the national political agenda. That scenario unfolds when the domestic problems of a nation somehow spill over its borders or when the domestic riches of a nation (minerals, markets, cheap labor, etc.) reach out and lure foreign powers in. Externalities generated by an offending state will not alone suffice to provoke foreign intrusions; it is only when those externalities impinge on a state's vital national interests that they would cause it to react intrusively. States may then choose to intercede either directly or indirectly through international organizations such as the IMF and OAS whose very emergence is a product of these state imperatives. Either way, high politics defines scenarios in which the international often trumps the domestic when it comes to promoting change. *Int'l > D*

By contrast, low politics defines those lower-stake issues where states have little or no incentive to interfere in the domestic affairs of others. They do not associate their own national well-being and survival with the fate of a foreign nation's internal struggles over issues such as poverty, unemployment, education, health policy, democratic deepening, or human rights. Moreover, political leaders see no electoral gains to be had by delving deep into these domestic matters of another country. Hence, states calculate few benefits but numerous costs to intervention.[2] They are also reluctant to intercede indirectly via international institutions, or to legitimate intervention via adherence to international norms, believing that doing so will create a precedent applicable to all states, themselves included. Accordingly, domestic forces for change often trump international ones in this scenario. *D > Int'l*

A state's self-interest then is obviously the starting point of this analysis since it is central to the definition of high versus low politics. But it takes political leaders to understand, interpret, and react to those interests. When foreign state leaders are galvanized into believing that their vital interests are at stake and are sufficiently motivated to do something about them, they usually occupy center stage. It will be exceedingly difficult for any given Third World state to ward off a powerful foreign nation or a collection of less powerful nations determined to intervene in order to advance their primary security, economic, and political objectives. Powerful states have overwhelming financial and coercive resources at their disposal. Collections of weaker states, sensing that their own vital interests are up for grabs, can sometimes band together within regional organizations and intervene as well.

However, when states do not perceive their key interests to be at stake, they will step aside or turn away, allowing domestic politics to dominate. In their absence, foreign nonstate actors also move front and center. Those individuals and institutions are driven more by principles and norms than by interests. Consequently, the key motivators for change shift from interests to ideas as we move from high to low politics. So too do the forms that influence takes, from the high politics reliance on hard power—the currency of financial leverage and coercion—to the low politics reliance on soft power—the currency of values and moral suasion.

Powerful states are certainly more than capable of pushing their weight around in the realm of human rights, the environment, and other low politics issues, should they choose to. They could, in theory, link progress on development, human rights, social justice, health, democratic reform, or the environment to the provision or withdrawal of aid, investment, trade, or military support. They seldom do, however, because the political will to do so is not there. All of their considerable resources that are brought to bear so impressively on security and economic issues are usually held in abeyance in low politics areas because those states surmise that the application of hard power will either not be worth the effort, be counterproductive, or be deemed inappropriate. Occasionally, hugely motivated activists can grab the attention of states just long enough to make a difference. But unless low politics problems generate externalities that cause foreign states sufficient and sustained concern, the attention span of those states will be short-lived, as they gravitate back to issues of greater national significance to them.

Boundaries, Motives, and Capabilities

The high and low political distinction should, we submit, give guidance for understanding the balance between international and national sources of political change in Latin America. The full framework for analysis will be elaborated below and in chapter 2. But before proceeding any further, it should be noted that the high-low politics distinction comes with a basic presumption: that there are separate external and internal political spheres. In this day and age, is that separation still valid? We live in a globalized era, and some would say that the boundaries between the domestic and the foreign have washed away (e.g., Ohmae 1995; Strange 1996; Greider 1997). Who or what is there to demarcate the domestic from the foreign? Countries are figuratively and literally wired into the global economic system like no time before. In an age when billions of dollars of finance capital can be shifted in and out of a country in a split second, not slowed for a moment by national controls, of what value is the distinction between a domestic and a foreign bank account? When MNCs increasingly outsource tasks to laborers in other nations, does it really matter whether the firm is located at home or abroad? And what of the ability of networks—be they comprised of media channels, activists, or terrorists—to operate freely across borders? Undeniably, people, information, and resources are crisscrossing state frontiers in unprecedented numbers and at great speed.

Although it is tempting to dismiss the domestic-foreign distinction, we would respectfully demur from this view. While the world is more interconnected than ever before, nation-state boundaries still matter. They matter because states and citizens still act as if they do. It is states that go to war, vote in the United Nations, and sign treaties. It is state politicians whose goal it is to advance national interests and who promote *foreign* policies. And it is citizens who rally around the flag when their nation is attacked, is at war, or competes at international sporting events. Behavior and identities are still profoundly shaped by the nation-state, probably more so than they are by the diffusion of mass communications, cultures, or economic ideologies.

The divide between the domestic and the foreign is never so simple as a well-marked geographical frontier. It is certainly that, but it is more. The domestic often migrates with the flow of its own people. Companies, diplomats, and members of the armed forces serve abroad with consequences for their host nations. A state's expatriates reside and work elsewhere, send income back to family members, and simultaneously affect the economic well-being of their host and homeland. With the "Mexicanization" of Southern California, residents there have dual loyalties, cultural references, and political interests. When anti-immigration biases there run strong, some residents—even citizens—can be treated as if they were strangers in their own land. The boundary between internal and external persists, but it often becomes blurred.

Perhaps most significantly, the line between what is internal and external shifts according to flows of influence. State and nonstate actors frequently attempt to extend their spheres of influence beyond and across national boundaries. Clearly, there are examples of where foreign influences are welcomed. In these instances, the international and the domestic may work in tandem to resolve a problem, as their actions reinforce one another. But on many other occasions, outsiders are not welcome. Often there is a tension between a government's need for decision-making autonomy, and the desire of outsiders to erode some of that autonomy. The push and pull of influence from the inside and from without can be characterized by an overall framework and two competing elements within it. Our framework, as mentioned before, is one of issue orientation. The first element is sovereignty—a state's powers of exclusive jurisdiction over its people and territory. The second is the abilities and desires of those outside the nation-state to transgress its sovereign borders in order to shape domestic affairs.

To use an analogy, if sovereignty is an immigration checkpoint, then foreign influence is a traveler with documentation. Checkpoints are not posted everywhere, nor are they equally endowed with resources and trained personnel. Some will let down their guard just enough to allow undocumented travelers through. But there are aliens who can more easily penetrate any given checkpoint, depending upon what kind of passport they are carrying. Others will have a more difficult time; they will be stopped, questioned, detained, and then turned away. Some of those will be more persistent than others and return for another try, equipped with bribe money, or fraudulent papers and a new identity. The analogy sums up the three key elements to understanding whether the sources of change in Latin America originate primarily at home or abroad: barriers, capabilities, and motivation.

• As a barrier, sovereignty is the tried-and-true principle that states regularly invoke when defending their rights to check external influences at their borders. Since all states can lay claim to the right to act with supreme authority over their subjects, sovereignty embodies the anarchical nature of the international system: there is no higher authority to appeal to. In this rough-and-tumble world where states are left to fend for themselves, sovereignty is a leveler; all nations are, in principle, endowed with equal amounts of it. In practice power often spells the difference between those who can girder their sovereign walls and those who cannot. Consequently, sovereignty is more than an idea: it has always been a mix of legal standards, mutual understandings, and power imbalances. While sovereign rights have been written into countless international and regional conventions, those rights are often honored only in the breach. More powerful states will often trample on the autonomy of other states while avowing their allegiance to principles of autonomy. Stephen Krasner has suggested that breaches of sovereignty have been so commonplace in world history that they have made a mockery of the principle (1999).

Many more would agree that while sovereignty is under siege, as a standard and practice it survives (Hashmi 1997). For every successful assault on sovereignty there is always an example where sovereignty has held its own, by dint of force, reason, or norms. Weaker states in particular bet on the fact that sovereignty as an international norm is still embraced widely enough to deter inappropriate interventions in their internal affairs. Thus, sovereignty is never as solid as a law always abided, but certainly not as soft as an idea conveniently disregarded.

There is also agreement that sovereignty is in flux (Barkin and Cronin 1994; Farer 1996; Philpott 1997). Laws, customs, and practices evolve over time. What was once thought to be the exclusive domain of states no longer is. The trend line is clear: state prerogatives have shrunk. While we fully agree that sovereignty is in flux, we wish to emphasize something else: Sovereignty does not throw up the same set of defenses from issue to issue. As a rule of thumb, it is a more formidable barrier in the realm of low politics than it is in the realm of high politics. Domestic actors generally have greater control over rights-based policies, or educational and environmental policies, while foreign actors will make their presence known more effectively on financial or security-related matters. Why that is has to do with the capabilities and motives of those who would attempt to breach another nation's barriers.

Take human or political rights as an example. There has undoubtedly been a steady erosion of legal protections for governments that violate the rights of their own citizens. Many would agree with Fernando R. Tesón who says that the "domain reserved to the exclusive jurisdiction of the state is now quite small" (1996, 50) when it comes to these issues. But this observation begs the question, are international influences likely to trump domestic influences? The answer, interestingly enough, is not often.

While barriers to entry may have been dramatically lowered via law and custom, the capacity of external agents to take advantage of those lower barriers has not risen proportionately. The principal foreign agents in the realm of human rights are NGOs, transnational activists, judges, and lawyers. Though these non-state actors are hugely dedicated, principled, and motivated, they lack the centralized power, coordination, and enforcement mechanisms necessary to easily turn their convictions into results. These organizations and individuals are numerous and are growing, but they are dispersed across vast regions, are usually resource poor, and most important, do not have at their disposal the coercive tools needed to bring perpetrators to justice, or the leverage needed to compel changes that states resist making.

If nonstate actors are to succeed they must, through material, political, or moral persuasion, capture the attention of state leaders. It is states that have clout. It is they who can pull various economic, diplomatic, and military levers necessary to press other governments into compliance with human rights norms. But because they do not perceive their own vital interests to be at stake, states are insufficiently motivated to fight for human rights protections abroad. Issue linkage is rare in this regard; only occasionally will states "go to the mat" for a humanitarian cause because they believe their security or economic interests are implicated. Consequently, human and political rights advocates will succeed, at best, only episodically—because seldom can they get foreign states to care enough about the transgressions of offending states to do anything about them. As Kathryn Sikkink admits, the "link to government is simultaneously the most powerful and least dependable aspect of the work of the issue network" (1993, 423).

At the receiving end, offending states are only occasionally troubled enough by negative international opinion or pressures to change their internal human and political rights practices. Much depends on their sense of exposure to the outside world, how much they value their international reputations, and their calculations of potential political or material gain from being cooperative. Their vulnerability to the outside world occurs only at moments, something to be discussed later on. Normally, however, states will resist the intrusions of foreigners, by refusing to conduct inquiries, hold trials, apprehend suspects, or honor extradition requests of other states. In the realm of low politics, sovereign states are usually equipped to hold highly motivated nonstate actors and less motivated state challengers at bay.

In the high politics arena, sovereignty poses a much weaker barrier to entry for external forces wishing to shape internal events. Like the traveler with the right documents, international agents can penetrate virtually any Latin American checkpoint. Here the problem is not so much an absence of legal precedent as it is the presence of very formidable, highly motivated actors able to breach international and regional agreements as they see fit. Within high politics, the gap between sovereignty's rules and realities is astonishing. Since World War II, all justifications for armed aggression by one state against another have been stripped away, save two: self-defense or military action authorized by the UN Security Council. The United Nations Charter makes this limitation clear as does article 19 of the Charter of the Organization of American States. And it is not just unprovoked armed aggression that is outlawed by the OAS, but as article 19 points out "any other form of interference or attempted threat against the personality of the State or against its political, economic, and cultural elements." Article 21 adds that the "Territory of a State is inviolable; it may not be the object, even temporarily, of military occupation or of other measures of force taken by another State, directly or indirectly, on any grounds whatsoever."[3] Both international and regional accords provide ample protection for Latin American states against foreign coercion of an overt or covert nature, aimed at destabilizing the political order.

Yet over the course of decades, the Unites States has violated these conventions on dozens of occasions, in the name of national security. The list of nations that have fallen prey to U.S. military, paramilitary, and covert interventions is well known: Guatemala, Nicaragua, Chile, The Dominican Republic, Brazil, Grenada, and Panama, and there are more. The pretext for intervention is an externality, and a familiar one: the domino effect. The rise of a left-wing insurgency or government in one state could precipitate similar developments in other states, creating a real regional security crisis for the United States. The sovereign rights of Latin American states to be free from coerced intervention into their security affairs are usually trumped by the imbalances of power between the hegemon and its weaker southern neighbors.

If we turn our attention to the economic dimension, then it seems clear that Latin American states lost the ability to chart their own economic course—free from the counsel of foreigners—nearly half a century ago. Again, the loss of economic independence cannot be attributed to a dearth of rules and conventions governing nonintervention. One could reach as far back as 1902, when the Drago Doctrine became accepted into international law. Named after the Argentine foreign minister, it established the principle that just as individuals could no longer be apprehended for indebtedness, states should no longer be subjected to the forceful repayment of loans at the hands of other more powerful states (Levine 1937). And the OAS Charter proclaims that every state has the right to develop "its economic life freely and naturally" and that no state can "use or encourage the use of coercive measures of an economic . . . character in order to force the sovereign will of another State and obtain from it advantages of any kind" (OAS 2004, arts. 17, 20).

No treaty or other international agreement ever bound states to permit the international financial institutions to pry into their fiscal and monetary accounts, as they have done. Never was there a shared understanding between states that an IFI like the International Monetary Fund had the right to not only condition receipt of credit on changes in macroeconomic policy, but to literally sit at the table—cajoling, intimidating, and warning ministry officials to tow the line or face the consequences. Yet since the mid 1950s, the IMF, backed by the power of creditor states, has operated in precisely this manner against weak debtor nations.

The most persuasive evidence that sovereignty has been permanently undermined in the economic realm is the fact that the theme hardly ever comes up in deliberations about neoliberal adjustment in Latin America. While that might suggest that there is now a widespread acceptance among Latin American states of their fiscal and financial vulnerability to external forces, it would be more aptly characterized as a mixture of some agreement and ample resignation. Material self-interest and the fear of failure to abide by the terms of externally imposed conditionality are at the root of submission to IFIs, as much if not more than some consensual understanding. In economics, as in security affairs, sovereignty is not only weak but obedient to the logic of consequence.[4]

To recap, our objective is to understand why influence over Latin American affairs tips in the direction of the international on some occasions and the domestic on others. Toward that end, we offer a comprehensive, issue-sensitive framework, so devised as to get us to the bottom of why barriers to external influence seem more formidable in some instances and less so in others. Embedded within that framework is the division between high and low politics, which helps us understand who the principal change agents are, and how capable and motivated they are. As issues shift from high to low domains and back again, so too do the central players, their motivations and abilities, and the forms of influence they resort to. With that information in hand, we are better able to assess when and why sovereign barriers to external influence are either successfully breached or not.

What does it mean to breach sovereign barriers? And how do we know that international influences have prevailed or not over domestic influences? This study considers neither the potential loss of a nation's legal sovereignty in the world community as sanctified by international treaties, nor a government's political right to rule over its inhabitants (Krasner 1999). We are, rather, concerned about political decisions—including government policies—and the degree to which they are or are not shaped by forces beyond their control and beyond the territorial limits of the state. More specifically, we are interested in determining whether domestic decisions are made that would not have been likely without foreign pressure, or conversely occur independently and with little or no regard for the external world.

Invulnerability or vulnerability varies by issues, and our challenge is to find those issue areas where the balance of influence seems to tilt decisively—if even just for a brief period—in one direction or the other, and then to account for that tilt. To know if the "foreign" matters, we first establish some sequence of related events that may suggest a cause-and-effect relation. When domestic actions follow on the heels of international pressures and appear to flow directly and logically from those pressures, that gives us an initial indication of causality. Timing is important. The shorter the lag between external action and internal reaction, the more persuasive the nexus is; the longer the lag, the more doubt is cast since other factors could have more readily intervened. If, however, it is domestic forces that prevail, the task is to note either that foreign pressures have receded or are absent from the scene, or that domestic actors completely disregard them.

Then again, how much does the foreign matter? Are external pressures crucial in some instances and irrelevant in others? Once having discovered a succession of international actions and domestic reactions, we can then assess what significance key actors and informed observers attach to them. Those actors may have acknowledged that external agents had a critical impact on internal events. In chapter 4 on democracy in the Andean region, we take note of political and media acknowledgments of the OAS mission's stunning effect on the first round, 2000 presidential elections in Peru.

Of course, domestic actors may take umbrage at external interference in their affairs and thus emphatically deny that foreigners have any influence upon them. In that instance, other measures of significance are needed. We could note the relative constancy of political life in a country that is suddenly disrupted by foreign intrusions. If a search for potential domestic agents of change turned up empty-handed, we could infer the external mattered. Alternatively, we could raise, as we do, the "what-if" question through the use of counterfactuals (Tetlock and Belkin 1996). What if political actions had evolved without any external intrusion? Would that evolution have looked appreciably different? By definition, these are educated guesses not verifiable certainties. But the counterfactual can be reasonably persuasive if based on a thorough understanding of the chronological past and the plausible course that political events would have taken without the introduction of catalysts from the outside. In chapter 5 on human rights in Chile, we assess what would have probably occurred in Chilean courts in the absence of judicial action against Augusto Pinochet in Spain and Britain.

Conversely, if the domestic prevails in a decisive way, we look for evidence of national figures promoting change while rebuffing foreign opposition or find instances where foreigners never bothered showing up in the first place. Chapter 6 on Central America demonstrates how Central American states forged their own regional security organizations without any overt U.S. input or interference whatsoever.

One final distinction must be noted. In this study, we prefer to focus on the more inclusive term "influence" than on intervention. Intervention normally refers to coerced or unwanted intrusions by outsiders into the territorial confines of another state (Finnemore 1996). Military interventions are of course the most common, but there are other kinds, including covert intelligence gathering, economic sabotage, and humanitarian rescues. Intervention has the advantage over influence of greater definitional precision but the disadvantage of excluding from our review the array of alternative noninterventionist methods by which outsiders compromise domestic decision-making autonomy. Sovereignty can be and indeed has been breached without intervention. States can for example enter into agreements with other states or international institutions that place limits on their decision-making autonomy, as chapter 3 on neoliberal reform makes clear, and as does the capsule study on drug trafficking in chapter 7. And as chapter 4 on democracy in the Andean region points out, governments regularly invite in foreign observers who then constrain their ability to manipulate elections as they see fit.[5]

The High-Low Politics Framework

This issue-sensitive framework gives scholars a general orientation for understanding shifts in the origins of influence on Latin American politics from near and afar. But change is seldom the simple outgrowth of a monolithic force symbolized by the terms "domestic" and "foreign." The domestic and foreign are themselves hugely complex constellations of actors and institutions with distinct though overlapping priorities, abilities, and values. When, in a given issue arena, the most powerful political and economic forces from abroad pressure for domestic changes, they may not do so in a uniform, consistent, and durable fashion. It is quite likely that we will discover variations in the pursuit of interests and the expression of influence across actors even as their overarching priorities converge. Across time, we may find that what was once a peripheral concern for states has become a vital necessity. Thus, for them issues will migrate over the divide from low to high politics. And across space, the international may become momentarily significant to a low politics cause as foreign nonstate actors unexpectedly muster strength, while the domestic has its moment in a high politics affair as foreign state actors briefly lose interest. We turn to succinct discussions on these dimensions in order to fine-tune the framework in ways that foreshadow the empirical discussions that follow.

Unpacking the Domestic and the Foreign

To speak of a foreign-domestic balance without reference to possible discord and detachment within these arenas only obscures the subject matter. It is implausible and often misleading to conceive of a "domestic" alliance standing in opposition to an equally unified "international" group. Each arena comprises actors who may hold conflicting interests, values, and strategies, and in each realm cooperation can be problematic.

For instance, international players in the field of human rights confront a host of coordination problems that partly explains their lack of capacity. The functional division of labor among nonstate agencies often limits their ability to grasp the whole picture. Some monitor abuses from the outside to pressure foreign states, others offer legal counsel, still others focus solely on lobbying the governments from the inside, and several, such as the Red Cross, eschew criticism to ensure access. Moreover, the single country or regional focus of most groups limits concerted action. All of these coordination obstacles conspire to weaken the clout of foreign nonstate actors and enable domestic actors to chart the path of human rights policy.

By contrast, in high politics U.S. hegemony concentrates decision-making authority in fewer hands, often rendering coordination troubles moot. And as noted by the neoliberal camp, the intensity and persistence with which states pursue their self-interests within the high politics sphere reduces the likelihood that they will be thwarted by collective action difficulties. Having said that, we must note an interesting distinction between security and economic issues. States are most unwilling to surrender control over security policy. The state alone is master of its security interests and perceptions, deciding if, when, and where to make its presence felt in the region; in Latin America this means that the expression of U.S. military hegemony fluctuates in tune with its own security imperatives.

But this flexibility and control is more problematic in economic issues, as illustrated in chapter 3, which discusses international support for neoliberal reform in Argentina, Brazil, and Chile. Economic interests tend to be more stable than security concerns due to the greater durability of trade patterns and investment destinations. Colombia is currently a security preoccupation to Washington. It may not be in twenty years. Mexico and Brazil are of economic importance to the United States now, and they will likely be twenty years hence. This durability is not difficult to understand. Even a hegemon cannot easily control where businesses trade and invest, but it must answer to these decisions as it seeks to promote the economic well-being of the country as a whole. And though increasing levels of interdependence have encouraged states to create international institutions such as the International Monetary Fund and the World Trade Organization (WTO) to address discrepancies and common concerns, these institutions can gain a level of relative autonomy, develop their own interests, and thus further crowd the field (Stein 1993). The fact that states must respond to business interests and accord institutions some autonomy means that foreign influence, while strong throughout Latin America, will be expressed differently from country to country.[6] For political reasons, states may want to throw greater economic support behind some countries, but this demands that business and international organizations be so induced. And decisions by a state's international enterprises may engender greater economic support for a state, even in the midst of political differences.

Movements from Low to High Politics

There are both opportunities and limitations for an issue to cross the low-high politics divide. Movement occurs when an issue that was once of remote concern to foreign states takes on greater importance to them. In the low politics realm, principles of sovereignty and nonintervention traditionally have kept states at arm's length from the internal problems of others. Nonetheless, at certain unique points in history, nations sometimes discover that their interests hang in the balance even on matters that typically reside in the realm of low politics. A sense of urgency overtakes them, propelling them to join with other nations to collectively intercede in the domestic politics of a state. These efforts are determined and sustained, placing them beyond the concept of an "international moment."

In fact, governments may increasingly associate a heretofore low politics issue with their vital interests, even survival. When they do, they often codify and institutionalize new standards of political conduct to justify ongoing regional interventions. Once norms become embedded within treaties and other collective agreements, it becomes more difficult for states to ignore them (Ruggie 1983). What was once inappropriate conduct for states (i.e., intervention on a given issue) now becomes entirely appropriate.[7] What was once the self-interest of the "other" now becomes the self-interest of "us."

But there are limits to how far states of a given region are prepared to rewrite the rules of collective engagement. When what afflicts one state becomes inextricably tied up with the self-preservation of others, then intervention into the domestic becomes easier. But sometimes it becomes more difficult, when intervention can bounce back to haunt other states if by interceding they expose deep flaws in their own systems. States would rather not judge regional neighbors too harshly for having failed to live up to certain standards, for fear that the spotlight would be thrown back on any of them next time around.

When states are so motivated by self-interest that they rewrite the rules of intervention to facilitate outside involvement, an issue can move from the realm of low to high politics. The example to be used in this book to typify such a movement is that of democratic defense. Democracy is a choice of regime, and regime choice has historically been a domestic affair. But increasingly, Latin American states are associating their own well-being with the well-being of others. If one democracy is threatened by a military coup, then others may be as well, because coups are contagious. Should the armed forces successfully usurp power in one country, then militaries in bordering states may try to emulate the same behavior. The more democracies that succumb, the easier each succeeding coup becomes. Likewise, if civilian leaders with questionable democratic credentials try to tamper with or cancel elections in one nation, then that serves as an example for other presidents with authoritarian leanings. To avert these fates, all democratic nations of the region have an interest in rallying to the defense of any one democracy or election in trouble.

These same states are much more reticent to push too far for democratic reform (also referred to as democratic deepening), fearing that they will cross the line from legitimate to illegitimate intervention in the internal affairs of another state, prompting retaliatory intrusions against themselves. It is not just that classic principles of nonintervention resurface. It is the somber reality that so many states of the region exhibit sizeable imperfections in their own democratic systems. Thus, they respond to problems of democratic deepening in a lackluster fashion so that reprisals are not taken against them next time around. What is the upshot of this? Democracy is torn between its high and low political components. The oftentimes competing pressures between these spheres produce a kind of equilibrium that is suboptimal. Because outside states shun movements to improve quality but resolutely protect democracy from threats to its very existence, the Western Hemisphere now embraces a system that shores up "low quality democracies" of decreasing legitimacy to their own populations. This development does not bode well for democratic consolidation.

A Departure from Normal Politics

The high-low politics distinction provides a baseline to compare more conventional scenarios with unconventional ones. Under conditions of "normal politics" we would expect self-interested foreign states and carefully supervised international organizations to hold sway in issues of security and economics. A nation's defense and its material needs should rivet its attention on the domestic affairs of foreign states; commitments to principles and norms should recede into the background. Conversely, we would expect domestic actors (state and nonstate) to be more influential on matters of democracy and human rights. Ideas and institutions should hold their own against interests, all else equal.

Of course in politics all else is seldom equal. Political change is often the product of unanticipated disruptions to the status quo by unlikely candidates. Issues normally shaped by internal factors can have their "foreign moments," and those usually dominated by outside forces can have their "domestic moments." Why is this so? Moments, as the term suggests, are brief periods of time when windows of opportunity open for agents who would normally be offstage to move front and center. These opportunities can be traced to specific historical periods, and to the motivations and capacities of domestic and foreign actors.

International moments feature enduring motivations and varied capacities. These are occasions when highly committed activists and NGOs from abroad are able to leverage relatively disinterested state actors into showing brief concern about low politics issues. While these activists and NGOs are highly and consistently energized, their ability to effect changes by themselves in the domestic politics of foreign states is limited. As stated earlier in the case of human rights, these nongovernmental actors are resource poor and do not have at their disposal all the assets needed to bring formidable pressures to bear on offending nations to compel desired changes. They will succeed only if they can grab the attention of key state actors—be these from judicial, legislative, or executive branches—who have some leverage. Persuading foreign states to act in defense of human rights, social justice, or the environment is not easy but once done can set in motion a chain of events that can boomerang back home (Keck and Sikkink 1998). To bring international moments into sharp focus, this book will devote a chapter to the theme of human rights.

By contrast, domestic moments are characterized by a dominant state's enduring capacity and cyclical motivations. Now any analyst of Latin American politics would approach the question of "domestic moments" in high politics with trepidation, due to the overbearing presence of the United States. And hegemony cannot be dismissed. But ironically enough, hegemonic potency itself creates opportunities for the domestic to emerge. As realists unhesitatingly remind us, military might responds to threats (e.g., Waltz 1979) and in the Western Hemisphere those threats wax and wane across time and space. Hegemonic expression, while potentially enduring, ebbs and flows with changes in perceived risk. Absent threats of sufficient magnitude, a hegemon will grow less attentive to a region. As it does, it allows for independent security arrangements to emerge from the region because it is simply less concerned with developments there. This book will explore this phenomenon with a case study of the rise of Central American security institutions in the post–Cold War era.

In international and domestic moments, the window of opportunity can close as quickly as it opens. International and transnational activists will be able to spark foreign state interest but not sustain it. The state's attention to low politics issues abroad fades as subjects more central to its own national well-being take precedence. Domestic moments will fade as well. Eventually, the hegemonic state will reassert its will, constraining or stifling Latin American efforts to carve out their own security niches. That will occur when the Unites States again perceives that its vital national security interests are at stake in the region.

2. Issues and Political Change

This book offers a unique perspective on how domestic and international forces intersect to create political change in Latin America. The need and appeal of this perspective appears self-evident after a survey of the literature on political change in Latin America. Indeed, it is the character of the field itself that prompted this work in the first place. It is a field that has numerous accounts of political, social, military, and economic developments in Latin America, but one that never pulls these together under a common framework, nor draws comparisons or explores whether there is an underlying unity to this diversity.

We begin with a look back at two broad and important literatures in Latin American politics: development studies and U.S. foreign policy studies. We take as our entry point the seeming disconnect between those foreign policy scholars who concentrate so straightforwardly on U.S. dominance and those developmentalists who shun the hegemon in favor of the domestic in their explanations of political change. These scholars, we assert, choose separate starting points not because they are in error, but because they deal with different subject matters lodged in different issue arenas. Hence, those pointing to U.S. hegemony typically base their assessments on high politics issues such as security or economics, while those that accentuate internal factors find corroborating evidence in the low politics of social, humanitarian, or democratic quality affairs. In the end, we agree that the dynamics of political change vary from case to case. But our goal is to explore the basis of that variance. Leaving the high politics of international affairs to foreign policy specialists and the low politics of domestic matters to developmentalists restricts the field's capacity to assess political change more broadly and systematically.

Foreign Policy Studies and Developmental Studies

The study of Latin American political change is rich and textured, but it is also rife with inconsistency. David Dent and Paul Sondrol note, "there continues to be little agreement on specific variables, theories or characteristics that are most essential for understanding the political landscape" of Latin America (Dent and Sondrol 2000, 399). Our particular quest for answers on the relative impact of domestic and international forces leaves us frustrated. The problem is not that analysts inconclusively debate the foreign-domestic balance, but that they largely omit such inquiry.[1] Assertions are made about the importance of one or the other, but seldom are the conditions specified under which internal forces matter more than external, or vice versa. Likewise, there is little discussion on how they interact with each other in situations where both hold some sway. By addressing these gaps, we seek to build bridges in an otherwise divided field.

Latin America presents an intriguing and formidable laboratory for the study of political change and the relative impact of domestic and international pressures. The pervasiveness of Iberian culture, a shared colonial heritage, the overwhelming stature of U.S. hegemony, and the common quandary of economic and political underdevelopment offer a firm foundation of symmetry found perhaps nowhere else on earth. Nonetheless, diverse streams of political change, duly documented in the literature, continue to characterize the region. It is this incongruity, diversity in conjunction with symmetry, that marks not only the politics but also the scholarship of the region. Why this is so is clearly grounded within the reality of U.S. hegemony. That reality produces two reactions. The first is to acknowledge the power imbalance by noting how the United States generates political and economic convergence among the weaker Southern states. The second is to take cover by exposing the tapestry of political and economic divergences in the region—for surely if such differences exist, hegemony, and the international, must be less overwhelming than we think.

The persistence of these two reactions has engendered two detached sets of scholarship—U.S. foreign policy studies and developmental studies. U.S. foreign policy studies begin with the question of hegemony and view independent domestic events and trends as aberrations. Developmental studies place more value on explanations set within Latin American states. While they occasionally tip their hats to the power of the hegemon to forge regional union, more often they are skeptical of its pervasiveness and accentuate historical, cultural, and institutional uniqueness from case to case.

Both literatures have tackled high and low politics issues, but their respective presuppositions have steered U.S. foreign policy studies toward the former and developmental studies toward the latter. The two actually held some resemblance during the 1960s and 1970s, when the debate between modernization and dependency theories subordinated the domestic to the international (Valenzuela and Valenzuela 1978). On the one hand, modernization theorists applauded the hegemonic diffusion of modern values to Latin America, which would propel those states toward free markets, economic prosperity, and democracy. On the other hand, dependency theory pointed to hegemony as a check on economic and political growth in Latin America, uncovering its exploitative features. While the two theories were elegant in their simplicity, they were inaccurate in their portrayals, failing to grant the domestic realm the credit it deserved.

As a tide of authoritarianism engulfed much of the region through the 1970s, reservations about the optimistic (and value-laden) tenets of modernization theory emerged. The field embraced a modified form of dependency theory, bureaucratic authoritarianism, which relaxed the assumption of economic stagnation to highlight how economic growth may be possible, but only at the cost of military dictatorship (Collier 1979). But the stepchild of dependency theory would itself be undone by the regional turn toward democracy in the 1980s.

The undue weight accorded to international forces on a low politics issue drove modernization theory and dependency theory to misconstrue the prospects for democratization. Neither approach sufficiently developed a satisfactory explanation of why outside states would unfalteringly prop up either democratic regimes (in the case of modernization) or authoritarian regimes (in the case of dependency theory). And those working during the death throes of these theories also failed to take up the task. In an astounding reversal during the 1980s, scholars simply took refuge in the domestic and began to discount completely the impact of international pressures. In this new transitions literature, democracy emerged as regime elites squabbled over political power and created opportunities for political change. International forces would really not come into play until the consolidation phase of democratization, and even here their role would be little more than supportive (O'Donnell and Schmitter 1986). Reason dictates that we look to the international environment when states undergo common political or economic shifts (Remmer 1997), but this logic found little appeal in a scholarly community twice bitten by its obsession with outside forces.

The democratic transitions work represented a turning point in developmental studies as scholars submerged themselves within the parameters of domestic processes and events, a trend that continues to this day.[2] Analysts in this literature freely rebuff hegemony and naked power and instead champion the roles of nonstate actors, ideas, and institutions as they set their sights on issues traditionally outside the limelight of international intrigue. As observed by Damián J. Fernández and Jacqueline Anne Braveboy-Wagner, "issues once deemed as low politics, such as the drug trade, immigration, and the environment, are now of high import" (2000, 577).

Are the mistakes of the past repeating themselves? Modernization and dependency failed by presuming too much of outside forces and were caught off-guard when events contradicted the strictures of their expectations. This literature may be making similar mistakes by now thinking too little of outside forces in low politics. By failing to question why the domestic all too often trumps the international in the realm of low politics, analysts are left unprepared to explain those situations in which the international may actually matter. Those instances, though uncommon, are significant and potentially enduring, as illustrated by the case of human rights in Chile. While human rights policies there have been largely internal matters, the European court verdicts on the Pinochet case jolted the Chilean nation and left their mark. Rather than celebrate the stochastic, we question what hinders outside interference. Is it the inviolability of the idea of sovereignty? Does the intractability of many domestic issues shield them from overt manipulation? Do outside agents lack the motivation to intervene? Or are foreign actors simply incapable of intruding? Once we define the obstacles, we are prepared to explain how they may fall, even if momentarily.

Meanwhile, the U.S. foreign policy literature seems too impressed with the power of external actors, and not impressed enough with the power of ideas and institutions in low politics. Norms are portrayed as mere rhetorical devices to enhance the power of the hegemon rather than tools of collective institution building, negotiation, and compromise that may level the playing field between North and South. For these analysts, norms are always self-serving for the United States, espoused on behalf of some other more fundamental goal (Kenworthy 1995). The "Western Hemispheric" or the "Pan-American" ideals were all important only in so far as they legitimated U.S. efforts to fortify its sphere of influence by preventing extrahemispheric rivals from stepping in (Molineu 1990, 15). Ideas and ideals help to cloak naked security and economic interests in the language of moral virtuousness (Cottam 1994). If some form of discourse—be it anticommunism, human rights, or democracy—can further those central interests, that discourse will be employed (Molineu 1990; Smith 2000; Schoultz 2001). But where touting these ideas clashes with overriding imperatives, they are easily forsaken.[3] Unlike studies of social activism in the developmental literature, there is very little confirmation of a strong constructivist view of norms. U.S. foreign policy specialists maintain that the hegemon can use principles like democracy and human rights but never be used by them.

When norms or ideas are presumed to reside only at a discursive level, it is easy for foreign policy analysts to dismiss them as artifacts of U.S. hegemony. But some norms and ideas are institutionalized through the rules and regulations that compose regional and international organizations. Neoliberal theory tells us that institutions raise the costs of defection and thereby constrain all who come into contact with them, including the powerful (Keohane 1984). Moreover, institutions create a formal equality that cannot be achieved outside of them: one country, one vote. That opens up the theoretical possibility that institutions may level the playing field in U.S.-Latin American relations and thus diminish Washington's clout (Tulchin and Espach 2001). Others herald the convergence of interests on democracy and market reforms and note how this allows for greater cooperation via multilateral forums and thus more influential Latin American input (Hartlyn, Schoultz, and Varas 1992; Farer 1996; Pastor 2001). Indeed, the Summit of the Americas, held in 1994, 1998, and 2001, spotlighted low politics issues as leaders throughout the region urged cooperative action on democratization, good governance, education, human rights, health, migration, and cultural affairs.

But one wonders if this kind of convergence on low politics themes is a weak if not deceptive test for institutional strength. Does the United States abide by negotiated rules and deals *because* Latin American states concur? We have yet to witness a strong test of institutional constraint, because the current ideas and agreements forged within regional institutions are in vogue; Washington policy makers perceive them as "user-friendly." How abiding will the United States be when its Southern neighbors dissent, and is Washington likely to respond unilaterally on those occasions? Within the literature, there is general consensus that the United States continues to reserve for itself the unilateral option (Bulmer-Thomas and Dunkerly 1999, 318–20) and that value convergence at best (and value imposition at worst), rather than institutional vigor, drives collective international pressure in defense of human rights or democracy (Pastor 2001; Farer 1996). Still, what is often absent in the literature is a critique of how U.S capacity and motivation to act unilaterally varies from issue to issue and across the high-low politics divide.

In the end, one is left unsatisfied with the analysis of low politics issues such as democracy and human rights. These topics captivate developmental scholars, who bury their heads in the domestic and drum up the relevance of nonstates, ideas, and institutions. On the other hand, low politics holds only a subsidiary appeal to foreign policy specialists, who fixate on the international and admit only brute force and self-interest. Conveniently, the roles are reversed when the high politics issues of security and economics come to the fore. This issue area receives greater attention from foreign policy specialists and their preference for explanations from the exterior.

Hence, the literature on security affairs discounts possibilities for the domestic in favor of outside influences. Martz and Schoultz proclaim the enduring stature of U.S. supremacy: "In the absence of a threat, hegemony is no less real by virtue of its obscurity" (1980, 13). The defeat of communist expansion may have removed a threat, but drugs, terrorism, crime, and other threats keep Latin America on Washington's radar screen (Hartlyn, Schoultz, and Varas 1992; Lowenthal and Treverton 1994). But others view control over security issues as problematic. These new threats do not provide the same rallying capacity as communist subversion for coherent policy making (Buchanan 1996; Desch 1998). Finally, Peter Smith (2000) argues that hegemonic regional exertions will fluctuate in accord with Washington's global interests. The inter-American system is a subsystem of the larger global order, and thus the impetus for change must always come from the outside, mediated through the offices of the U.S. government. Consequently, even though U.S. power in the hemisphere is uncontested and greater than ever, it does not follow that Washington will consistently flex its muscles and demonstrate its power.

We are more persuaded by the view that hegemony over security affairs is episodic—a factor of U.S. motivations and capacities that are themselves subject to change. But while foreign policy analysts focus on hegemonic vacillations for its own sake (i.e., for what this means for U.S. control of security affairs in the region), our attention is directed to the possibilities that unfold for security affirmations from within Latin American states. By examining the *domestic consequences* of hegemonic fluctuations, rather than hegemonic fluctuations themselves, we go beyond foreign policy studies that remain focused on U.S. power and interests.

In the high politics issue of economic interests, analysts find it difficult, if not impossible, to ignore foreign pressures. Nonetheless, most studies reject a simple conceptualization of global convergence, in which all states tread a similar path of competitive capitalism. In a nod to the persistence of politics, they instead write of regional convergences directed by a hegemon (Stallings 1995; Loriaux et al. 1997). In the Western Hemisphere, the United States exerts its own regional influence over neoliberal reform with carrot-and-stick maneuvers (Smith 2000; Williamson 1990).

Yet even in an issue girdled by international forces, analysts have found room to underline domestic constraints and opportunities. The "second-image reversed" approach (Gourevitch 1978; Keohane and Milner 1996) found its way into Latin American studies (Frieden 1991; Haggard and Kaufman 1992; Schamis 1999; Naim 2000). Here, domestic political and economic institutions constitute intervening variables that mediate international forces and allow for national variations in economic policy choices. Sebastian Edwards (1997) concentrates more forthrightly on domestic forces when he portrays neoliberal reform as the product of distinct "learning by doing" and "muddling through" policy processes within Latin America. The work on neopopulism and corporatism also seeks refuge in the domestic despite tremendous global economic pressures. Caudillo-style political traditions with roots in the region's Iberian heritage transform neoliberalism's impact (Weyland 1996; Bulletin of Latin America Research 2000).

Our study tends to concur with the view that the domestic often mediates the foreign in economic affairs. While our issue-based analysis leads us to emphasize the robust motivations of outside actors to intervene in this high politics issue, it also allows us to highlight how the cast of characters differs from that found in security affairs and thus to recognize dynamics unique to economic issues. Namely, in economic affairs, the international stage is crowded by the respective interests of private business, foreign government, and international financial institutions, most prominently the IMF. These actors see different stakes from country to country, and this produces very different experiences with neoliberal reform, as exemplified by the cases of Argentina, Brazil, and Chile in this book. Interest divergence means that "the international" will grant leverage to some states and ensure little for others, and profoundly affect the prospects for reform.

Our survey of the scholarship reveals two disparate literatures that, when combined, fail to proffer a coherent theory of political change. Leaving the high politics of international affairs to foreign policy specialists and the low politics of domestic matters to developmentalists restricts the field's capacity to assess political change more broadly and systematically. By assuming that the chief impetus to change will come primarily from the international or the domestic, and from self-interests and power or ideas and institutions, the underlying bases for influence are left unexplored. Moreover, one is unable to expose those instances where outcomes are the product of an interaction between the two. The work on transnational social activism offers only a partial answer to this disjuncture as it depicts how these actors foster cooperative efforts across state borders (Keck and Sikkink 1998; Khagram, Riker, and Sikkink 2002). Missing is an identification of how domestic and international interests collide or unwittingly coalesce on certain issues, as illustrated in our analysis of the Andean countries, where the regional community often acts with conviction on matters of democratic survival or procedure but eschews the low politics of democratic quality. The outcome, low-quality democracy, is not the intent but is in fact supported by the international community, demonstrating that the international does hold some weight in the largely domestic issue of democratization.

The scholarship on political change in Latin America provides little direction for those seeking answers to the relative impact of domestic and international forces. Scholars are all too content to reside within their own respective niches. While this specialization has produced a cornucopia of valuable accounts, it has stunted our broader understanding of the forces behind all kinds of political change. There is a paucity of theory on how and why the foreign or the domestic trumps the other, the opportunities each has for influence in the other, or how they interact. An issue-oriented approach, based upon the distinction between high and low politics, allows us to impose some order on this clutter. By revealing where foreign states are and are not motivated to influence domestic politics, by identifying how the set of engaged actors shifts from issue to issue, and by recognizing how each issue area transforms the process by which change unfolds, we can go a long way toward addressing the discord. Though we do not expect cacophony to become symphony, an issue-based approach represents a clear overture to a better understanding of the energy and texture behind political change in Latin America.

Elaborating the High-Low Politics Framework

Issues, Actors, and Power

The literature illustrates how both international and domestic forces leave their stamp on political change in Latin America. But to proclaim that both matter merely places a veil of consensus on a scholarship still struggling for answers. Good questions are the midwife of good analysis, and at this point it is clear that the real question is not whether outside or inside factors matter, but the conditions under which they do. The dissection of political change into issue areas unearths these conditions. When divided into high politics and low politics, issues demarcate two distinct political arenas that respond to different sets of actors, capabilities, and motivations behind change.

Over three decades ago, Theodore Lowi argued that we should move beyond considering how "politics determine policies," to how "policies determine politics" (1972, 299). Though addressed to the study of public policy, the suggestion is no less relevant to issues of comparative and international analysis. Issue areas, like policies, represent a valuable focal point insofar as political behavior is determined by expectations (Lowi 1964, 688). As political actors look to different issue areas they gauge their capacity to influence, reflect on their values, tally expected benefits, strategize, and act accordingly. For this very reason, international influence is readily rearranged and varied as one moves from one case of political change to another. In military operations against drug cultivation in Latin America, external influence is measured bilaterally: Washington's security assistance, driven by its keen desire to stem the flow of narcotics into the United States. But in the aftermath, when attention is turned to crop substitution or agricultural extension ventures, international development organizations and transnational social activists move to the fore. By virtue of their drawing power, issues thus determine who the principal protagonists will be (Lowi 1964, 688).

Issues also shed light on how power relations can alter from case to case. Power finds its roots in the soil of military might, economic wealth, legal precedent, strategic and bargaining prowess, or normative appeal. Classic realist works cite state-level attributes such as military preparedness, industrial capacity, and population as power resources (Morgenthau 1967, 106–158). Neoliberals look more squarely to economics to note how interdependence creates sensitivities and vulnerabilities even in militarily dominant states (Keohane and Nye 1977, 23–37). And contemporary work on transnational social activism underscores the power of consultation, protest, symbols, and accountability. These movements exercise a form of "soft power" as they monitor deviations from behavioral standards set by norms (Brysk 1994; Keohane and Nye 1998; Sikkink 2002). Clearly, the sword, purse, and principle all matter, but each of these resources works better in some fields than others, be it combating insurgencies, renegotiating debt payments, settling territorial disputes, or redressing human rights abuses. As Robert Keohane and Joseph Nye reminded us decades ago, economic and military power as agents of coercion are not as fungible as they once were (1977, 27–31). Power changes its form as we move from issue to issue, and the formidable actors in one context become less so in another.

The separation of issues into those of high politics and others of low politics draws into sharp relief how different problems attract distinct sets of actors and power resources. High politics lures outside states seeking to protect or advance their well-being. States closely monitor institutions and push aside ideas and norms that run counter to their self-interests (Evans and Wilson 1992). Low politics issues just do not have the same appeal and are often viewed as too distant or conversely potentially ensnaring. High politics is about states, self-interest, might, and material assets. Latin American states can ignore outside actors only at their own peril, which all too often means that the "foreign" will not only contend with, but will more often trump, the "domestic." Low politics is about nonstate actors, values, and soft power. In low politics, nonstate actors find more room to maneuver, institutions will not necessarily submit to the pressing needs of states, and ideas and norms will evolve to hold self-interest at bay. Here the domestic trumps the international. High politics and low politics represent distinct political spheres with different agents, agendas, and avenues of political change.

Issues, Institutions, and Ideas

Just as which actors are significant and which are powerful are questions best answered with reference to issues, so too are questions regarding the role to be played by institutions and ideas, which operate differently in high and low politics. There is a burgeoning literature on the roles institutions and ideas play in political change.[4] Though much has been addressed in these works, the additional consideration of issue orientation further advances our understanding of the contextual conditions under which institutions and ideas hold more or less significance.

For instance, in high politics states may discover that to advance their interests on their own is tough going and that they are better served by cooperation. To this end, they create international institutions predicated on collaboration and in doing so grant those institutions some discretion (Keohane 1984; Axelrod and Keohane 1993) while limiting their own. In agreeing to submit themselves to the organizational rules, norms, and decisions that others submit to, their bet is that institutional adherence will work to their advantage (Ikenberry 2001). Should it not, then what was given can be taken away. When the stakes are high, and when the push against the self-interests of nations comes to shove, a state is likely to either retract its support for the institution or rein the institution in by limiting its autonomy (Keohane 1993). Institutions act similarly to the felt ropes of a movie theatre line—states accept their strictures in tranquil times. But when an emergency erupts and threatens national interests—when somebody shouts "fire"—states rethink their adherence and grow more willing to breach institutional confines.

But what of low politics? Here an environment lacking consistent relations across state boundaries fortifies institutions. Because there is often no real history of contact or any sense of convention on these issues, actors cannot reasonably presage each other's intentions and abilities when they do intermingle. But because institutions are rule and value driven, they serve as reference points for actors, fostering predictability in these situations of occasional interaction (Steinmo, Thelen, and Longstreth 1992). Compare this to high politics, where states remain keenly aware that national interests may come into play at any moment as they design and then act within institutions (Ikenberry 2001).

The variable impact of institutions in high and low politics is captured by John Ikenberry's (1998) assessment of neoliberal rationalist explanations of institutions as too "thin" (they emphasize agency over structure), and constructivist explanations as too "thick" (they emphasize structure over agency). "Thin" approaches work better in the environment of high politics where self-interested states may at times run roughshod over institutions. That means powerful agents will more easily reconfigure institutional rules to suit their own needs or, conversely, ignore those rules entirely. "Thick" approaches hold more relevance to low politics, where actors depend on the predictability afforded by institutions. Thus, states will more likely submit to an organization's conventions and decisions. As we unpackage the context in which institutions operate, we reveal the conditions under which they are either more expendable or durable. Institutions do matter, but issue-based contexts matter more.

Issues also shape the roles played by ideas and norms. Stephen Krasner (1978) grants unceremonious significance to ideas and norms when he notes that ideology rises to the fore only in the absence of threats to the national interest (which implies that they can be easily overrun). In the high stakes game of high politics, states bring self-interest to the table while often snubbing principles that do not serve them.[5] Thus, in the face of efforts to declare war illegal, states hold fast to doctrines of self-defense, collective self-defense, and even expansive notions of anticipatory or pre-emptive self-defense. And while negotiating trade agreements, states hammer out loopholes to sustain protectionism despite professed commitments to free markets. In the Western Hemisphere, the United States has created institutional mechanisms to curb or circumvent OAS-led efforts to shape norms of regional behavior. Through the Rio Treaty, Interamerican Defense Board, the Defense Ministerial in security affairs, and the Summit Process in economic affairs, the United States will push for outcomes more to its liking than availed by the established machinery of the OAS (Buchanan 1996; Rosenberg 2001).

But ideas and norms come into their own in the sphere of low politics. Here states are more apt to take a hands-off approach, granting opportunities for nonstate agents to inspire norm-driven political change. Lacking military capabilities or the economic resources of states, nonstates seeking influence find norms to be the instrument of choice. Transnational social activists help construct international norms from their own sets of collective beliefs or expand the application of existing norms to new issue areas (Khagram, Riker, and Sikkink 2002, 15–16). They also gather information, monitor state behavior, and "mobilize shame" toward states as they document transgressions from existing international norms (Thomas 2002, 72–74).

Such norm-based strategies often mean less in high politics, where precepts are more likely to mirror the interests of states and the ability of nonstates to shape state behavior via norms remains a "hard case" for political analysts (Price

1998, 613). Hence, in her constructivist interpretation of military intervention, Martha Finnemore finds that the relevant norms "are strongly if not entirely shaped by the actions of powerful states that actually have the capacity to intervene" (2003, 5). On the other hand, the dynamic of influence is more nuanced in low politics. States remain fortified by principles of sovereignty, but international organizations and transnational activists hold reservoirs of knowledge and even retain some capacity to act independently (Gordenker and Weiss 1995, 364; Spiro 1995). Sovereignty still shields low politics from the international, but the battle to retain, or remove, that shield pits transnational activists, international organizations, and states against each other in a struggle over the meaning of norms and ideas. In this struggle, nonstates sometimes triumph (Keck and Sikkink 1998, 35–37).

Is There Issue Linkage?

Once separated into high and low political realms, issues are enormously useful to comprehend the differential impact of actors, power, institutions, and ideas in predictable ways. But what of the stability of issues themselves? Do states act as if there is a real separation between issues? Or are the lines blurred as states harness military and economic power to simultaneously pursue a multitude of goals? If they are in fact blurred, then powerful states should have no difficulty transgressing the sovereign confines of others, regardless of the issue at hand. No student of U.S.-Latin American relations can look upon the "sanctity of sovereignty" without skepticism. This doubt is fed by Washington's growing use of security and economics-based rationales to intrude into the low politics affairs of weaker states. For instance, the 1994–1995 and 2004 U.S. and UN interventions in Haiti to stop human rights abuses were also justified by apprehension over refugee flows to the United States and the security and economic alarms these were setting off. Likewise, the preoccupation with the oil pipelines of Colombia in its civil war and the anxiety about violations of democratic procedures in oil-rich Venezuela provide grist for the mills of those looking to the sway of material self-interests. If powerful states indiscriminately intervene on behalf of their high politics concerns, perhaps the realists have it right: the world really is one in which "the strong do what they can, while the weak suffer what they must" (Thucydides 1951, 331).

If sovereignty is no more of a barrier to state intervention when it comes to human rights or the rule of law than it is to security or economic appeals, then such issue distinctions lose their value. When is this true? The answer is, only on occasion. Unless domestic social and political problems generate powerful externalities (like refugee flows) that lure outside states in, then those states will devote scant attention to low politics issues. The externality must impose clear, immediate costs that are felt throughout the foreign country. Externalities of less magnitude fall victim to political calculations as political leaders find it difficult to justify sustained involvement in another country's low politics affairs. These issues only rarely make and remain on the national agenda.

For example, the United States continues to pursue an expensive military option in Colombia to face down narco-traffickers and left-wing guerrillas. It collaborates deeply with the Colombian armed forces which have been accused of countless human rights transgressions. But the United States has resisted calls for it to suspend its military aid and training program, pending human rights improvements. There are simply not enough political inducements or costs for Washington to mind the plight of Colombian victims of the civil war. That would likely change only if and when the Colombian émigré community in the United States constituted itself as a powerful lobbying force capable of pushing its concerns higher up on legislative and executive agendas.[6]

Sovereignty remains relevant and will pose a more formidable barrier to entry on human rights than it will on security. Although Krasner (1999) portrays a history of disregard for sovereignty in which "might makes right" seems to rule the day, such conclusions are deceptive. Methodologically, they suffer from selection bias insofar as they fail to measure violations of sovereignty against all those instances in which sovereignty held its own (Philpott 2001, 306–8). Moreover, we should not throw the baby out with the bathwater by dismissing the claim that international intrusions into the domestic may represent more the evolution than repudiation of sovereignty (Sørensen 1999). The very fact that breaches of sovereignty garner attention and generate controversy indicates that this boundary still holds relevance. Hence, the high-low politics division is still valid because sovereignty survives and seems more permeable on certain issues than it does on others. The United States was reminded of this when the Bush administration's failure to condemn the April 2002 coup attempt in Venezuela unleashed widespread criticism from Latin American leaders sensing support for the overthrow.

If issue linkage at times blurs a clean separation between high and low politics, that is an empirical question and more the exception than the rule. These exceptions occur when an externality of sufficient magnitude pulls a powerful state across the high-low politics divide. The first four chapter cases affirm that there still exists enough real world separation between low and high political arenas to warrant analytical distinction. But in order to more directly address the conditions under which externalities and issue linkage come into play, we devote a fifth empirical chapter to the low politics issues of environmental policy, immigration, and drug trafficking. These problems occasionally entice some foreign influence, but not on a sustained basis.

Applying the High-Low Politics Framework to the Casework

Our framework, and its application to our cases, can be neatly summed up with the aid of a property space, depicted below. The "high politics-low politics continuum" indicates whether an issue is associated with a country's vital, national interests. The continuum between international and domestic sources of change indicates who the likely change agents are. Within this space we situate various issues that will be addressed by this book. So for example, neoliberal reform sits in the realm of high politics, where international influence is usually dominant. Democratic deepening lies in the realm of low politics, where we find that domestic influences consistently prevail over international ones.

The diagram also depicts two kinds of movements within this space. One is permanent, where an issue such as democratic defense is moving from the low to the high end of the continuum. The other is temporary and gets at the notion of a "moment." Here for example, human rights remain a low politics issue, but there are occasions when international influences take on greater significance. The same is true for environmental degradation. The vertical dashed line, running from domestic to international issues, depicts international moments of change in these otherwise low politics arenas. And, likewise, there are times when the domestic can matter in the high politics realm of regional security—an issue traditionally dominated by the United States and its international agenda. For that we note the vertical dashed line running from international to domestic issues. Finally, some issues, though characteristically residing in the realm of low politics, generate enough externalities to lead them to be treated as if they

Figure 2.1. *Sources of Political Change: The High-Low Politics Continuum*

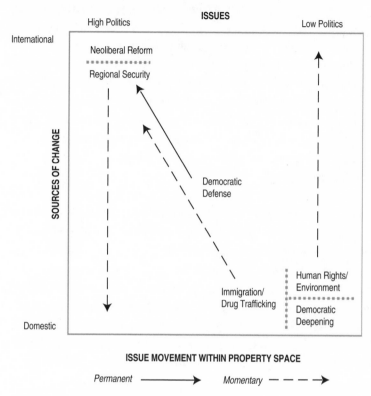

were high politics affairs, often done by linking them to matters of vital, national interest. Nonetheless, the linkages are forged under unique circumstances and often prove transitory. Hence, these issues generate a dashed diagonal line from domestic, low politics to international, high politics.

Core Propositions

An issue-based approach unearths a number of unique observations in the field of political change by way of the case studies to be presented in the pages that follow. These cases are bound together by a set of core propositions that emerge from the theoretical discussion in chapters 1 and 2. Those propositions are as follows:

States, driven by self-interest, have a greater incentive to intervene in high politics than low politics issues. If there is a defining maxim to our study, it is that for states, high politics means high stakes and low politics means low stakes. States will generally intervene in the domestic affairs of others in the region only when they perceive that doing so is necessary to advance a prominent political goal or to preserve and sustain key security and economic interests. Absent these goals, states lose interest in the internal affairs of foreign states, either because gains to be had from intervention are negligible or the costs are too high. When they lose interest, nonstate actors often move to center stage. Only on occasion are foreign states sufficiently cajoled into intervening for a low politics cause, be it human rights or the environment.

Sovereignty poses a more formidable barrier to entry in the realm of low politics than high politics. Foreign states motivated to protect their vital interests will often muster the financial, coercive, or political means to hurdle the sovereign walls of other states, often in clear disregard for historical norms of nonintervention. But those same states will think twice before infringing on others' self-governing rights when it comes to low politics issues. Meanwhile, foreign nonstate actors may be very inclined to effectively intervene on behalf of a just cause but lack the leverage to do so on their own. Hence, domestic political actors, operating behind sovereign walls, normally reign supreme in the realm of low politics.

Institutions and ideas enjoy more autonomous influence in low politics than in high politics. Greater autonomy allows institutions and ideas to define propriety and persuasion respectively as the central means of influence. They are, in other words, the conduits of soft power. When allowed to evolve on their own, institutions and ideas can potentially present challenges to states in their pursuit of vital self-interests. Hence, in high politics, states often willfully contain, manipulate, or push them aside, as they harness hard forms of power.

Domestic moments occur in high politics when foreign states episodically lose their motivation to intervene. The United States' ability to guard its own sphere of influence in the Latin American region has remained unchallenged for centuries. While that is unlikely to change, what does change is its motivation to defend its sphere. Domestic moments arise when regional threats to security dissipate, causing the hegemon to temporarily relax its guard. Thus, the domestic moment is issue sensitive—it is a response to a specific kind of dynamic that appears and disappears primarily in the security realm. It should also be noted that a change in the hegemon's motivation creates a necessary—not sufficient—condition for domestic action. When an opportunity emerges, it is not always seized.

International moments occur in low politics when nonstate actors acquire a capacity to intervene. Nonstate actors are highly motivated to engage in low politics issues. Theirs is forever a problem of capacity, and one that they cannot easily resolve on their own. Activists and NGOs must implore states to join their cause through moral suasion. Once they do, they gain considerably more leverage over the internal affairs of other nations. And yet such influence is transitory, as states turn away from their cause and toward issues of greater centrality to them.

An externality must generate immediate costs at the national level if an issue is to move permanently into the realm of high politics. Externalities raise concerns for outside states. Nonetheless, the costs imposed by externalities must be immediate, rather than long term, and hold national, rather than regional or local, consequences. Absent one of these conditions, an issue may still be treated as if it were a high politics affair if it is linked to some pre-existing high politics issue (such as economics or security), or if special historical conditions propel the issue into the national limelight. Sovereignty still remains a formidable barrier to negotiate, and the tenuous nature of these conditions ensures an inevitable descent from the high politics plane.

Methodology and Case Selection

The cases examined in this book were chosen both to maximize the range of issues under study and to cover as much geographic space in Latin America as possible. It is only by selecting cases that run the topical gamut that we are able to sort out the general relations and causal forces behind political change in Latin America. It allows us to get beyond the confines of narrow subfield emphases to consider concepts and explanations with broader reach. If, indeed, there is a pattern to why international influences matter more in some instances and the domestic in others, it can be found only by examining problems across the high-low politics divide, as we will do.

Our principal cases comprise neoliberal reform in the Southern Cone and

Brazil, democratization in the Andean countries, human rights in Chile, and regional security in Central America, along with briefer studies dealing with the environment, immigration, and drug trafficking. The study of neoliberal reform represents an issue entrenched within the area of high politics, where the forces for political change can largely be found in the self-interests of powerful outside states, corporations, and international financial institutions and where the consistency and coordination of these interests create a rather steady pattern of economic relations for each Latin American state. The Andean case spans the high-low politics divide and tells two stories: one of strong regional action in defense of threatened democracies and one of nonaction in the face of democratic deficiencies. The studies of Chile and Central America return us to issues rooted specifically in low or high politics, though both concentrate on how deviations from the rules governing influence come about. Our analysis of human rights policy in Chile takes us to the field of low politics, where the balance of influence typically tips to the domestic. Here we expose the peculiar conditions under which "international moments" can upend domestic primacy. The discussion of regional security institutions in Central America harkens back to the high politics pattern found in our case on support for neoliberal economic reform, where international forces prove ascendant. But here we again document how deviation, in this case a "domestic moment," surfaces to raise new concerns. The final empirical chapter combines discussions on the environment, immigration, and drug trafficking to illustrate the utility of the framework for issues that challenge easy placement within the high-low politics categories. Each generates externalities of significance, but not enough to secure a permanent high politics seat.

These case studies are intended to illustrate—not prove—the theoretical notions laid out in this chapter. They do so in methodologically explicit ways. The study is structured in the sense that it poses the same set of questions for each case—questions derived from a common theoretical frame (George 1979). So, for example, we ask of each: Is change directed mainly from the inside or outside? How much of a barrier to external influence does sovereignty pose? What are the respective motives and capabilities of the primary actors? And are those primary actors states or nonstates? Of course each of the narratives is, in many ways, substantially different, which is to be expected given the range of topics, events, and countries under review. But rather than treat these narratives as unique stories—which they are not—we bring them together under the rubric of a unified framework. In doing so, we are able to reveal different values for the same set of variables.

Moreover, the purpose behind presenting several studies is not so much to replicate our findings as it is to point out different components of the same overall construct. Each case fulfills its function by flushing out dimensions that others cannot. Because each presents only a partial view, whether it be from the "high" or "low" end of the political spectrum, sustained movements or temporary moments of oscillation between high and low politics, or issues that defy simple identification with either category, none of these chapters can stand alone. Together however, they comprise a full view of the construct in all its dimensions. In this respect the methodological approach is close to what Theda Skocpol and Margaret Summers (1980) have in mind when they refer to the writing of parallel histories. Finally, explicit comparisons between the cases will be reserved for the concluding chapter. There, we will also assess what consequences our framework may have for the academic fields of international relations and comparative politics, and for policy making in the region.

3. Neoliberal Reform in Argentina, Brazil, and Chile

We begin our study of political change with an issue steeped in foreign enticements and vital national interests—international support for neoliberal reform. High politics characteristics are prominent under these conditions: the supremacy of external forces, the use of hard power, the relative insignificance of social movements and other actors who rely on soft power, and the subordination of ideas and institutions to state interests. International support for neoliberal reform provides a good entry point for our case studies because, of all the cases, it most closely approaches what we have termed "normal politics" within the high-low politics framework. There are no moments in which the balance of influence unexpectedly tips to the domestic, nor are there issues that defy easy categorization within that framework. But the analysis of international support for neoliberal reform does convey a core puzzle—how diversity coexists alongside uniformity within Latin America. For in an arena where the international looms so large and indeed proves determinative, there is still considerable variety in neoliberal experiences from country to country: Brazil finds leeway to experiment even as it receives support, Chile must jockey for attention from foreign players, and Argentina is left by the wayside. Why does this medley exist within the strictures of high politics?

Our model helps to untangle this puzzle by demonstrating how issues shape the capabilities and motivations of key actors. The tremendous wealth of foreign players, and an economic model that prescribes active engagement with the global economy, paves an accessible path of international influence that winds its way throughout the region. Important international actors tread this path with distinct political, economic, and institutional motivations. The hegemon favors those states pivotal to its political and economic designs, international businesses chase profits, and international financial institutions work to balance pressure from stakeholders with their own institutional imperatives. For any given country, their motivations may diverge, even clash. Nevertheless, because each offers critical contributions to neoliberal reform, all are required for neoliberal success. This necessity ensures a constant struggle for cooperation as foreign actors look to one another to nourish their interests. And this is a struggle that the strapped states of Latin America find difficult to sway. Political leaders in the region thus face the following dilemma: they must open a route of international influence if neoliberal reform is to succeed, but who travels on that route is largely out of their hands. In this way, uniform pressure and diverse outcomes coexist.

High Politics Support for Neoliberal Reform

Neoliberalism is an economic model founded upon a minimalist state, the market allocation of goods and services, and unhindered exposure to foreign trade and investment. The doctrine is championed by its beneficiaries in international business, embedded within the foundational documents of the International Monetary Fund and World Bank, and promoted in Latin America by the United States to such an extent that it plays a constitutive role in what has been dubbed the Washington Consensus (Williamson 1990). Throughout Latin America, neoliberal reform is a high politics cause. Anxieties over profit margins, desires to open new investment opportunities, growing concerns over economic contagion, and the clear tie between economic expansion and national interests ensure that foreign actors remain intensely involved in economic reform efforts throughout the hemisphere.

The capacity of the international in this issue is awesome. Whether through private foreign direct or portfolio investment to supplement inadequate domestic ventures, verbal expressions of support from outside countries to instill investor confidence, the establishment of trading and investment agreements to open new markets, bilateral arrangements sympathetic to the developmental needs of Third World countries, or the willingness of IFIs to extend loans when needed and free of burdensome conditions, the international arena must be considered when evaluating the prospects for neoliberal reform in developing countries. While current scholarship lucidly addresses the structure of this dependency, how its process, coordination, and character contribute to reform success or failure has yet to be successfully incorporated into a broader theoretical framework of foreign and domestic influences.[1]

The interesting questions surrounding this issue arise as we move away from questions of capacity and focus more squarely on motivations. It is true that the gains to business, aspirations of the U.S. government, and mandates of international financial institutions stand unambiguous and united on neoliberal reform in general, while discrepancies emerge as these actors deliberate whether to support the reform efforts of particular countries. For international business, each Latin American country may hold potential profits, but differences in investment opportunities, natural resources, market size, growth potential, standing investments, and other financial considerations clearly make some countries more attractive than others. For the U.S. government, greater access to the emerging markets of the South furnishes new opportunities, and integration in the hemisphere further solidifies the hegemon's leadership position. But economic relations rest within a web of foreign policy concerns, many of which may conflict with efforts to deepen economic relations. A hegemon can afford to use economic relations as both the carrot and the stick, and Washington may simply deem certain countries negligible, ignoring them altogether. Finally, while international financial institutions profess a steadfast commitment to neoliberalism, the combination of government and business pressure along with the rigors of standard operating procedures ensure that they too exhibit distinct and varied motivations across countries. Moreover, where the IMF finds itself less hindered by business and U.S. pressure, it is able to advance its own interests.

The divergent motivations of these three actors—business, government, and IFIs—ensure a steady stream of foreign influence throughout the region, as well as unique combinations of outside involvement from country to country. Though the United States has the wherewithal to rally support in the international for any given country, often it prefers not to, or is reluctant, due to political differences or global priorities, which tend to discount the region's significance. But transnational corporations and international financial institutions can move in to represent the international and sometimes even adjust Washington's focus. Indeed, because the United States and private business are so integral to international support and successful neoliberal reform, crisis becomes almost inevitable when they are inattentive and this heightens IMF participation. In certain countries, U.S. inadvertency can be reversed as private investors create economic linkages that modify the national interest, or as extensive IMF activity compels U.S. immersion as the cardinal decision maker in this organization. All told, Latin American countries find it difficult to avoid international influence as they embark upon neoliberal reform; nonetheless, the blend of foreign engagement can differ drastically from country to country.[2]

Whatever the makeup of the international, its weight is not significantly diminished by the principle of sovereignty. As a matter of fact, Latin American politicians eager to implement neoliberal reform for their own benefit have eased international engagement. These leaders used market-based reforms to dislodge entrenched economic interests and to open electoral niches (Remmer 1998; Armijo and Faucher 2002). And insofar as neoliberal reform promises a remedy to deep-seated economic malaise, many Latin American societies have been willing to bear the costs of economic change (Weyland 2002). But no matter the domestic origins of neoliberal policy initiation, political leaders find that its ultimate success relies on backing from the outside. And with foreign involvement comes foreign influence—influence that burgeons as reforms encourage investment, dependencies on new markets and financial flows intensify, and episodic crises deepen IMF engagement. Sovereignty proves no match for the march of self-interests that constitutes both sides of the foreign-domestic balance on this issue. Indeed, should political leaders reconsider the neoliberal turn, they find little relief from evolving legal principles in international economics. Dispute settlement mechanisms in the WTO and regional arrangements, agreements on trade and investment rights, and the bylaws for IMF superintendence all tilt the balance away from national autonomy. The neoliberal path is a steep decline for developing countries; once the first few steps are taken, control over the stride and tempo is easily lost.

To grasp the permutations of the international on this economic issue, we focus on foreign support for neoliberal reform efforts already underway. That some countries find themselves graced with international assistance while others must clamor for attention is undeniable. But clearly, rewarding the devotion to economic principles is not the driving force behind foreign decision making. If it were, one could reasonably expect international backing to fluctuate with neoliberal policy compliance and stability; the evidence, however, indicates otherwise. We propose that certain states, due to their market draw or political utility to powerful states, gain support beyond what their policy compliance and stability would predict. The existence of these "privileged states" is not inconsequential to reform efforts in neighboring states. As privileged countries garner more international support, less remains for others, and their prospects for neoliberal consolidation diminish in tandem. Also, because privileged states receive such attention, investors have come to expect periodic expressions of confidence from foreign governments and IFIs. When none is forthcoming, a state will be regarded as less desirable, irrespective of its conformity to neoliberalism. The net result is that nonprivileged states may in fact find themselves receiving less investment than their policy compliance and stability would otherwise predict.

But who decides which states are advantaged and which are to be left in the shadows? Private businesses, IFIs, and powerful foreign governments (primarily, but not exclusively, represented by the United States in the case of Latin America) bring different interests to the table, and none of them alone can set the course of international influence. How foreign actors coordinate their goals (or fail to do so), how they persuade each other to rally in defense of one country or another, and the effects of incomplete assistance are crucial elements to consider in assessing international sustenance of neoliberal reform. This study affirms how the valuable metaphor of a "foreign-domestic balance" of influence cannot be used to presume unity in thought, motivation, or strategy on the part of the international. Even where the international hovers formidably, as it does in the high politics realm of economics, this potency may mask underlying coordination difficulties and distinctive motivations.

An analysis of international championing of neoliberal reform, with emphasis on the impact of market draw, political utility, and coordination, resolves extant puzzles surrounding the role of the international in the neoliberal experiences of Brazil, Chile, and Argentina. Despite lower levels of policy compliance and stability in Brazil than in Argentina through the 1990s, market draw allowed Brazil to accrue more foreign backing. And while a compliant, stable Chile seems to confirm a straightforward policy-based model, the argument presented here affirms that political factors also matter. That country easily falls from Washington's view as other, more important nations come into focus. But pull factors are also at work—Chile spotlights the gains to be had by conformity with the Washington Consensus and represents a chip as the United States confronts the bargaining power held by the Brazilian-led Mercosur coalition, which covets full Chilean membership for its own purposes. Argentina, lacking the market opportunities of Brazil and political utility of Chile, finds itself in an unfortunate position. Despite considerable showings of neoliberal concurrence, international support for the country falls behind the levels secured by its neighbors. Indeed, strategic calculations raise the possibility that the United States saw Argentine economic failure as opportune, insofar as its decline tore at the fabric of Mercosur and undermined Brazilian leverage in hemispheric free trade negotiations.[3]

The focus on coordination, and the mingling of economic and political interests, also illuminates important distinctions among the cases regarding the march of international neoliberal advocates from business, government, and IFIs. Over time, both Brazil and Chile receive attention from all three actors. But because economic interests prevail in the case of Brazil, while political neglect or even rivalry mark U.S. governmental behavior, private business takes the lead but finds it difficult to consistently gain Washington's ear. More often than not, she answers only in times of crisis, when Brazil's economic importance suddenly emerges in presidential press conferences and fears of contagion from the crash seem to arise from nowhere. Compare this to Chile, which lacks a critical mass of private investors but is politically useful to the United States as a showcase for the Washington Consensus and because of its allure to Mercosur. Here the U.S. government takes the lead role by spurring commercial interchange. While such expressions may be just as sporadic as the relationship with Brazil, engagement is not determined by crisis. Rather, Chile is captive to the vagaries of the U.S. global political agenda. The country is important by default. When other events and issues emerge, be they in China, the Middle East, or Iowa, Chile recedes to the background. Generally, we can characterize Chile as a case of U.S. policy *steering* while Brazil represents a case of U.S. policy *responsiveness*.

While economics is key for Brazil and politics for Chile, Argentina again stands apart. Here, U.S. policy could best be described as relatively *indifferent* to displays of compliance and pleas for assistance. As economic malaise deepened through the latter 1990s, the IMF, in accord with its mission as a lender of last resort, moved in to assist the country, although under strict conditionality due to the lack of concomitant support from private business and the United States. Indeed, without pressure from business or governments, the fund placed its own interests first and tried to use the Argentine case to prove its worth and legitimacy. Toward this end, the IMF backed policies that over time proved to be flawed, to exemplify its consistent standards, gambling that the country could ride out the storm. But because international support hinges on the conduct of all three parties, the IMF could only postpone (and may have even intensified) an economic crisis in Argentina. Lacking significant market draw and political utility, Argentina discovers that international support is, at best, piecemeal and imposes hurdles to neoliberal consolidation not found in Brazil or Chile.

External Actors, Neoliberal Reform, and Coordination

Neoliberal reform sets a country on a path of immediate costs, with only the prospect of long-term benefits resting over the horizon. Reductions in government subsidies and transfers stimulate political protest; the emphasis on economic efficiency infuriates those who witness the sacrifice of other values, such as equity, environmentalism, cultural protection, and national security. The relaxation of trade and investment markets opens exacting challenges for domestic businesses and competitive pressures, and labor reforms produce job losses and insecurities. In addition, foreign portfolio investment creates new financial vulnerabilities, greater access to imports contributes to trade imbalances, diminished capital controls open the door for flight, and structural unemployment grows as the country moves toward its comparative advantage, or at least away from an economic structure designed by government policy. It is thus not surprising that international advocacy in the form of financial assistance and low conditionality correlates with the sustainability of neoliberal reform (Remmer 1998). International sustenance gives governments greater flexibility to respond to such concerns and thus loosens the bindings of a strict orthodox approach to neoliberal reform.

From an analytical perspective, international advocacy should be viewed as a package distributed by private business, foreign states, and IFIs. Each contributes something different, yet all are necessary for successful change. Private businesses disseminate technology, underwrite research and development, generate exports, create jobs, cultivate labor skills, and extend the pool of investment capital. States communicate political support, which sows the seeds of confidence that is so important to private investors. More powerful states also help by drafting conciliatory trading arrangements and affirming commitments to aid the country should its economy slip. IFIs assist flexibility in neoliberal reform through low-conditionality lending, complimentary reports to promote investor confidence, and by being lenders of last resort.

In theory, these three actors mesh like pieces in a puzzle to form a triad of international influence over neoliberal policy. In practice, their initiatives and interactions are more complex and are even open to dispute, warranting further scrutiny. For example, in the case of Latin America, one might question the efficacy of IFIs as lenders of last resort in the face of mounting private investment flows through the 1990s. Pamela Starr (1999) documents how the tide of private investment has corroded the capacity of IFIs to offset instabilities threatened by capital flows (table 3.1).

The shifting mixture of capital flows holds real political consequences for economic reform efforts. For the IMF, these transformations can undercut its ability to coordinate relief efforts as it acts as a lender of last resort. In the 1980s private bank lending and official developmental assistance greatly outweighed the funds channeled through portfolio and foreign direct investment (FDI), which had the effect of limiting the number of significant foreign actors. According to Lorenzo Pérez, assistant director of the Western Hemisphere Department at the IMF: "In the 1980s you could go to New York, and call 10 banks—American, European, Japanese—maybe even 5 banks. And you sit down and say this country has problems, you are the main banks, you have to do something for them and we'll do something for them. Now you cannot do that because there are so many [investors]."[4] Privatization, the opening of stock markets to foreign capital, greater issuances of government bonds, and relaxation of capital controls had the dual effect of increasing the number of foreign investors while decreasing the ability to negotiate common strategies. Hence, in 2000, the use of IMF credit from the General Resources Account stood at $6.27 billion in Latin America, hardly enough to offset potential instabilities from the $61.6 billion in portfolio and foreign direct investment that year (the numbers for 1999 were $14.42 billion and $74.6 billion, respectively). Disbursements from the World

3.1. Capital Flows to Latin America (annual averages in billions of US$)

	1977–1982	1983–1989	1990–1996	1997–2000
Net Private Capital Inflows[a]	26.3	−16.6	44.4	52.4
Net Foreign Direct Investment	5.3	4.4	16.4	57.8
Net Portfolio Investment	1.6	−1.2	29.2	13.5
Bank Lending and Other Debt	19.4	−19.8	−1.2	−18.9
Official Flows	19.0	9.2	8.1	11.4

Sources: Data for 1977–1996 from IMF International Financial Statistics Yearbook, compiled in Starr (2000, 135). Additional 1997–2000 data from IMF International Financial Statistics Yearbook, compiled by the authors.
   a. Net foreign direct investment plus net portfolio investment plus bank lending and other debt.

Bank totaled $1.97 billion in 2000, and complete net financial flows with all multilateral institutions rested at -$6.7 billion (repayments on IMF debt produced a net negative sum) (World Bank 2002). Official developmental assistance, with numbers now hovering under $10 billion per year, indicate that government actions also hold little prospect for countering the growing tide of private flows.

But numbers can be deceptive, especially when removed from their dynamic context. In particular, though the relative decline of IMF and official flows may be stark, these channels may serve the purpose of triggering or stalling further investment. In fact, the IMF can claim that is more important today than it has ever been due to the surveillance function it performs: "When countries had fairly closed capital markets and weren't really drawing on external resources, in some ways getting this clean bill of health from the fund was much less important than it is now, when countries do have significant external financing needs because they're undergoing large public investment. So in some ways the fact that capital flows are much larger now than they were 10–15 years ago increases the importance of the fund surveillance."[5] Surveillance occurs most prominently through annual "article IV consultations," which send teams of IMF observers to borrowing countries to assess the implementation of recommended or binding reforms. To enhance this surveillance mission, the IMF has increasingly pushed countries to publish the complete staff reports of these consultations.[6] Among the countries studied here, only Brazil remains reluctant.

IMF signals its approval or disapproval via the scrutiny of performance. This role stands as a reasonable reply to those who see IMF influence as drowning in the deluge of alternative private finance. The only problem is that scholars have had great difficulty identifying this signaling function in practice, however reasonable it appears to be in theory. Analyses at both the aggregate and case study level show little support for the presumed catalytic effect of IMF actions on further private investment (indeed, many studies show net losses, as IMF money is used to repay existing debt), though there is some corroboration for its impact on bilateral and multilateral public sources (Bird, Mori, and Rowlands 2000; Bird and Rowlands 2002). And on the basic economic impact of IMF agreements, scholars have found only scant evidence of positive economic gains, and some studies find correlation between IMF deals and economic losses (Przeworski and Vreeland 2000; Vreeland 2003). One advantage, however narrow, is that the adoption of an IMF program does seem to be associated with concessionary debt rescheduling (Marchesi 2003).

While an agreement with the IMF may not guarantee economic prosperity, this is not enough to diminish the weight we accord to the fund as a foreign actor. At the very least, in countries suffering from economic malaise IMF packages satisfy the short-term interests of political leaders with the momentary relief offered by additional official flows and debt rescheduling. But what is most important to our study is that Latin American governments continue to behave *as if* IMF funding remains salient to economic development and the advancement of neoliberal reform, even when eclipsed by private flows and regardless of their actual catalytic or long-term impact.

The IMF's continued significance must be noted because IMF negotiations themselves should grow more politically charged and caustic, largely as an unintended consequence of two efficiency reforms gradually instituted since the late 1990s and officially adopted in September 2002. One policy change is "streamlined conditionality," or a paring down in the number of structural benchmarks listed in a conditionality agreement, so that only its most critical components remain. In the past, countries might have completed only twenty-six of thirty benchmarks and still received a passing grade. The IMF found it politically difficult to sanction a country that could claim success on the vast majority of its conditionality benchmarks. But all too often those goals left unachieved were among the most crucial. The other policy change deals with the notion of program "ownership," which calls for governments to propose their own bases for conditionality. In a clear reaction to growing criticisms of IMF intrusiveness, the idea is to have the agreements "produced by the government rather than imposed by the fund."[7]

While the changes may advance efficiency aims, they can also be expected to agitate debate and deepen divisions within borrowing countries. Streamlined conditionality, irrespective of the longer-term performance gains expected by IMF officials, heightens the demand that the most politically and economically costly measures be implemented. Ownership, by placing the burden of proposal creation on borrowing countries, denies political leaders the scapegoat strategy of pointing to IMF imposition to separate themselves from the implementation of deleterious measures and thereby deter political protest (Vreeland 1999). Latin American societies will now more likely view their political leaders as complicit engineers of austerity, rather than reluctant victims of IMF demands.

Just as the IMF remains a significant actor in the world arena in the face of expanding private interests, so too do governments. Though many pundits see state capacity and autonomy being choked by the vagaries of globalization, Robert Gilpin notes that governments remain formidable insofar as they "constitute the necessary political foundations for a stable and unified world economy" (2000, 13). They draft the rules and sit on the governing boards of international economic organizations, they assuage domestic protest through distributive policies as economies open to greater competitive pressures, and their public pronouncements calm and sway millions of investment decisions each day. They impose a semblance of order on what would otherwise be a chaotic, unstable, and ultimately doomed process of globalization.

For Latin America, U.S. hegemony remains a reality. As Heraldo Muñoz (2001) argues, growing official assistance from other powerful states such as Japan, mounting private capital flows, and trade and investment linkages that now branch far beyond the Western Hemisphere have undoubtedly shortened the long shadow cast by Washington. But the ebb in its relative influence has done little to undercut the daunting position held by the United States in the pecking order of outside actors. General economic trade and investment dependencies show that Latin America needs the United States much more than the United States needs Latin America. As illustrated in table 3.2, Latin America, excluding Mexico, looks to the United States for 21.7 percent of its exports, while the United States in turn sends just 7.9 percent of its total exports to the region minus Mexico. The differences are yet more humbling for Argentina, Brazil, and Chile individually. To compound the situation, Latin America finds that this "asymmetrical significance" also holds in its relations with Japan and Europe, which gravely attenuates Pollyannaish strategies of playing off regions against each other (Smith 2000, 341–44).

A final question concerning international actors deals with the autonomy of the IMF. Is the organization a mere puppet of the United States and international business, and thus undeserving of independent status in a model of foreign influence? With nearly 18 percent of the fund's vote, the United States enjoys a hefty decision-making advantage,[8] and the location of the IMF in Washington, D.C., eases lobbying efforts and opens ample staffing opportunities for U.S. personnel, further broadening what Jagdish Bhagwati (1998) tagged the "Wall Street-Treasury Complex." Are the Dependistas correct in their view that the foreign is but a monolithic actor? After all, Tony Killick (1995) found a statistical association between IMF loans and reversals in private capital flows, suggesting that it regularly bails out international capital interests.

3.2. Trade between the United States and Latin America as a Percentage
of All Exports for 2001

	Exports to:	Exports from:				
	United States	Argentina	Brazil	Chile	Latin America	Latin America except Mexico
United States	—	0.5	2.2	0.4	21.8	7.9
Argentina	10.9	—	—	—	—	—
Brazil	24.7	—	—	—	—	—
Chile	18.5	—	—	—	—	—
Latin America	59.0	—	—	—	—	—
Latin America except Mexico	21.7	—	—	—	—	—

Source: *Direction of Trade Statistics Yearbook* (2002).

While U.S. and private financial influences cannot be denied (see Thacker 1999; Gould 2003; Stiglitz 2002), both must contend with the formidable inertia of a large-scale bureaucratic organization, which ought not to be taken lightly. Even as the Third World came into its own, and through the course of oil shocks, stagflation, and debt and currency crises, the IMF has remained surprisingly dedicated to the core of its original mission (Joseph 2000). Due to the technical nature of conditionality agreements and surveillance, the IMF remains a staff-driven institution. The Executive Board allows select member states considerable oversight, but expertise is clearly weighted toward the bureaucracy, giving it significant leverage (Woods 2001, 87–88). Ultimately, this inertia loads the deck in favor of action when called for by IMF standard operating procedures and helps to explain why, for example, Argentina secured assistance in 2001 (however contingent) even in the face of U.S. reticence. In the end, states can do more to steer IMF favoritism when it engages than to deter the organization from imposing its procedural standards of involvement when requested by member states. And while private financiers may influence lending levels and the contours of conditionality, their impact on the decision itself to grant assistance is more circumspect. General studies that seek systemic, determinative political influences on IMF behavior have been, and are likely to remain, inconclusive, because politics tends to manifest itself differently from case to case (Bird 2001). Only a nuanced analysis that goes beyond political pressures and economic interests and comes to terms with institutional fortitude can accurately capture the fund's singular role and rightfully identify how it combines with powerful states and companies to form a triad of international influence over neoliberal reform efforts.

Policy Compliance and Stability in Argentina, Brazil, and Chile

The United States, IMF, and international business embrace a common mission to promote neoliberalism worldwide. The United States espouses this mission as explicit policy, IFIs view free market capitalism as integral to economic development, and large-scale private businesses are obvious beneficiaries of open markets. One might therefore assume some correlation between international support and neoliberal policy compliance and stability in Argentina, Brazil, and Chile. But the evidence indicates otherwise. Efforts by scholars to index neoliberal reform in Latin American countries illustrate the disconnect. The widely cited study by Samuel Morley, Robert Machado, and Stefano Pettinato (1999) quantifies trade reform, financial liberalization (both domestic and international), tax reform, and privatization and places countries on a scale from 0 to 1.0. The "general reform index" gives the average of these five scores. Tables 3.3 and 3.4 extract the most recent (1995) data from the study to indicate the relative standings of Argentina, Brazil, and Chile among the seventeen total countries examined. The data clearly portray Argentina and Chile as having progressed

3.3. General Reform Index (1995)

Uruguay	.891	Bolivia	.816
Argentina	**.888**	Mexico	.807
El Salvador	.872	**Brazil**	**.805**
Dominican Republic	.862	Ecuador	.801
Costa Rica	.847	Colombia	.792
Peru	.845	Honduras	.780
Chile	**.843**	Jamaica	.767
Guatemala	.838	Venezuela	.667
Paraguay	.834		

Source: Morley, Machado, and Pettinato (1999).

3.4. Structural Reform Categories and Scores for Chile, Argentina, and Brazil, 1995 (rankings in parentheses)

	Commercial	Financial	Capital	Privatization	Tax	Avg. Rank
Argentina	.934 (13)	.986 (1)	.986 (3)	1.00 (1)	.534 (10)	5.6
Chile	.984 (2)	.983 (2)	.745 (15)	.840 (7)	.663 (4)	6.0
Brazil	.930 (14)	.971 (5)	.639 (17)	.813 (9)	.674 (3)	9.6

Source: Morley, Machado, and Pettinato (1999)

3.5. Readiness Indicators

	2001 Rank	Readiness Indicators	1994 Rank	Readiness Indicators	Rank Difference 1994–2001
Chile	2	4.30	1	4.13	−1
Argentina	7	3.84	7	3.59	0
Brazil	22	3.14	14	3.38	−8

Source: Schott (2001).

further than Brazil in structural reform. Table 3.4 lists the scores and rankings for the three countries in each of the categories examined.

Data from a study by Jeffrey Schott (2001) also reveal the distance between Argentina and Chile on one hand, and Brazil on the other. Schott gathered data on price stability, budget discipline, national savings, external debt, currency stability, market-oriented policies, reliance on trade taxes, and policy sustainability and scored countries on a scale from 1 to 5. His interest is the readiness of Latin American economies for entry into the anticipated 2005 Free Trade Areas of the Americas (FTAA), hence the label "readiness indicators." As illustrated in table 3.5, from 1994 to 2001 Chile and Argentina retained their high positions in the rankings among the thirty-two eligible Latin American countries, while Brazil actually fell into the lower half of the scale.

Also of note in the Schott study is his measure of policy sustainability. This indicator measures "the ability of the domestic political process to allocate the gains from trade so as to maintain support for economic reforms" (2001, 18). It uses data (not shown in table form here) from Freedom House rankings and the Human Development Index and in doing so provides a gauge of political reform

3.6. Indicators of Investment Climate in Argentina, Brazil, and Chile

	Unofficial Economy (% of GDP)	Regulation[a]	Bureaucratic Quality[b]	Rule of Law[c]	Property Rights[d]	Corruption[e] (1996/2000)
Argentina	21.8	2	3	4.06	2	2.81 / 3.5
Brazil	37.8	3	4	3.38	3	3.56 / 4.0
Chile	18.2	2	3.13	4.44	1	6.05 / 7.5

Sources: Unofficial economy as % of GDP: Loayza (1996)
Regulation: Johnson and Sheehy (1997)
Bureaucratic quality: Political Risk Services (1997)
Rule of law: Political Risk Services (1997)
Property rights: Johnson and Sheehy (1997)
Corruption: Transparency International (1997, 2001)
   Note: These measures were collected from the database created in Johnson et al. (1998)
   a. Scored 1–5, higher score indicates "less free"
   b. Scored 0–6, higher score indicates greater autonomy from political pressures; score is average over 1990–1996 period
   c. Scored 0–6, higher score indicates stronger rule of law; score is 1990–1996 average
   d. Scored 0–5, higher value indicates lower property rights
   e. Scored 1–10, higher score means freer

and social development. Progress in these areas emerged as key concerns for policy makers in the United States and IFIs in the post–Cold War era. But here again we find Brazil, with its 2001 score of 3.13, far behind Argentina (3.88) and Chile (4.00).

Further indicators that one might expect to influence international support are listed in table 3.6. Here, Chile leads the pack, and while Brazil does score better than Argentina on measures of bureaucratic quality and corruption, its lower marks on the remaining indicators make it difficult to argue that the investment climate was any more hospitable than that provided by Argentina. Indeed, comprehensive measures of economic freedom from the Fraser Institute, a conservative think tank, scored Argentina at 8.4 (ranked 12th in the world), Chile 8.2 (ranked 18th in the world), and Brazil at a distant 5.9 (ranked 85th in the world) (Gwartney and Lawson 2001).

All told, the data would lead one to expect more international backing for Argentina and Chile, and a more cautioned approach to Brazil, if principled adherence to economic policy guided the decisions of international actors. But as detailed in the case studies, events have proved otherwise. Private business marched unabated to Brazil through the 1990s, lured by its massive market and rich bounty in resources, despite a neoliberal path cluttered with reversals and curtailments, and a hallmark economic plan (the *Real* Plan) that found little initial support in the United States and IMF (Kearney 2001). And when crisis hit the country in 1998–1999, the United States and IMF readily extended support, even as Brazil experimented with its own policy approaches. This support stands in stark contrast to Argentina, which found heavy conditionality levied upon it throughout the 1990s even as it aggressively pursued "by the book" neoliberal reform. In 1995–1996, the country received tepid support as it worked its way through a recession, and after economic stagnation reemerged in 1998, critical comments from the United States undermined investor confidence, while IMF support came only after bitter bargaining. The draw of neoliberal reform seems strongest in the Chilean case, a country that remains a magnet for foreign investment. But political factors should not be overlooked. Outside Mexico, no country within the hemisphere has received greater attention from the United States, which has gone to great lengths to portray Chile as a model of neoliberal reform and an unquestionable success story. The country was targeted as the next North American Free Trade Agreement (NAFTA) member, and U.S. negotiators worked eagerly to promote and ultimately pass the U.S.-Chile Free Trade Agreement. But Chile's importance waxes and wanes as U.S. foreign policy shifts, confirming that economic factors tell only part of the story.

This first cut on the relationship between neoliberal reform and international support exposes a number of puzzles. Why has international support been so forthcoming for Brazil, but so timid for Argentina, where reform began earlier and proceeded further? Recognizing that advances in neoliberal reform alone are insufficient explanations, why has Chile assumed so prominent a position in U.S. policy? And finally, if international support depends upon participation from states, IFIs, and private businesses, how do these actors coordinate their efforts, and what happens when support is extended incompletely? With explanations based on policy compliance and stability found wanting, we revisit theory for further guidance.

Market Draw and Political Utility

If the commitment to economic principles by itself fails to explain international sustenance for neoliberal reform, what is missing? As a high politics issue saturated by self-interested motivations, economics offers no surprise that narrow profit opportunities and political objectives play a role. To grasp these other dimensions of foreign impulse, we refer to market draw and political utility. These factors are key to understanding the variations in external support for Argentina, Brazil, and Chile because the three countries possess distinct blends of relevance to outside actors in terms of these two variables.

Market draw refers to the range and depth of investment opportunities a country has to offer. The concept is, in large part, a proxy for the enticements of factor endowments. The larger a country's population, the greater its diversity of resources, and the more lucrative its array of investment opportunities, the more attractive it will be to private business (Agarwal 1980; Schneider and Frey 1985). The lure of market draw has come into question of late, as analysts theorize on the impact of globalization. John Dunning (1999) argues that greater access has led business to move from resource- and market-seeking strategies to efficiency-seeking strategies that pay greater attention to investment climates. Ari Kokko (2002) adds that new production strategies wrought by telecommunications and information technology have allowed smaller countries to compete for investment as never before.

But, apparently, the zeal to theorize on novel ramifications of globalization has outpaced the actual impact of globalization. In their survey of empirical analyses of FDI determinants, Peter Nunnenkamp and Julius Spatz (2002) find a near consensus on the significance of traditional market-based factors such as GDP, population, and access to natural resources. Moreover, their own analysis of twenty-eight developing countries over the past two decades indicates that "surprisingly little has changed so far: traditional market related determinants are still dominant" and "the notion that trade policy has increasingly shaped the distribution of FDI among developing countries finds little empirical support" (2002, 26–27). Joaquín Vial agrees in his study of capital flows to the Andean countries, noting that among the numerous determinants of foreign investment, "distance from corporate headquarters and size of end market amply dominate all other hypotheses" (2002, 13).

Why do businesses not reward strident neoliberal reform with investment flows? One might expect private capital to support those who open new markets and investment opportunities. The puzzle exists only so long as one envisions international business as an indivisible, unitary actor. But protectionist walls divide firms between those on the outside and those who profit from, and may even grow desperately dependent upon, market barriers. It may not seem rational for all privately owned firms to increase investment in a state reluctant to initiate neoliberal reform, but the decision to invest by any one business able to secure a position behind the wall often is. As a matter of principle, corporations favor open markets, but as a guide to action, business is driven by profit. Restricted markets may reduce these prospects for international business as a whole, though some opportunities remain. They do attract investors, and companies already benefiting from protection continue to enjoy their status. For countries with market draw, the relative opportunity may be lower than for other smaller but more open economies, but the absolute opportunity makes for a greater flow of investment.

Once capital begins to flow from the private investor's home country, political implications follow as new interstate linkages emerge or existing relationships deepen. Contrary to globalization theorists eager to pronounce the death of politics (e.g., Kindleberger 1969; Ohmae 1995), the state does not stand by passively as trade and investment intensify. Robert Wade is correct when he notes, "the world economy is more international than global" (1996, 61; also see Weiss 1998). With more and more economic ventures and relationships, pressure grows on businesses' home governments to advance the economic well-being of the host country. Clearly, powerful companies will lobby their governments to protect their investments. But beyond the narrow interests of any one MNC, the state begins to promote concessionary lending and favorable trade agreements, sensing its own stake in the host country's economic future, as investment and trade pathways grow more crowded. The state goes to bat for itself ("the national interest"), with individual businesses auspiciously placed in scoring position. Herd effects further intensify the relationship, as savvy investors anticipate state action. In this way, individual profit seeking, interest group pressure, state interests, and herd effects conspire to ensure that powerful, capitalist states support countries for reasons other than their advances in market reform.

Whereas market draw entails a process by which business leads and government follows, political utility reverses the sequence. As Albert Hirschman (1945) noted long ago, economic exchange is embedded within the matrix of national power relations. More to the point of U.S. power and the global web of investment, Gilpin holds that "the multinational corporation has prospered because it has been dependent on the power of, and consistent with the political interests of, the United States" (1975, 41). While we need not presume absolute control, we can reasonably argue that governments, in pursuit of their own national interests, actively steer business decisions with investment and trade incentives. If a country holds significant value to a state's hegemonic designs, that state will readily express its support by aiding the country.

Government actions work as an insurance mechanism to cultivate business confidence. Investors know that not only will this increase the likelihood of conciliatory trading and investment relationships, but also that in the event of economic crisis, the state will be more likely to contribute to and coordinate support packages from international lending agencies and other countries. That powerful states will also use their potency to sway multilateral lending agencies is widely acknowledged. When asked to rank the criteria that determine the allocation of IMF packages, queried officials promptly placed the political significance of the country first, followed by commitment to reforms, and depth of the crisis.[9]

The impact of market allure and political utility attenuates the association between international support and principled commitments to neoliberal reform, and thereby hinders the ability of many third-world states to attract investors through policy choices. In this issue area, the domestic must heed the international as the country seeks economic assistance. Countries fancied for their political usefulness, but lacking in market attraction, reap the rewards of a steering policy. Expressions of confidence by hegemonic states and the granting of conciliatory economic arrangements deliver a boon to these countries and foster an amicable relationship so long as the country proves functional to political designs.

Those countries set apart by market allure, but lacking in political usefulness, receive different treatment, one where the hegemon is reactive, not proactive. Due to their combined market attractiveness and status as a subregional power, these countries may in fact rival the great power at the regional level and may be more prone to experiment with policy choices unfavorable to the hegemon. Despite the political tension, the powerful state may be induced to support the market-endowed country due to investment patterns carved out by private business. Politics and economics face off in their classic dual. The hegemon is poorly motivated to back the subregional power that is politically less useful and a potential rival. Yet, when economic crisis hits, the scale is tipped toward economics—business lobbyists marshal their forces and the state yields to the yoke of its economic relations.

A policy of indifference stems from the absence of political utility and market attraction. On a regular basis, the great power sees no compelling economic or political reason to support such countries, nor does it receive significant pressure from business to do so. This disregard leaves international influence to the IFIs, and more specifically the IMF, which is hardly induced to act creatively or with conciliation as it addresses the economic crisis. Here the fund advances its own interests first, due to the lack of immediate pressure from government and business.

The Extension of International Support

The experiences of Argentina, Brazil, and Chile with international support through the 1990s corroborate the arguments outlined in this study. Each country represents a different combination of market allure and political utility. It is duly noted that the model fashioned above was done so with ideal types in mind and that the countries in this study do not represent ideals. The cases were selected for their comparative characteristics (their alikeness situates them well for most similar systems research designs) and their contribution to the literature on Latin America. While it would be folly to argue that Argentina has no market allure, it rests below a threshold of importance to the United States, such that depicting it as a low market draw does make sense. Likewise, while Argentina and Brazil have some strategic value to the United States, Chile has more due to its position between the United States and Brazil as the movement toward a Free Trade Area of the Americas progressed through the 1990s, and because of its status as exemplar for the Washington Consensus. The term political utility should not be confused with political importance. Finally, while we characterize Brazil as further behind neoliberal reform than Argentina and Chile, this does not diminish the great strides achieved by that country (Kingstone 1999). It is the country's high ratio of international support to level of neoliberal reform when compared to Argentina and Chilean rations that drives our inquiry.

Brazil and Responsive U.S. Policy

In terms of economic stature, Brazil is the giant of Latin America. Its position as the largest recipient of FDI flows in Latin America was attained in 1996, when it surpassed Mexico. Its 1999 GDP represented 38 percent of the total for the nineteen countries of mainland Latin America. Mexico followed at 24 percent;

then Argentina, 14.5 percent; and Colombia, 5 percent. Also in 1999, the country accounted for 38 percent of all gross capital formation in Latin America and 36 percent of all income paid to the rest of the world by the region.[10]

Politically, the country has traditionally portrayed itself as a subregional rival to the United States, making it less politically attractive to Washington. The transition to democracy in 1985 and the eventual move toward neoliberalism by Brazil seemed to augur more harmonious relations, but proposals for a regional free trade agreement in the 1990s ensured that the issue of regional hegemony would remain lively, especially as Brazil promoted its own regional scheme in Mercosur or a broader South American Free Trade Area (Soares de Lima 1999). Brazil cannot coerce the United States and impose its own economic designs on the region, but it does hold some leverage of consequence. The country's economic size makes its membership in a hemispheric arrangement vital to the integrity of any agreement, and its paramount role in Mercosur allows it to exert leadership in South America (Hakim 2002).

Yet, the notion of subregional rivalry is ultimately a one-sided affair. In reality, neglect is the more enduring quality of the political relationship with Brazil cultivated by the United States. While this may represent an underhanded strategy to dampen competitive aspirations, more likely it is emblematic of Washington's historic approach to all of Latin America as a backyard—the region has always been subsidiary to events and issues far afield.

So how has Brazil's high market draw but low political utility shaped the nature of economic support from the outside? Brazil represents a good case of business interests leading U.S. policy. In day-to-day affairs, the country holds little currency in Washington policy circles. Its legacy of underdevelopment lowers its prestige, and politically it acts as the France of Latin America. But market allure matters. An economic structure of growing investment linkages ensures that Brazil receives occasional nods of attention, however late and sporadic. Such instances surface when economic crises hit the country and U.S. business interests prod Washington to protect their investments. U.S. officials then feel compelled to act, even in the midst of political or economic policy differences. A brief survey of Brazilian crises, economic policy choices, and ensuing reactions in the international realm illustrates these dynamics. Whether it be commercial banks during the debt crisis, or the more diverse array of investors currently seated in the country, private business proves to be the critical foreign actor for Brazil. And while U.S. government support—increasingly through the IMF—invariably follows, Washington acts begrudgingly and is quick to retreat, expressing little appetite for a lasting relationship.

The 1980s is referred to as the "lost decade" for developing countries due to the ravaging impact of the debt crisis. Brazil was no exception. Under the 1964–1985 military regime, the country grew increasingly dependent on foreign savings to finance growth that was itself slowing. To curb this dependence and attendant debt service obligations, and in hopes of reversing a mounting trade deficit, the authoritarian government implemented strict adjustment policies as the decade opened. The consequent 4.4 percent decline in the 1981 GDP represented the first real negative movement in the economy since World War II. As the crisis deepened, Brazil looked to the IMF to roll over its debt, at the cost of severe austerity measures from 1981 to 1983. A slight recovery ensued in 1984 as power passed to a new democratic regime in 1985, but unemployment, inflationary pressures, and an external debt level ranging from 40 percent to 45 percent of GDP continued to haunt the Brazilian economy (Dinsmoor 1990).

Brazil's new government could not dispense austerity like its military predecessors. The new democracy's desire to maintain popular appeal probably sparked what would be a much more confrontational stance toward foreign creditors (von Doellinger 1995). The Cruzado Plan would be the first of several "nonorthodox" programs implemented from 1986 to 1991, to the chagrin of the IMF. These policies attempted to address inflation through various price freeze strategies and soften the blow for the popular sectors by leaving government spending and private consumption intact. They all failed miserably (Nazmi 1995). But the significance of these programs lies not in their failures, but in their demonstration of the kind of latitude Brazil enjoyed to experiment. Such is the boon of market draw. It seemed that foreign creditors could do little more than seethe from the sidelines as economic malaise threatened the repayment of their loans.

Events came to a head in February 1987, when President José Sarney declared a moratorium on interest payments to debt obligations to force rescheduling talks. In his study of the seventeen-month suspension, Howard Lehman (1993) documents how Brazilian leverage was able to offset the pull held by the banks and force a mutually agreeable settlement—one that saw favorable interest rate spreads for rollover debt and extensions on existing loans.[11] Just as important, he also illustrates the propensity of private business to speak for the international in concluding "banks were willing to cast aside the traditional linkage of an IMF austerity package with a new money accord in order to be repaid" (1993, 149).

The case was not atypical. Werner Baer, in his seminal study of the Brazilian economy, also recognizes how this country's crowded international avenues of lending and investment act as a two-way street: "there is an interest by these companies and creditors to keep the economy growing and to have it achieve a strong balance-of-payments position. This has been used by the Brazilian government to get favorable considerations in expanding its trade and obtaining new credits" (2001, 234). Indeed, though neoliberal principles found their way into Brazilian policies through the 1990s, officials remain adamant in their assertion that these were not imposed by the IMF or U.S. Treasury, nor drawn from a neoliberal conceptual framework. Rather, they were the product of experimentation by Brazilians themselves as they worked through different strategies to dampen inflation and jump-start growth.[12]

And the record backs up this claim. Though not obliged to adopt IMF dictates, but only to "consult with" the fund (Lehman 1993), the Sarney administration called for more orthodox policies through 1988 to combat inflation, did so half-heartedly, then retreated more plainly back to heterodoxy—in no small part due to Sarney's desire to curry favor as elections approached (Sola 1988). And by July 1989, Brazil reignited its defiant stance, when it imposed another moratorium on interest payments that would last to July 1991.

The appointment of Finance Minister Marcílio Marques Moreira in May 1991 during the administration of Fernando Collor de Mello (1990–1992) foretold a more enduring turn toward neoliberalism. His tenure ended the "confrontational phase" (von Doellinger 1995) of debt renegotiations with the completion of several agreements—a July 1991 understanding to end the moratorium and begin repayment on interest arrears; a $2.1 billion stand-by arrangement with the IMF in January 1992; and in July 1992, a $44 billion renegotiation of Brazil's entire foreign debt. Moreira also initiated substantial trade reform, the beginnings of a privatization program, a deregulation push, and economic policy that took a clear orthodox turn, though these policies proved so contentious and were implemented so imperiously by Collor that they spurred widespread alienation throughout Brazilian society (Weyland 1993).

Coming on the heels of Collor's experience, which included an impeachment on corruption charges, it is little wonder that President Itamar Franco decided to tread more lightly on the issue of economic reform, despite lingering inflation. In May 1993 the impetus for action fell to Franco's fourth finance minister in seven months, Fernando Henrique Cardoso, whose stewardship of government from the ministry was a secret to no one. Cardoso launched several austerity measures, though constitutional mandates on the budget stymied many. Before leaving the ministry in April 1994 to run for the presidency, Cardoso had his team draft the *Real* Plan to organize the attack on inflation and work through the constitutional hurdles (some of which were uprooted through constitutional reform). The economic package, implemented in July 1994, succeeded in the battle against prices, much to the satisfaction of Brazilian society. Because the plan became permanently tied to Cardoso's legacy in the Finance Ministry, it spiked his popularity and proved critical to his victory in the October 1994 presidential election.

Despite its triumph over inflation, the IMF and U.S. government did not embrace the program. Viewing with dismay Brazil's inflation, high interest rates, and a growing deficit, the IMF originally pushed its standard prescription of tight monetary policy—reduce spending and raise interest rates. Brazil took another route by stabilizing its currency with a peg to the dollar. The move brought international credibility to the Brazilian currency, dulled inflationary pressures, and dampened interest rates, which in turn reduced a government deficit largely driven by interest payments. Unable to ignore the success of the plan, the IMF and United States soon expressed lukewarm support.

The country did well from 1994 to 1996, but the plan demanded a daunting balancing act that simply could not be sustained in the long run (Cardoso 2000). In short, the peg to the dollar overvalued the currency, putting a damper on exports. So long as foreign investment marched to Brazil to finance the deficit, all was well. A privatization scheme, relaxed investment rules, and openings to portfolio investment sustained the strategy but just could not keep pace, as Brazilian exports grew less and less competitive. The cautious turn by international investors after the 1997 Asian currency crisis, and the sharper apprehension that followed the August 1998 Russian currency crisis, finally pulled the rug out from under this formula. The remedy seemed easy enough—devalue the *real*. This policy was pushed by the IMF as negotiations commenced over a crisis package to offset the Russian fiasco. But the stand to protect the peg found a strong proponent in Gustavo Franco, president of the Central Bank, who convinced the Cardoso government to stay the course. A crisis ensued as investors retreated, and Brasília was forced to repurchase *reais* as quickly as they were sold in order to maintain the peg. The Central Bank saw its foreign reserves plummet from $70 billion in July 1998 to $40 billion by November 1998.

It was in this setting that the United States marshaled a $41.5 billion IMF stabilization package. Though marketed by the Clinton administration as an anticipatory move to forestall contagion from the Asian and Russian crises, the action was anything but this. Economists had warned that the *real* was "dangerously overvalued" in late 1997; hence, by November 1998, "Brazil had been 'walking on razor's edge' for some time" (Ferreira and Tullio 2002).[13] The reality was that Washington had its sights elsewhere—on South Korea, on Russia, on China—as the crisis unfolded.

Aside from illustrating how the international so generously responds to countries with market allure, more specifically the November 1998 package underscored a change in the roles played by international actors in the case of Brazil. Previously, when the issue was debt repayment, commercial banks took the lead, as noted. But with new linkages in portfolio investment, substantial increases in foreign direct investment, and an increasingly globalized economy threatening contagion effects, the number and range of economic interests now promised classic collective action problems. Hence, it is no surprise that in the lead-in to the November 1998 package, the lobbying efforts exerted by U.S. banks to extend a supportive package were matched by their own reluctance to contribute.[14] While the banks hold significant stakes in Brazil, they understandably hesitate when asked to carry the load for the new multitude of economic actors, compelling the U.S. government, and ultimately the IMF, to take a stronger role—at the behest of the national economic interests. Shifting financial flows through the 1990s reveal this makeover in how the international addresses Brazil. In 1991 commercial banks extended 60.1 percent and the IMF 1.3 percent of all foreign credit to Brazil. By 1998, these numbers had recalibrated to 29.9 percent and 21.6 percent, respectively (Baer 2001, 233).

Fortunately, Brazil was able to work its way through the crisis, though typically enough to the beat of its own rhythm. The November 1998 Letter of Intent signed at the IMF implied a commitment to the peg as the fund relented to Brazil's position. But continued selling and the move by Itamar Franco, now governor of Minas Gerais, a Brazilian state, to declare a moratorium on internal debt ensured that the crisis would continue. In response, Brazil made a unilateral decision to abandon the peg in mid-January. Though the United States and IMF felt betrayed, knowing that extended criticism would threaten recovery, their condemnations were short-lived.[15] Moreover, Brazil atoned for the transgression by meeting fiscal adjustment targets, tightening monetary policy to control inflation, and achieving a surprising recovery that allowed the country to make early repayments in 2000. But the United States has remained detached and continues to enter the fray only when crisis calls. A 2001 sell-off of the *real* due to the Argentine crisis, and another as jittery investors pondered the impact of Lula's election in October 2002, were met by additional IMF packages of $15.5 billion and $30 billion, respectively.

The aid comes, despite a swelling external debt that rivals levels seen in the 1980s and a current account deficit that keeps the country vulnerable to capital flight. Officials from Brazil, the IMF, and the U.S. Treasury champion Brazil's ability to meet, and even surpass, primary budget surplus (government expenditures *less* payments on the debt) targets set by the IMF, but some analysts wonder if they are doing little more than rearranging the deck chairs on the *Titanic*. John Williamson (2002) argues that solvency remains feasible so long as Brazil retains its primary budget surplus target at 3.75 percent. But Mark Weisbrot and Dean Baker (2002) note that such calculations rest on lofty assumptions, such as an average real interest rate of 9.2 percent (the eight-year average is 16.1 percent, and 2002 saw interest rates of over 21 percent), a growth rate of 4 percent (the eight-year average is 3 percent), and a *real* that rises 1.5 percent annually against the dollar.[16] Pessimistic analyses are also found in the press. In August 2002, the *Financial Times* reported, "some economists have begun to argue that Brazil's debt burden is unsustainable at current rates."[17] Still, Washington is all too eager to give Brazil a passing grade and move on with little thought for longer-term solutions. A case in point is the hemispheric free trade negotiations, which could aid Brazilian exports, yet remain mired in debate.

Indeed, after a decade of neoliberalism, and the recent spate of U.S.-engineered emergency packages, one might expect warmer, more sustained relations between Brazil and the United States on the issue of free trade. But with Washington only periodically expressing its good graces, Brazil sees no reason to shoulder the onus of cultivating relations to the detriment of its own interests. At the 2001 Summit of the Americas, an event soaked in the spirit of cooperation, Cardoso surprised many with his frank assessment of ongoing hemispheric trade talks in his keynote address:

A Free Trade Area of the Americas is welcome if its creation is a step toward providing access to more dynamic markets; if it indeed leads to common antidumping rules; if it reduces nontariff barriers; if it prevents the protectionist distortion of sound sanitary norms; and if, while protecting intellectual property, it also furthers the technological capabilities of our people; and also if it goes beyond the Uruguay Round to redress the inequalities resulting from those negotiations, particularly with regard to agriculture. Otherwise, it would be irrelevant or, worse, undesirable.[18]

Brazilian officials interviewed repeated this pessimistic tone as they explained the depth of the differences between the two countries. Trade disputes are not simply a matter of protected industries in each country. If this were the case, horse trading could alleviate tensions. Rather, the points of friction are "more normative in nature," enmeshed in fundamentally opposed views on dispute settlement mechanisms, countervailing duties, subsidies, and dumping allegations.[19] And insofar as particular protected industries do move into the limelight, it just so happens that Brazil's most competitive exports threaten some of the strongest sectoral lobbies in the United States—oranges, sugar, textiles, and grains.[20] Divisions remain and they are unlikely to go away, especially with the ascent of Workers' Party candidate Luiz Inácio Lula da Silva to the presidency. While Lula has made clear moves to calm international markets, he is just as steadfast in his defense of Brazilian national interests and his own progressive agenda. When Lula's government organized a defiant coalition of developing states at the September 2003 WTO meeting in Cancun and refused to toe the line in discussions with the United States leading to the November 2003 Free Trade Area of the Americas meeting in Miami, it was simply placing greater resolve behind customary Brazilian foreign policy.

But, oddly enough, the United States continues to show its support for Brazil, albeit in sporadic, belated fashion, showing no real desire to establish a lasting interchange so that problems could be headed off before they reach the crisis stage. This relationship can only be explained with reference to the combination of political irrelevance and economic import held by Brazil. Particular bureaucratic linkages between the countries that shift as Brazil moves from stability to crisis buttress the consequent responsive policy. More precisely, on a daily basis, the Ministry of Foreign Relations, Itamaraty, represents Brazil (the ministry even holds full responsibility for negotiating trade relations). Itamaraty has long been recognized as a repository of the Brazilian intelligentsia, fierce in nationalism and circumspect toward U.S. proposals. Luiz Carlos Bresser-Pereira, who as finance minister in 1987 jostled with Itamaraty's cold reaction to U.S. free trade initiatives, opined critically, "Itamaraty does not understand the new times and dismisses U.S. integration because of old nationalist and developmentalist ghosts" (1996, 203). The routine interlocutor for the United States should be the State

Department, but the fact is, the State Department has little regard for Latin American affairs, let alone Brazil. Its concerns rest more squarely in Europe, the Middle East, Russia, and China. Hence, in normal everyday affairs, Brazilian nationalism is met by neglect from the United States.

But things change dramatically when economic crisis hits. Itamaraty stands aside as the Finance Ministry and Central Bank come to the fore to negotiate and are met by their counterparts in the U.S. Treasury and IMF. Unlike the nationalist intellectuals of Itamaraty, technocrats staff these Brazilian institutions, and many hold close personal relations in Washington, D.C., or an Ivy League background. Conditions are tailor-made for amity. But crisis management tends to be short, and as the finance officials go their separate ways, so too does the spirit of harmony. These, then, are the machinations behind the on-again-off-again tendency in U.S.-Brazilian relations.[21] Politics, be it the politics of neglect or rivalry, keep economic interests at bay—most of the time. Like a sleeping giant, the U.S. government must be rousted from its dreamy state. And when this happens, Washington responds with vigor, suddenly conscious of its surroundings. But the giant tires easily and once again slumbers as the crisis dissipates, only to reawaken when the next calamity transpires. A queried economic counselor in the Brazilian Embassy captured the essence of the responsive policy approach: "Brazil will be surveyed so as to not provide the fulcrum of the next crisis, but that is all."[22]

Chile and Steering U.S. Policy

Chile plays a unique role in U.S.-Latin American relations. A far cry from Brazil, which is large enough that it is less of use and more of concern to the United States, and unlike most countries in Latin America, which are too small to rouse U.S. hegemonic designs, Chile holds a middle ground that grants it meaningful strategic purpose in the region. Too small to be a threat, yet not too small to be irrelevant, the country is of importance to the United States partly because of its ability to affect the balance of leverage within Latin America. Chile is instrumental to U.S. designs in two respects. First, the country's decades long embrace of free markets and democratic reform, and its success in these areas, purportedly affirms the virtue of the Washington Consensus. Also, an ideological alliance with Chile based on free markets and democracy gives the United States a beachhead of influence on the South American continent, one that can be used to offset Mercosur as a counterpart to NAFTA, or Brazilian designs more specifically, and grant the United States more influence over the Free Trade Areas of the Americas (FTAA) process.

But is Chile really that important? No serious scholar of U.S. foreign policy would champion Santiago as the hub of U.S. activity in the world arena, and that is not the intention here. Chile rests in Latin America, and for Latin America, context and contingency mean everything when it comes to U.S. foreign policy. The region is subsidiary to broader U.S. interests and perceived threats. As an example of U.S. hegemonic prowess at the turn of the century, as a battlefield between U.S. and Soviet interests during the Cold War, or as an economic market under NAFTA and the FTAA to counter the advance of the European Union, Latin America must be tethered to some other concern to enter the limelight. Hence, Chile finds that it must bow to the dismissive dynamics of U.S. foreign policy. The country does command some political utility, but it is subject to the ebb and flow of U.S. regard for the entire region. Chile, then, is a country that is important by default.

What this means is that U.S. relations with Chile tend to be defined by political concerns. Unlike Brazil, the country lacks a critical mass of U.S. business interests ready and willing to lobby Washington aggressively on its behalf, nor is there a broad web of economic linkages to capture the attention of U.S. officials as they pursue economic policy with an eye to the national interest. All told, it cannot be argued that market draw drives the international when dealing with economic issues in Chile. Instead, political themes entwine the story of foreign involvement with Chile's neoliberal progress through the 1990s and beyond. And in this political story, it is no surprise that the United States takes the lead role, while business and IFIs step aside.

In June 1990, President George H. W. Bush publicized his Enterprise for the Americas Initiative to expand trade and investment throughout the hemisphere. Though devised to address the debt crisis under the rubric of "trade, not aid" or, in the eyes of some analysts, to add to the message sent by NAFTA developments and rattle mulish Japanese and European trade negotiators at the then-stalled Uruguay GATT Round (Wyatt-Walter 1996, 85), the proposal caught the immediate attention of Chile. Officials from the country took the opportunity to solicit and hopefully institutionalize greater openness with its largest trading partner.[23]

The United States welcomed the enthusiasm. Trade negotiations commenced within a few months, and the governments organized the Bilateral Council for

Trade and Investment to think through a free trade agreement (Mares and Rojas Aravena 2001, 85–87). And as deliberations over NAFTA progressed, U.S. officials began to float Chile as a prime candidate for expansion. The push to engage Chile was above all a political decision, designed to reward the country for its neoliberal accomplishments. John O'Leary, U.S. ambassador to Chile, reflects this position: "Chile *earned the right* to be first on free trade with the United States by its leadership in championing democracy, economic freedom, human rights, transparency, and the rule of law" (authors' emphasis).[24] And by rewarding Chile, the United States would provide an incentive for other Latin American states to follow the U.S. dictates codified in the Washington Consensus.

And it is no mystery why Chile was chosen to be the poster child of neoliberal success. This one-time bastion of import substitution economic policy largely introduced neoliberal shock treatment to the Western Hemisphere during the 1970s under the Pinochet dictatorship (Foxley 1983). By the time of democratic transition in 1989–1990, the country gained renown as an economic success story, and the commitment to continue the neoliberal program after the return to civilian rule only increased its stature in the eyes of the United States. This political assessment, rather than the lobbying efforts of business, or anxiety over economic ties, provided the impetus to free trade efforts on the part of the U.S. government.

Receiving Washington's blessings was good news. But politics can be a capricious business, as Chile would soon discover. And to succeed while entering the fray with low market draw demands a Herculean effort. Chile did discover an ardent advocate in the U.S. Treasury, but economic reform alone could not sway officials from the U.S. Trade Representative or Department of Commerce, who look first and foremost to global trade patterns when they anoint a country with economic distinction. Thus, little more than principle buttressed the free trade proposal as it made its way up the steps of the Capitol, and, as in all legislative processes, principle tends to lose its momentum rather quickly. The measure soon fell prey to environmental concerns energized by NGOs critical of Chile's fishing industry, health and safety issues unleashed by the fictitious detection of cyanide in two grapes imported from Chile, and the absence of a strong legislative sponsor driven by the potential economic benefits of his constituency. Finally, and most important, even those supportive of free trade in principle found their political capital depleted by the NAFTA negotiations (Mares and Rojas Aravena 2001, 85–91). Indeed the debate over NAFTA proved so contentious for

Democrats and Republicans that "there was a gentleman's agreement, encompassing both parties, to postpone any further progress on Chile's accession to NAFTA until after the U.S. presidential election in November 1996" (Wiarda 1997).

The delay proved costly to Chile. Turmoil in Mexico through 1994, from the Chiapas rebellion to political assassinations, led U.S. politicians to reconsider risks associated with developing stronger ties to the markets of the South. With the stakes surrounding free trade now perceived as greater than ever, Congress showed its resolve by withholding presidential "fast-track" authority in 1994.[25] But the Clinton administration pressed on, perhaps viewing free trade as the best issue to undermine the new Republican majority elected in November 1994.[26] Clinton, in an extensively leaked proposal, marked Chile as next in line for NAFTA expansion at the December 1994 Summit of the Americas. The invitation was premature. Beneath the pomp and circumstance of the Summit, the Mexican peso crisis began to fester. The weakening currency sent Mexico's economy into a tailspin through 1995 and took with it Chile's hopes of NAFTA accession. In Washington, free trade with Latin American countries was no longer just a political hot potato—it was a blistering coal.

U.S. partisan politics assured that Chile would remain on the back burner, even as fears of the "tequila effect" subsided. Congressional Republicans stymied fast-track authority, along with Chilean confidence in any trade proposal. But the 1998 Summit of the Americas, this one in Santiago, once more placed hemispheric free trade at the top of the agenda. Again, it would be government, not business, that would provide the initiative. At the Summit, U.S. and Chilean officials agreed to drop conclusively the issue of NAFTA accession and to concentrate instead on a bilateral arrangement. To that end, Clinton and Chilean president Eduardo Frei used the summit meetings to organize the Joint Commission on Trade and Investment (JCTI). Ambassador John O'Leary notes, "Without the JCTI, it would have been awfully difficult for me to have helped maintain the momentum toward the Chile FTA [free trade agreement]. . . . It played a key, catalytic role."[27]

Personnel from the Office of the U.S. Trade Representative and the Foreign Ministry of Chile, along with the ambassadors of both countries, composed the JCTI. No business or NGO groups participated in the three annual meetings held from 1998 to 2000. The Commission was integral to the mission of reviving the confidence of business communities miffed by the past dallying of U.S. trade promotion. For government officials, it offered a clear, substantive indicator of political will that forced both sides to address pressing concerns. The 1999 meeting was celebrated as a breakthrough when Chile agreed to include environmental and labor issues in any forthcoming arrangement. Circumstances were primed for an FTA announcement, but yet again the shifty eye of Washington politics would dampen Chile's prospects.[28]

For the United States, events surrounding the WTO loomed far more imperative than bilateral trade negotiations with Chile. Civil disturbances outside the December 1999 Seattle meetings, and the failure of these talks to produce any substantive agreements, compelled Washington to marshal all of its forces toward raising the credibility and fortitude of the organization. Things grew more difficult through 2000, when the Clinton administration came out in favor of Chinese accession to the WTO. The administration expended a great deal of political capital fending off the unflagging pressure from traditional Democratic constituencies in labor unions, environmental groups, and human rights activists. Would Chile be left behind once again?

The line of reasoning advanced thus far places Chile on the fringes of U.S. political priorities. The country is, and always will be, ancillary to larger U.S. interests. Roberto Matus, economic counselor at the Embassy of Chile in Washington, is keenly aware of this:

Small country, small market, strategically not important, so what do we have to do? We have to position ourselves as a relevant actor, because we are not naturally a relevant actor, like is China, or would be Brazil. And what do we do to position ourselves? We position ourselves to be a valid actor in this [U.S. foreign policy] arena. To do that you must have a certain political stability, you must have certain consistency in your economic development, and you must have also some kind of consistency in your social development.[29]

The strategy is circumscribed and the outcome is uncontrollable. Chile can do little more than behave mindfully, wait patiently, and hope that the United States finds a role for the country in its grand designs. Unlike Brazil, the problem for Chile in economic relations with the United States is not the specter of Chilean products flooding U.S. markets and riling sectoral interests. Rather, Chile faces the challenge of simply being noticed. It is telling that in interviews with economic counselors from both Washington embassies, Brazilian officials rail against the innate protectionist climate in Congress, while the official from Chile maintains, "I would definitely reject a statement that says that the [U.S.] Congress is reluctant to moving forward with a free trade agreement with Chile.

Our reading of direct contact with Congress is accommodating." Setbacks are instead explained by "all kinds of exogenous factors [that] affect this process and not something direct against Chile."[30]

But being subsidiary can also have its benefits. Chile easily falls from the agenda when other issues tug at Washington's interests. Nonetheless, the country, insofar as it follows the "mindful strategy" elucidated above, may also find itself swept up by broader foreign policy goals of the United States. And this is precisely what happened by the end of 2000, as WTO affairs threatened to smother Chilean hopes. Another grand foreign policy goal was in the works, and the United States saw a clear role for Chile to play: FTAA negotiations. This goal helped to offset the adverse effects of WTO matters.

Though mindful behavior first positioned Chile for prominence (although contingent) within U.S. foreign policy in the early 1990s, the country garnered further political utility as FTAA negotiations lingered on. Three factors—irritation from many Latin American leaders over what seemed to be growing chariness on the part of U.S. officials, the success of Mercosur, and mounting protests from Brazil—combined to lower U.S. repute and influence. For the United States, Chile could help on two fronts. First, an agreement with the country would shore up Washington's credibility. An FTA could be portrayed as a stepping-stone to the FTAA. Also, by courting Chile, the United States could keep the country one step away from Brazil and increase its leverage in the negotiations.[31] In the FTAA negotiations, Brazil pushed for, and won, a slow approach, betting that with time it could expand Mercosur, even to the point of creating a "SAFTA" (South American Free Trade Agreement), as a counterpart to NAFTA (Carranza 2000). Chile would be a prized player in Mercosur because of its geographic proximity and bustling economy. But through the 1990s, the prospects of NAFTA membership fed Chilean reticence to join Mercosur. Moreover, the common external tariffs of the customs union are higher than Chile's uniformed rate (6 percent in 2003). Nevertheless, the country was granted associate membership. Brazil's foreign minister, Luiz Felipe Lampreia, related Brazil's reaction to the U.S.-Chile FTA when he declared that the agreement would be "incompatible with Mercosur" and threaten the status of Chile's negotiations toward fuller membership, and added that Brazil might file for trade compensation.[32]

Hence, WTO issues delayed, but did not derail, the U.S.-Chile FTA. The JCTI talks culminated in a November 27, 2000, telephone conversation between Bill Clinton and Chilean president Ricardo Lagos. On November 29, both governments announced that work would begin on a draft U.S.-Chile FTA.[33] A draft was hammered out, and though the war in Iraq and Chilean protests in the UN Security Council threatened to deflate the process, the negotiations were saved by the lifeline now firmly established between them and broader U.S. foreign policy goals.[34] The Chile-U.S. FTA is one small, albeit integral, step in the push to retake the initiative in the global trading system (Bergsten 2002). And in Latin America, in the midst of the FTAA negotiations, deputy U.S. trade representative Peter Allgeier notes that the accord is "an incentive for others to move ahead."[35]

So, in the end Chile did gain a free trade agreement with the United States. But the path was not wrought by economic rationale and the strenuous efforts of economic lobbying groups. It was the vacillations of U.S. foreign policy. Chile could only wait for the spotlight to move its way and accept that it was a spotlight to be shared. Washington, and its fickle politics, represented the international as Chile worked its way toward neoliberal consolidation.

Argentina and Indifferent U.S. Policy

market draw,
does what its told
but doesn't get the
.customers
it wants

A 1991 media report on the status of Argentina's debt rescheduling talks noted "good behaviour does not seem to be getting Argentina anywhere" with the IMF or commercial banks.[36] A decade later, despite a wholesale turn toward neoliberalism and a foreign policy stance slavishly dedicated to Washington, surprisingly little had changed on the part of international support for neoliberal reform in the country. In 2001–2002, while unemployment topped 20 percent, GDP growth sunk into negative double-digit figures, inflation reached 41 percent, and Argentines watched in disbelief as their bank deposits were frozen, U.S. officials undermined business confidence with gruff comments, the IMF cut loan disbursements, and the United States rubbed salt into Argentina's wounds by placing countervailing duties on Argentine exports cheapened by the crisis. The foreign response seems startling on the face of it. Unlike Brazil's experiential approach to economic policy through the 1990s, Argentina fell in line much more quickly and showed no inclination toward subhegemonic rivalry. And compared to Chile, Argentina offers a consumer market population 2.4 times greater (37.5 million to 15.5 million), a GDP fourfold larger ($268.3 billion to $66 billion), and a per capita GDP 1.5 times bigger ($6,940 to $4,590).[37]

But the political contrast with Brazil and economic comparison to Chile only underscore the point that international support must be analyzed with an eye toward both politics and markets, and their respective international mainstays in government and business. For as we have seen, though Brazil has veered from the Washington Consensus, a nexus of economic linkages to the United States ensures support. And though Chile is situated below Argentina in economic importance, its political utility helps.

In defense of Argentina's market draw, some might point up the substantial increase in FDI flows through the 1990s. But unlike in Chile and Brazil, most FDI flows were "safe" investments, located in the nontradables sector (i.e., production not liable to global competition) or in oligopolistic industries. One study estimates that 70 percent of investment flows to Argentina between 1990 and 1996 were directed to privatized state industries such as gas, electricity, and telephone services that hold natural monopolies (Chudnovsky and Lopez 1997; also see Lopez 1998). Secure investments dampen the inducements of engaged international businesses to plead for outside support. Adding to the difficulties of low market draw is the fact that, like Chile, Argentina sits below a threshold of substantial importance as an economic partner to the United States. Whereas Brazil ranked as the thirteenth largest U.S. trading partner ($29 billion in imports plus exports) in 2001, Argentina ranked thirty-fifth ($6.6 billion) and Chile ranked thirty-seventh ($6.1 billion).[38] Seeing no international business corps pleading on behalf of Argentina at the height of the peso crisis in December 2001, the *New York Times* could run the headline, "American Investors in Argentina Mostly Taking Losses in Stride."[39]

And what of political utility to the United States? There is perhaps no other country in Latin America, including Mexico, which has made such dramatic foreign and economic policy turns in the past twenty years. For much of the post–World War II era, Argentina was at loggerheads with the United States. The country's contemplation of Axis support during the war as a display of defiant independence was a prelude to its leadership position in the Nonaligned Movement, its pursuit of nuclear weaponry, and its pariah status under the 1976–1983 military regime. Its devotion to import substitution economic policies had a similarly antagonistic effect in the economic arena. But by the 1990s, the differences could not have been greater. Argentina became a leader in personnel contributions to peacekeeping operations, gained the distinction of "Major Non-NATO Ally" from the Clinton administration, and was widely applauded for its substantial strides in neoliberal reform by the United States and IFIs (Escudé and Fontana 1998).

These dramatic shifts notwithstanding, the United States turned a cold shoulder to Argentina during the 2001–2002 crisis. Hence, it is reasonable to assert that perhaps no level of compliance could overcome one hard reality—Argentina simply lacks political usefulness for Washington's aspirations. The temporal dimension is important here. In the early 1990s, Argentina vied with Chile as a poster child of neoliberalism and therefore held the potential to play a similar role in U.S. designs, earning, like Chile, the Midas touch of Washington's promotions in policy, business, and media circles. But from the U.S. perspective, participation in Mercosur and warming relations with Brazil foreclosed Argentine political utility. Chile mattered, if only periodically, because it was a needle in Brazil's side and exemplified the Washington Consensus. Argentina was cozy with Brazil and offered nonessential padding to the showcase position already captured by Chile.

So what happens when a country holds only slight market draw and negligible political utility, as in the case of Argentina? In this predicament, the international still matters. Economics is an issue of high politics; the interests of states and business are intense. It is then little wonder that states, with ardent business support and collaboration, established a network of organizations in the Bretton Woods system to regulate trade, finance, and investment. Enough has been written on how these institutions address cooperation problems—they have spawned an industry in neoliberal institutionalism—but the scholarship has overlooked another function. Namely, that the institutional progeny of Bretton Woods—the WTO, IMF, and World Bank Group—serve as a safety net to disseminate neoliberal doctrine in countries shunned by indifferent states and corporations. And in the case of neoliberal reform, the IMF has increasingly taken the lead as other agencies await the verdict of its article IV consultations. Thus, where market draw and political utility fail to impress, the IMF steps up as lead actor in the triad of international influence. And bereft of demands for flexibility to address the narrow economic and political interests of business and government, the fund marches to the beat of its own interests and doles out the most doctrinaire of neoliberal precepts.

So it was up to the IMF to take the helm as the international exerted influence over Argentine economic affairs. And it did so while considering how the Argentine case could affect the predicament the fund found itself in at the turn of the century. At this time, the IMF faced criticisms on two fronts. One came from borrowing countries, whose disapproval of IMF intrusiveness was bolstered by the mishandling of the Asian currency crisis. The other surfaced from a surging antiglobalization movement and the growing anxiety of creditor countries over the mounting size of crisis bailout packages. Both of these groups, however unrelated in their interests, placed pressure on the IMF to prove its legitimacy and merit.

And the fund took both lines of criticism seriously. The debt crisis dragged the IMF into the internal politics of Third World countries as never before, when conditionality arrangements tightened to justify record disbursements and acquired status as credibility signals. After the debt crises of the 1980s gave way to the financial crises of the 1990s, the engagement continued, but so too did the liability of the IMF. And with involvement came responsibility. The scrutiny proved disastrous for the fund during the 1997 Asian currency crisis, where its policies shouldered some of the blame for aggravating an economic downturn. The ferment of criticism made its way into the institution itself, which put forth a flurry of self-conscious policy papers, created an Independent Evaluation Office, and devised new strategies of engagement—such as ownership and streamlined conditionality.

Criticisms that doubted the very legitimacy of the institution represented a more severe blow. Support by the Clinton administration for several bailouts in the 1990s provided fodder for Republican critics, who were also taken by the moral hazard argument of how lending to "irresponsible" governments gives incentives for further misdeeds.[40] Grumbles of protest turned to shouts of condemnation by 1998, when corrupt government administrators in Russia spirited away a sizeable portion of a $4.8 billion IMF disbursement to overseas accounts. The cries were redoubled by the induction of the Bush administration, which brought with it many officials engrossed by the risks of moral hazard.[41] Adding to these elite-level barbs, the civil disturbance at the 1999 WTO meetings in Seattle turned up the heat on all economic multilateral institutions from the mass level, especially as protestors moved to target the annual World Bank-IMF meetings, and as the antiglobalization movement developed (ironically) a worldwide network (Wucker 2002, 52).

But responding to both lines of protest presented a dilemma. The heightening aversion to strict conditionality and intense engagement coming from borrowing countries stood at odds with the pressure to legitimate from creditor countries, which demanded a demonstration of heavy IMF participation in an economic recovery or solid success story. And this is where the case of Argentina fit into the grander designs of the IMF. Having been deeply involved in the country's neoliberal reforms throughout the 1990s, the IMF could share the laurels of economic achievement. But a 1998 downturn threatened this development. A pegged exchange rate system tied the hands of government as the trade deficit deepened, and austerity spurred political protest in a population already reeling from unemployment hovering at 15 percent. Nonetheless, these were the policies supported by the IMF through the decade, and to reverse course now would surely invite further condemnation. Also, movements from the status quo would raise new protests of intrusiveness. Hence, as the 1990s came to a close, the IMF took on the Argentine case as a gamble (Wucker 2002, 52). Stay the course, and hope that worldwide demand for Argentine exports would increase, that confidence in emerging markets would return, that the interest rates spiking Argentine debt would decline, and that Argentina's most important trading partner, Brazil, would remain healthy. None would come to pass.

Though external shocks played an important role, faulty policies frozen in place under the gamble contributed significantly. Poor decision making by the Argentine government placed the country in a vulnerable position, but the IMF fastened the straightjacket. At the core of these poor decisions was the commitment to a pegged exchange rate (Feldstein 2002). In April 1991 the Convertibility Plan linked a new currency, the peso, to the dollar and restricted the growth of the money supply. The scheme eradicated Argentina's infamous inflation rates and raised the country's credibility in global financial markets. Impressive economic growth ensued, averaging 8.5 percent from 1991 to 1994.[42]

But wise choices are creatures of circumstance, and as conditions change, so too should they. Though the peg brought stability, its link to a climbing dollar damaged Argentina as time passed, which became apparent during the 1995 Mexican peso crisis. The increasingly overvalued peso had generated a current account deficit, leaving the country dependent on the influx of foreign capital to balance its books (Pastor and Wise 1999). But the tequila effect wreaked havoc on Argentina's newly opened financial markets, and threw the economy into a tailspin as foreign investors grew skittish on emerging markets. With a diminished flow, Argentina had to finance the trade deficit from its international reserves, which fell from $682 million in 1994 to a deficit of $102 million in 1995.[43] The closing stages of the privatization program also narrowed the availability of capital, and the subsequent rise in interest rates hampered economic growth. Unemployment rose from 11.7 percent to 15.9 percent, and government, strapped by petering tax revenues and swelling interest rates, watched foreign debt begin a precipitous rise that would take it from $98 billion in 1995 to $146 billion by 2000 (*IMF Financial Statistics Yearbook* 2001).

Why not dispose of the peg? The dread of inflation, so deeply ingrained in the Argentine psyche, cannot be denied, but narrow interests were also at play (Starr 1997). For Menem, Convertibility represented his victory over inflation. A movement from the peg could undermine this legacy. Moreover, the link to the dollar emerged as a political statement—a sign of Argentina's newfound commitment to U.S. foreign policy. International business in the country also had a clear interest in stabilizing exchange rates to ease transactions and enhance the credibility of their investment proposals. And the middle classes enjoyed a windfall of imports cheapened by the strong peso.

From the international field, 1995 marked a turning point in assessments of the Argentine economy. Whereas neoliberal reform initially elicited a shower of applause from Washington, foreign business, and the IMF, the economic dip led many in these same circles to take a closer, more critical, look at Argentine economic policy. The burgeoning debt had in fact received an external shock previous to the tequila effect, when the U.S. Federal Reserve raised short-term interest rates in February 1994. But the IMF placed the onus squarely on the Argentina government, warning through 1994 that unchecked spending threatened fiscal surplus targets agreed to under conditionality arrangements.[44] The demands for "fiscal restraint" continued through the 1990s, and U.S. government officials and analysts soon picked up the mantra (e.g., Mussa 2002).[45] "Fiscal irresponsibility" now stands as an official explanation for the crisis, but is it a reasonable accusation?

Proponents of the fiscal irresponsibility contention note that the government budget fell from a surplus of $2.73 billion pesos in 1993 to deficits of $1.37 billion in 1995, $4.28 billion in 1997, and $6.79 billion in 2000. But the aggregate expenditure figures mask the weight exerted by debt payments, which were harnessed to the escalating interest rates. Interest payments as a percentage of government spending increased from 6.8 percent in 1993 to 16.8 percent in 1999 (Baer, Elosegui, and Gallo 2002). In fact, primary spending (which excludes payments on debt interest) did not change significantly during this time. In 1993 it stood at $45.1 billion pesos (19.1 percent of GDP), and moved only slightly to $47.6 billion (18.4 percent of GDP) in 1995, $53.9 billion (18.4 percent of GDP) in 1997, and $53.7 billion (18.9 percent of GDP) in 2000. Though corruption and wasteful spending did play their role, the exogenous shock cannot be denied or downplayed. The capital flight of the Mexican peso crisis reappeared during the 1997 Asian, 1998 Russian, and 1999 Brazilian crises, which challenged payments on existing loans. A vicious circle materialized, as investors grew skeptical, sending the country's credit ratings downward and thereby further raising interest rates and payments.[46]

The debate over the role played by fiscal spending continues in academia and among pundits. Michael Mussa, a former staff member of the IMF, dismisses the impact of interest payments by simply declaring, "public debt is public debt" (2002, 15). Others convincingly question how one can sustain charges of government profligacy while poverty rates reached 50 percent; social, health, and education programs deteriorated; spending on the armed forces crumbled; business subsidies were withdrawn; and government bureaucracies were cut to the bone (Healy and Seman 2002; Palast 2003).[47] Traditional Latin American populism in fiscal policy was nowhere to be found. Only by recognizing how both domestic and international factors interplayed can we reach above the fray of this debate (Corrales 2002).

First, we should recognize that criticisms of Argentine policy choices are not wholly off the mark, especially in references to tax reforms, judicial renovations, labor restructuring, and calls for greater transparency and "good governance," more broadly speaking. But the critical comments from abroad skirt the fact that neoliberal reform, especially when implemented under a democratic regime, always moves in fits and starts, often leaving the vestiges of interventionist policies in its wake (Etchemendy 2001). It is a painful process and follows a road potholed by entrenched interests. Brazil, once so rife with corruption that its president was impeached, and plagued by its own fiscal rebellions in the provinces, received the benefit of the doubt, despite recurrent and brash rebukes of neoliberal principles. The country drew ample support from the U.S. government and IMF and thus was able to place its house in order over time. But such was not the case with Argentina. With the vicious circle of increasing debt payments spinning in the domestic sphere, confidence-boosting calls from the U.S. government and constructive engagement by the IMF would have represented a genuine remedy from the outside. But Argentina lacks political utility and market draw, and so it also lacks an audience for its appeals.

Argentina did gain a short respite from the downturn triggered in 1995. Austerity demanded by IMF conditionality reports dragged the country out of the depression. GDP growth moved from -2.9 percent in 1995 to 5.5 and 8 percent the following years. But the effects of austerity, in the form of neglected investment and continued high unemployment, did not prepare the country for what was to follow. In 1998, growth slowed to 3.8 percent, as the ill effects of the Convertibility Plan deepened. Washington's strong dollar policy took the peso with it, inflating the prices of Argentine exports in most European, Asian, and Latin American markets. Recession in Brazil, which regularly purchased some 30 percent of Argentina's exports, hit the country especially hard in 1998 (the devaluation of the *real* in January 1999 would later deal a fatal blow). The current account deficit almost doubled from $6.9 billion pesos in 1996 to $12.3 billion in 1997 and then moved to $14.6 billion in 1998. It only declined thereafter as recession worked its way back into the economy and reduced imports.

By 1999, escalating competitiveness problems provoked by the Convertibility Plan supplemented the vicious circle of debt repayment still unfolding. International actors could have played a crucial role to escort Argentina from the crisis, but they did not. President Menem had been invited to give a keynote address at the October 1998 IMF-World Bank meetings, as Fund officials maintained their hopes that the status quo could ride out the storm. The IMF pronounced its support for Convertibility, locking the policy in place. As noted by Michelle Wucker, "every time Argentine officials talked about giving up the dollar-peso peg . . . investors showed their displeasure by selling Argentine bonds" (2002, 50). In December 2000, a $40 billion loan package was extended with the expectation that Argentina would stay the course. A press release issued by the IMF to announce the package remarked on how important it was that the government "protect the country's convertibility regime."[48]

The IMF's gamble would find little assistance from the newly inaugurated Bush administration. Argentine exports cheapened by the lack of demand were met only by charges of dumping and countervailing duties. This reaction denied the country vital foreign exchange, but more important, it sent a steely message of callousness for Argentina's plight. And at just the time when Argentina announced a zero-deficit plan to instill investor confidence, U.S. treasury secretary Paul O'Neill remarked in a July 2001 *Economist* interview that Argentina "has been off and on in trouble for 70 years or more. They don't have any export industry to speak of at all. And they like it that way. Nobody forced them to be what they are."[49]

The peg was growing unsustainable, even as the IMF opened a new $7.6 billion loan in August 2001 in a last-ditch effort to save it. Argentine citizens saw the banking crisis coming and sped to withdraw their deposits to convert pesos to dollars in advance of a devaluation. A statement by the IMF on December 18 that it had "lost confidence" in the government of Fernando de la Rúa and would halt a scheduled loan disbursement sealed Argentina's collapse.[50] The country defaulted on some $95 billion of its $141 billion in foreign debt. De la Rúa would resign on December 20, 2001, amid widespread street rioting that left over thirty dead. Adolfo Rodriguez Sáa assumed the presidency, only to last seven days, and his successor, Eduardo Duhalde, clearly positioned himself as a caretaker, with the chief goal of presiding over elections within a year.

Confirming the central role of the IMF, the United States made it clear that the fund, and not it, would address the crisis. In July 2002 Otto Reich, assistant secretary of state for Western Hemisphere Affairs, stated that "the United States is prepared to assist Argentina bilaterally, *after* an agreement with the IMF is reached," and in a trip to Argentina that same month, Secretary of the Treasury Paul O'Neill went out of his way to lower expectations and portray the visit as just one in a string of several he had lined up.[51] U.S.-Argentine relations continue to reel, in stark contrast to the 1990s. At his inauguration in May 2003, President Nestor Kirchner solicited "an ample, serious and mature relationship with the United States" and backed up the call with an emphasis on Mercosur and Brazil as foremost priorities in foreign policy. The Bush administration, in a move regarded as a snub, sent Mel Martinez, secretary of Housing and Urban Development, to represent the United States at the ceremony.[52]

Argentina's low market draw and lack of political utility has ensured for it a very different neoliberal experience from those secured by its neighbors. Through the 1990s and beyond, the country would not be granted the leeway accorded to Brazil, nor the endorsements secured by Chile. In its quest for international support, Argentina finds only the IMF is there to lend a hand, in accord with its own institutional interests, when not pressured by overbearing creditor states or the international business community.

The International and the Future of Neoliberal Reform

Neoliberal reform entails significant costs. Without international support, the prospects for success decline considerably. Although the conventional wisdom might expect international actors, with clear preferences for the spread of neoliberalism, to nurse its consolidation, they will not do so based on a host country's policy compliance. Foreign assistance is instead better explained by the combination of political utility and market draw. These variables also reveal the dynamics by which that support is expressed.

Political utility and market draw expose the political and economic motivations that both drive and distinguish international actors. Countries such as Chile, which possess only political usefulness, find that powerful states lead in turning on the flow of international support. But this flow is susceptible to periodic obstruction, as political agendas change and the country easily slips from the hegemon's attention. Market allure offers a more enduring linkage to the international arena, as international business lobbies on behalf of the country and outside states discern bonds to their own national interests. Nonetheless, when a country with subhegemonic designs holds the allure of a great market, as with Brazil, the hegemon will offer support only reluctantly. Like political utility, market draw by itself yields intermittent support, but the dynamics answer to economics rather than politics. Chile's opportunity to obtain favor from the international is dependent on the political vagaries of U.S. foreign policy. On the other hand, Brazil gains notice when its economy falls into crisis. Finally, Argentina illustrates what happens when a country offers neither political utility nor market attraction. In such cases the IMF takes the lead and disburses support unencumbered by the immediate interests of business or powerful states. Here, the self-interest of the IMF plays a more important role.

The combinations of political utility and market draw portend distinct chances for neoliberal consolidation. The acclaim received by Chile from the United States government sends signals to the international community that can only help, episodic as they may be. But the country lacks the insurance of a large market, should its economy slip at a time when it is off the U.S. foreign policy agenda. Luck is at play here, but the prospects are good so long as the country mindfully follows the dictates of Washington. Brazil's market draw grants more latitude as the country charts its own neoliberal path, but a tepid relationship with the United States hinders the constant flow of support. Crises act as wake-up calls, and the international answers belatedly, but dutifully. Brazil is able to pursue neoliberal consolidation with greater autonomy than Chile, which, like a roller coaster, rides through peaks and valleys as it remains on track. Argentina faces the greatest obstacles. It cannot depend on occasional nods of support, it must answer to the most orthodox of neoliberal expectations, and should it falter, it cannot expect generous aid.

Together, the cases illustrate the significance of the international in the high politics of neoliberal reform. Washington, the IMF, and international business possess resources vital to reform efforts. Analysts have persuasively identified the decision to pursue reform as essentially domestic in nature, but they have identified the success of that reform decision as one that is dependent on international backing. True, some countries do have some bargaining power based on political or economic appeal, but the opportunity to haggle is checked by the requisites of foreign sustenance. Ordinarily, the ability of a Latin American state to gain favor has more to do with cooperation dynamics in the international realm. It requires finding an advocate in international business or the hegemon to pressure the other to be supportive. Chile looked to the United States, Brazil found allies in international corporations. Still, support is uneven, configured more by the capacities and motivations of foreign actors than those of Latin American states. Finally, there are those states, such as Argentina, that lack a patron. The international remains prominent for these states as business and the hegemon send their surrogate, the IMF, equipped more with sticks than carrots to ensure compliance with neoliberal tenets. For all, the script is unyielding—Latin American states that embark on neoliberal reform open a door to considerable international influence. And once opened, this door cannot easily be shut.

Independently, these cases show how our framework of political change allows us to tease out differences between cases, even on this high politics issue where one might expect greater uniformity in the face of overbearing outside influences. The focus on both capability and motivation is the key. Capability tells us that the international will be of consequence on this issue—of that there should be little doubt. But an analysis that stops there would fail to explain why and how Brazil, Chile, and Argentina have charted such different journeys. Different concerns motivate foreign actors as they contemplate granting economic assistance, country by country. In neoliberal reform, the international matters, but it appears differently as it roams the hemisphere, raising or lowering the prospects of consolidation in tandem. If there is one safe prediction for the destiny of neoliberalism in Latin America, it is that the region will exhibit a greater mosaic of compliance and that this future will be orchestrated by the international.

4. Democratization in the Andean Region

D emocracy has moved from a wave to a way of life in Latin America. It is hard to believe that a little over two decades ago, the region was still overrun by authoritarian regimes. The by now familiar democratic third wave washed ashore in 1979 in Ecuador and spread across the continent with blazing speed. By 1990, all countries save Cuba and Haiti had democratic governments in place. The causes have been exhaustively studied and need not be repeated here. But one pattern does stand out: internal factors mattered more than external ones. While there was certainly some positive contagion effect once a critical mass of countries had turned democratic, for the most part the fact of democratic reemergence, its nature, and timing had much more to do with the dynamics of political and economic change within countries than outside of them.

Still, in a region so dominated by the United States, many naturally asked whether Washington, which aided and abetted the overthrow of countless civilian governments in decades past, could have had anything to do with their reemergence. This matter too has largely been settled. According to leading scholars on the subject such as Abraham Lowenthal (1991b) and Thomas Carothers (1991), while rhetorically the United States has often espoused democratic change, in practice its efforts to promote it have been timid, vacillating, and at times counterproductive. Whether via coercion, sanction, or diplomatic persuasion, the United States would usually only advocate on behalf of democratic change when ulterior motives were at play: to dislodge an unfriendly authoritarian regime, to justify its extrication from a country in which it had already been deeply ensconced, or to respond to domestic political pressures back home (Lowenthal 1991b, 259). Even then, its efforts were either uneven, lackluster, or not sustained. As far as the third wave is concerned, the best that can be said for the United States is that it did not stand in the way of democratization efforts in

South America but rather applauded these from the sidelines (Carothers 1991). Concerted diplomatic pressure was successfully brought to bear by Washington only against the Chilean dictatorship, and even there Chileans themselves were much more instrumental in affecting change.

Historically, democratic construction resided in the province of low politics. Foreign states—either individually or collectively—neither discovered a right to intervene in the regime choices of another state, nor saw a benefit in doing so, except in those cases where their own security or economic well-being was clearly at risk. As Lowenthal concludes, "external factors, including U.S. policy, are usually of secondary or tertiary importance in determining a Latin American nation's prospects for democracy" (1991b, 260). For these reasons, the changes that occurred beginning in the late 1980s[1] and that have continued into the 21st century are truly remarkable. In a little more than a decade, democracy has gone from being an internal matter of states to a subject of intense deliberation in regional forums. Once protected by norms of nonintervention and sovereignty, regime choice has now been subject to outside scrutiny. Politicians and scholars speak regularly of a "democratic right," one to which individuals and countries are entitled (Frank 1992). Whereas before sovereign power conferred automatic privileges on those who wielded it—irrespective of how autocratic they may have been—today, that power is no longer inviolable, but subject to recall should those in office not protect the democratic rights of their citizens. If those rights are violated by those in power, and citizens have no means of redressing their grievances domestically, then it becomes incumbent on the regional community to help restore democratic practices. To do so, that community would have to intrude into the domestic affairs of the state in question.

Elected governments themselves may be under siege from antidemocratic forces. They too have rights and can—and often must—appeal for help from external organizations to forestall coerced takeovers. Here, external intrusion may be initiated via request of the victimized government that has no means to fend off imminent assaults by the military or other armed groups. Whether by imposition or invitation, regional and international institutions, and especially the OAS, are increasingly making the internal affairs of Latin American nations their business, challenging long held notions of what used to constitute the exclusive domain of the sovereign state. In doing so, regional organizations and their members seem to be pushing democracy toward the realm of high politics, making it a foreign policy issue that states associate with their own vital interests.

The OAS is composed solely of member states and is beholden to their wishes. The institution is not greater than the sum of its parts, and its leaders are not legally authorized to act on their own. At the end of the day, it is states that must decide whether it is in their best interests to intercede into the domestic affairs of other members to fight for democracy. That they have increasingly chosen to do so over an extended period of time is the strongest indication that democracy is becoming a high politics theme. Indeed, states have signed a series of historic regional accords to collectively safeguard democracies because in large measure they have associated their own survival with doing so. By locking themselves into a series of agreements, resolutions, and protocols, OAS members have also altered notions of what is "appropriate" foreign policy conduct such that it is now more difficult for them to brush aside pleas for intervention to save or reinstall democratic regimes.

Yet, there is a limit as to how far governments are prepared to go in their defense of democracy abroad. While states of the region seem willing to rush in when the very survival of a democracy is in the balance, or when free and fair elections are at risk, they are more reticent to push too far for reform, fearing that they will cross the line from legitimate to illegitimate intervention in the internal affairs of another state, prompting retaliatory intrusions against themselves. For this reason, a distinction must be made between the defense of democracy, which members aggressively pursue, and democratic deepening, which they tend to avoid. The combined energies of members that are so effectively harnessed to rescue democracy on the verge of collapse turn into problems when members are confronted with issues of democratic quality. OAS actions embody this distinction. The organization tends to calibrate its response to democratic problems, adopting more vigorous measures to rescue a democracy in crisis, or to ensure that elections will be held as promised, and more tepid measures when trying to improve the quality of democratic practice once an election is over.

The OAS Comes of Age

As recently as the 1980s it would have been nearly impossible to predict democracy's movement from the realm of low to high politics, let alone the role of the Organization of American States in achieving that transformation.[2] After all, the countries of the region had constructed the entire inter-American system—

with the Organization of American States at its center—on the principles of non-involvement in the domestic politics of nations. The preamble to the OAS charter makes clear that the OAS will be primarily involved in matters pertaining to the relations between states, not within them: "The American States establish by this Charter the international organization that they have developed to achieve an order of peace and justice, to promote their solidarity, to strengthen their collaboration, and to defend their sovereignty, their territorial integrity and their independence" (OAS 1997, 3).

Article 19 of the OAS charter says "no state or group of states has the right to intervene, directly or indirectly, for any reason whatever, in the internal or external affairs of any other state" (OAS 1997, 6). Several other articles of the charter make reference in one way or another to a state's right to be free from external interference. The Latin American states that formed the OAS understood full well that while the principle of nonintervention applied to all states, the primary target was the United States. The vulnerable countries of the South believed that the charter language, finally endorsed by Washington itself, would serve as a legal deterrent to U.S. military incursions.[3] Consequently, it could be said that the founding of the OAS in 1948 was a strategic move by Latin American states to draw the United States into collective agreements that they hoped would curtail Washington's unilateralism.

Whatever the intent of the Southern states, the fact remains that the OAS would become anything but an effective deterrent to U.S. intervention. The organization did nothing to stop the United States from covertly toppling elected governments in Guatemala in 1954 and Chile in 1970–1973; from invading the Dominican Republic in 1965, Grenada in 1983, and Panama in 1989; and from breaking with Latin America to support Great Britain against Argentina during the Malvinas War of 1982. Understandably, by the early 1980s if not sooner, most seasoned observers were convinced that the OAS was, if not an explicit tool for the projection of U.S. power, then certainly an organization that could do little more than proclaim collective principles while failing to translate those principles into action. By the end of that decade, Ronald Scheman concluded somberly, "At present, because the Organization has neither power nor means to act, political issues are not negotiated: positions are staked out and resolutions adopted. In this environment, debate goes on in the abstract" (1988, 187).

The absence of institutional power to confront U.S. intervention was not the only problem afflicting the OAS. There was also the clash of principles. A "right to democracy" is a regional norm whose genesis dates back to the founding of the OAS (Muñoz 1998). The preamble to the OAS charter, written in 1948, stated that "the true significance of American solidarity and good neighborliness can only mean the consolidation on this continent within the framework of democratic institutions of a system of individual liberty and social justice based on respect for the essential rights of man" (OAS 1997, 3). This single mention lacked specificity and did not commit the member states to any course of action. Nonetheless, with this language in place, as Heraldo Muñoz explains, the participants of the Bogotá conference that launched the OAS had gone from making "declarations on behalf of democracy to [specifying] norms of a binding nature" (Muñoz 1998, 4). Whether obliged to act democratically or not, states that abridged that principle could rest assure that other states would look the other way, given the charter's strong, unambiguous defense of two other principles. The first, already mentioned, is that of nonintervention. The second principle is that of political pluralism, one enunciated in article 3 of the charter, which states that "Every State has the right to choose, without external interference, its political, economic, and social system and to organize itself in the way best suited to it" (OAS 1997, 3).

For decades, the OAS could never get much beyond this normative contradiction. Any effort by some members to act on behalf of democratic rights would be stifled by others who stood on behalf of sovereignty and the freedom of states to choose their own political destinies. In fact the OAS was not unique in this regard. For decades neither the United Nations nor any international body for that matter could push the pro-democracy agenda too hard without coming face to face with principles of sovereignty, pluralism, and free political choice.[4] Over time the political and legal world changed, and the barriers to intervention began to break down.[5] By the 1990s a consensus had emerged that rights of democracy went hand in hand with rights to intervention; the former could not flourish without resort to the latter. Still, principles can be applied only by politicians. The commitment to actually implement and enforce the new prodemocratic and interventionist precepts would always depend on the will of those in power. Understandably then, the organization's ability to promote democratic practices was inextricably bound to the kind of regimes represented in its Permanent Council and General Assembly. When military regimes emerged in the early 1960s and then consolidated their grip on most of the continent by the early 1970s, the OAS was not heard from (Muñoz 1998).

What lifted the OAS out of obscurity in the 1980s was a change in its constituency. The great majority of members had become democratic by the end of the decade, permitting a new convergence to develop around the principle of democratic defense. Each country could boast that its new leaders had been freely and competitively elected, that the institutions of democratic governance had been restored, and that basic respect for human rights returned. Of course, Latin America had seen democracy before, yet had never exerted much collective will to defend it. Why would anything be different now?

First, the region had become traumatized by the legacy of violence left by the authoritarian regimes of the 1970s. The costs in terms of human suffering had been great enough to convince members that there could be no justification—not economic, not social, not political—for a reversion to dictatorship. Also, the Cold War had come to a close, which removed an ideological excuse for Washington to prop up autocratic regimes in the region. That left democracy as the only preferred game in town and meant that Latin American states could be reasonably sure that Washington's post–Cold War global agenda would not conflict much with efforts to promote a democratic region. Finally, each new democracy became more focused on the problem of stabilizing civil-military relations. More attention had to be paid to how governments could ensure that their armed forces would unconditionally respect civilian authority and that the military coup would become a relic of the past. One means of ensuring that was to reawaken the notion, already expressed within the OAS charter, that the solidarity of American States could rest only on a democratic foundation. Any military threat to one elected government would violate that solidarity by placing at risk all other elected governments. After all, were a military coup or coup attempt in one state to go unanswered by the OAS community, it would send a green light to other militaries that they could overrun the constitutional authorities of their nations without bearing a huge cost in terms of regional isolation and condemnation. Thus, because each country's self-interest lay in preventing a military coup elsewhere, a cooperation problem had been resolved, at least in principle.

If, however, the problem were to be resolved in practice, the OAS would have to devise new rules and equip itself with new powers to accommodate the new priorities of member states, or risk becoming irrelevant to the political forces swirling around it. The organization would have to cross over several thresholds before discovering a new relevancy. One threshold was justification and was actually achieved back in 1979, when the OAS denounced Nicaragua's deplorable human rights record, placing the blame squarely on the Anastasio Somoza regime itself. In criticizing the regime the OAS justified rendering a harsh judgment about a member's internal political system (Acevedo and Grossman 1996, 137–38). Although the organization also called for democratic elections, it would not be part of that solution because just one month later, Somoza would fall to the Sandinistas. The other two thresholds to cross were those of specification and reaction. What were the specific problems, and what steps would a nation have to take, if it were to remedy those problems on its own? If it failed to do so, what would the OAS response be? Here, the OAS lost an opportunity to strengthen its cause when it criticized Manuel Noriega for canceling the results of the May 1989 elections but failed to articulate what it would do to return Panama to democratic rule. This inaction helped pave the way for the U.S. invasion in December of that year (Acevedo and Grossman 1996, 139).

The Panamanian episode was clearly an embarrassment for the OAS and threatened to derail its progress. But the OAS got back on track in an impressive way in 1991. In what would become the organization's defining moment, the OAS General Assembly adopted Resolution 1080 on June 5 that specified a problem and empowered the organization to react effectively. That resolution bound the OAS secretary general and Permanent Council to take immediate action in the event of a "sudden or irregular interruption of the democratic political institutional process or of the legitimate exercise of power by the democratically elected government" of any of the OAS member states (OAS 1991). An ad hoc meeting of the ministers of foreign affairs of the member states, or a special session of the General Assembly, would have to be convened within a ten-day period for the purpose of taking appropriate measures in response to the crisis. Resolution 1080 has to date been applied four times: Haiti, 1991; Peru, 1992; Guatemala, 1993; and Paraguay, 1996. In addition, the OAS Permanent Council was convened to discuss coup threats in Venezuela in 1992, and Ecuador in 2000. The key innovation of 1080 was its requirement that a threat to a democratic regime trigger the organization's automatic and immediate response. Members would not have the option to dither about, endlessly debating the merits of reacting. The organization's reactive capacity would be further strengthened the following year with the adoption of the Protocol of Washington. That protocol would allow for the suspension of a member state, by a two-thirds vote of the General Assembly, should its democratic government be overthrown by force (OAS 1992). The process of institutional strengthening culminated on September 11, 2001, with the signing of the Inter-American Democratic Charter.[6]

By the beginning of the twenty-first century, it was clear that the OAS had acquired the political will, legal machinery, and institutional wherewithal to rescue democracies under siege and to deter future conspiracies against them. Latin American militaries and their civilian allies had to think twice about coercively seizing power, knowing that were they to do so, the regional community would respond quickly and decisively.

If the regional community could effectively respond when a democracy's very survival was up for grabs, what then of problems of a less dramatic but serious nature? What would the OAS do were a Latin American leader to tamper with electoral machinery or ballot results? Elections are still the central drama in democratic politics. While few equate elections with democracy, most would suggest that their cancellation would be tantamount to regime change. No democracy can be reduced to an electoral battle but neither can any exist without those battles. So much is at stake in an election: the rights of citizens to choose their leaders, the rights of politicians and parties to express their views, the chance for an opposition to come to power, and the chance for a nation to rejuvenate itself after bouts of economic decline or political deadlock.

For these reasons, defense of elections is becoming a high politics affair in Latin America; the region will not tolerate their suspension and has insisted that they be conducted freely and fairly. Accordingly, there has been an unmistakable strengthening of electoral monitoring missions. What were once short-term visitations aimed at passively observing the balloting process have been transformed into longer-term stays, with large teams of observers actively engaged in supervising the entire process, training election officials, reporting irregularities, and even mediating disputes between incumbents and opponents (Middlebrook 1998). Beginning with the elections in Nicaragua and Haiti in 1990, broader authority has been conferred on observation teams to peer beyond the actual tallying of votes to observe and report on electoral laws, commissions, campaign financing, registration procedures, and access to media outlets (Middlebrook 1998).

Once elections are over, the dynamic changes dramatically. Assuming that observers have deemed the elections to be open and impartial, then the regional community will acknowledge the enormous legitimacy automatically conferred on the new leader by virtue of having won a democratic contest. But even when questions about the propriety of the elections linger, foreign state attention does not. Once elections are decided, and the new leader prepares to assume power, the die is cast. External actors withdraw, believing they have lost the leverage they enjoyed when power, in the midst of an election, was more fluid. Now that matters are settled, the newly elected leader or the governing coalition may tamper with democratic institutions without setting off alarms at OAS headquarters that could trigger collective action of one sort or another. Thus far, neither resolution 1080 nor the Democratic Charter has been invoked in response to the erosion of judicial autonomy, the weakening of congresses, or the loss of civil liberties and political rights.

These kinds of problems have to do with an erosion of democratic quality. When there is a steady and progressive weakening of democratic representation, accountability, institutions, and nonelectoral processes—even as the overall architecture of the democratic system is preserved—the region finds it enormously difficult to muster the will to respond. This brings us to the final threshold—that of deepening—and one that the OAS and the regional community have yet to cross.

Barriers to Regional Influence over Domestic Politics

Less attention was paid to democratic quality issues in the 1980s because the return to democracy itself was an exciting and major accomplishment. But as the decade of the 1990s wore on, it became clear that the democratic community, which on the surface seemed solid and monolithic, disguised serious deficiencies that cut across the conceptual line between procedural and substantive features of the system. The sense was that governments in the region had become less efficacious, representative, and accountable than they once were. Deadbeat congresses that failed to legislate, autocratic presidents that disregarded the letter of the law and ruled by decree, legislative-executive feuds that resulted in deadlock, remote judicial systems that were beyond the pale of average citizens, ossified political parties that lost touch with their bases, and in general governing institutions that seem unresponsive to the needs of ordinary people—all of these contributed to a decline in democratic quality.[7]

That loss of quality had vertical and horizontal dimensions. Vertically, there was a serious lack of accountability to the voting public. Doubts were raised about whether institutions of government were responding to the will of the governed. The general sense among scholars was that the foundation, stability, effectiveness, and appeal of parties, not to mention other interest-articulating aggregating institutions, had deteriorated over the course of the decade (Hagopian 1998). The horizontal dimension to this problem was best captured by Guillermo O'Donnell's concept of delegative democracy where chief executives acted as if they were no longer accountable to the other two branches of government (1994). Traditional systems of checks and balances that might have held *caudillo*-style presidents in check were undermined. Presidents circumvented the will of the congress, packed the high courts, robbed judges of their autonomy, tightened their grip on the mass media, and repressed others who were critical of their authoritarian inclinations, while drawing closer to their military, security, and intelligence forces.

The decline in quality of democratic governance has been serious enough to give rise to qualifications. Democracies are delegative, fragile, semi, pseudo, quasi, illiberal, and partial in nature (Collier and Levitsky 1997).[8] Adjectives are adjoined to nouns to identify different ways in which systems were not completely living up to their democratic billings. Freedom House scores reveal a slippage in adherence to democratic political rights and civil liberties between the early and mid-1990s for example. Of twenty-one Latin American republics rated in 1990, the nonpartisan group found that thirteen could be considered free, meaning they afforded political organizations and individuals full rights of participation, competition, and expression. By 1995, only seven were so categorized, while fourteen were considered to be only partially free or not free. By the end of the decade there had been some improvement and yet still ten of twenty-one republics were considered to be only partly free. Larry Diamond took the Freedom House scores and devised more refined categories, ranging from liberal at the top, to near and semidemocratic in the middle, to authoritarian and state hegemonic at the bottom. Based on this exercise, he concluded, "If we look beyond formal constitutional structure, it could be argued that more than half the major states of the region . . . fail to qualify as democracies (Diamond, Linz, and Lipset 1995, 53)."

Diamond may be too harsh in his conclusions based on partial data. Be that as it may, it can be safely said that nearly all the OAS member states exhibit sizeable imperfections, giving rise to a new problem. These flawed democracies have incentives not to press the organization to adapt firm measures against some other member for having failed to live up to democratic standards, fearing that the spotlight will be thrown back on them next time around. These are governments that are unwilling to risk being scrutinized for failing to uphold standards higher than they themselves have achieved, because they fear the repercussions. It is not that their vital material and security interests will be threatened, since we are dealing with low politics issues. But those democratic regimes do still incur costs in the form of foreign condemnation and shaming (Keck and Sikkink 1998). Countries concerned with their credibility in the eyes of the regional and international communities would rather not have their own democratic deficiencies subjected to close scrutiny.

It certainly is true that dilemmas of democratic deepening—representation, accountability, efficiency, fairness, and so forth—could eventually weaken a regime to the point of demise at the hands of insurgent civilians or coup-prone officers. If that were to occur, it would pose direct challenges via contagion to the survival of neighboring democratic regimes and others in the region. Why then would OAS members not anticipate low politics difficulties triggering high politics crises by acting presently to help a fellow member strengthen its democratic institutions and procedures? The reason is that political leaders are myopic; they worry about the short term, not the long term. While weakened democracies may prove troublesome sometime in the future, political survival in office (Ames 1987) dictates that politicians respond convincingly only to the crises at hand, not to difficulties on the far horizon. From that vantage point, democratic presidents cannot summon the political will to press for strong OAS measures to help deepen democracy in a member state.

But neither does any one country want to invite negative attention by appearing to obstruct all efforts, lest it lose credibility in the eyes of others. Consequently, all members agree that the OAS takes tepid, nonenforceable measures, allowing problematic democracies to escape from close scrutiny or penalty. The one country that could safely push for stronger adherences to democratic ideals would be the United States. But should the United States go at it alone and, moreover, act in a heavy-handed way, it would rekindle memories of Washington's unilateral thrusts into the region, causing a backlash that would be counterproductive. As a result the United States, along with its Southern neighbors, has responded in lackluster fashion when democratic quality is at stake.

It was not just the problem arising from the regionwide departure from democratic ideals that poses a barrier to external intervention, but the colliding standards upon which the OAS community itself rested, at least until passage of the

Inter-American Democratic Charter in 2001. In fact, departures from norms of democratic governance could be squared with the aforementioned principles of political pluralism found in the OAS charter. An "offending" state could remind the rest of the community of article 3 giving it the right to choose its own political system, reinforced by article 17, which says, "Each State has the right to develop its cultural, political, and economic life freely and naturally" (OAS 2004). Admittedly, this same article did qualify this right by also stating, "In this free development, the State shall respect the rights of the individual and the principles of universal morality" (OAS 2004). But this language left a lot of wiggle room for states to adopt their own versions of democracy, regardless of how imperfect they might be. Without a yardstick with which to measure democratic adherence, it was rather easy for governments in the region to get by with questionable practices. Principles of political pluralism conspired with principles of nonintervention to erect imposing barriers to rendering judgments about, let alone taking actions against, democratic infractions.

How could the OAS community commit itself to a principle of political pluralism and at the same time a principle of political uniformity, namely that democracy is the only acceptable form of government? Only if it were to enforce the second principle in a way that would not violate the first; it would have to concern itself with the fundamental survival of democracy more than its quality, the procedural minimum more than the substantive maximum. It would have to give each state the benefit of the doubt in defining for itself what is a permissible proximity to democratic standards, recognizing that no state adheres to a set of ideal standards. Certainly if the principle of plurality is honored, then some incremental departure from ideal norms of democracy would be a small offense to say the least, a far cry from the dramatic reversals that befall a state that becomes a victim of a military coup. In fact, to have helped a country step back from the precipice of dictatorship, as the OAS, and the United States and other states, did with Ecuador in January 2000, would be to earn a huge victory, one that would deflect attention from any democratic ills that predate and persist beyond the crisis.

The problems with Peru's 2000 elections—one of the objects of study here—occurred before passage of the 2001 Democratic Charter (OAS 2001). That charter laid out a set of essential elements to representative democracy, which in theory should lessen the doubt that the regional community is committed to specific, uniform, and nonnegotiable standards. It remains to be seen just how effective the charter will be at resolving the contradictions between democracy and pluralism. It also remains to be seen how often members will invoke the charter to resolve problems that lie beyond the electoral realm.

In sum, the region faces three kinds of democratic dilemmas: survival, electoral procedure, and quality. The OAS calibrates its responses to each, as shown below in figure 4.1. It has a range of options available to it, from declarations of concern or condemnation at one end, to punitive sanctions at the other. In between, the organization can call for extraordinary meetings of the ministers of foreign affairs to signal the gravity of the situation and a deeper commitment; it can send observer or fact-finding missions to the country, which produce reports and make recommendations; it can state demands for change; set timetables for compliance; threaten punishment; and enact punishment. A specific option will be selected based on the nature of the democratic infraction, as shown across the top of the diagram. The progression is not linear; it moves from the "either/or" of democratic survival, to procedural issues (are elections being held, and are they free and fair?) in the middle, to quality issues at the other end (democratic accountability, institutional strength, separation of powers, etc.). When the very survival of the democratic system is clearly at risk, the organization reacts decisively, in defense of its member states and what has become their high politics

Figure 4.1. OAS Responses to Democratic Dilemmas

Nature of Democratic Problem

	Democratic Survival	Democratic Electoral Procedure	Democratic Quality
Declarations of Concern	•	•	•
Ministerial Meeting	•	•	•
Observers Sent	•	•	•
Recommendations Made	•	•	•
Demands Made	•	•	
Timetable Set	•	•	
Punishment Threatened	•	•	
Punishment Enacted	•	•	

Frequency of OAS Involvement: High ↑ ↓ Low

stakes. When the democratic system is challenged in a less fundamental way, then less forceful measures are chosen, as shown in figure 4.1.

The "bullets" indicate actions taken, which vary by institutional venue and consequence. As the measures taken become more significant, they are used less frequently. For example, a more tepid response might constitute an OAS declaration of concern arising out of its Permanent Council, which meets regularly and comprises the OAS ambassadors. The organization will respond as such whether the problem is one of democratic survival, procedure, or quality. A somewhat stronger response would occur if the same message were conveyed by the ministers of foreign affairs, who have higher diplomatic status and who meet infrequently. Greater weight still should be afforded a declaration from either body that mandates the OAS to take direct actions in response to a problem, and stronger still where demands are placed or punishment inflicted on the offending nation. Even at its most determined level, the OAS is limited by the fact that it can recommend but not impose punitive measures on an offending government. Application of recommendations is voluntary and nonbinding (Muñoz 1994).

But as the strength of the response increases, the occasions upon which it occurs decreases. It is clear that the OAS will resort to the more draconian measures only when the democracy's survival is unambiguously threatened, either by a military coup, suspension of elections, or some similarly dramatic interruption of the constitutional order (i.e., *autogolpe*, the illegal usurpation of power). As the problem of a democracy deepens, OAS involvement grows shallower.

This is not to say that the OAS is completely inactive when questions of democratic consolidation are in play. The organization may lend its good offices in support of the government's professed desire to strengthen its own democracy. For example, the OAS's Unit for the Promotion of Democracy has frequently collaborated with Latin American administrations, parliaments, and NGOs to fortify institutions, promote democratic values, and provide technical assistance.[9] But the UPD is also the institutional embodiment of the organization's reluctance to intrude too deeply into the domestic affairs of member states. It is under severe budgetary constraint, which in the year 2001 meant it had literally no more than $83,000 to spend on each of the twenty Latin American republics. Those scant resources permit it to operate mainly at local and regional, not national, levels.[10] And it is a purely collaborative body that "complements, assists, and supports the internal efforts of member states," but which cannot pressure or leverage those states at all.[11] In sum, democratic deepening is a low politics affair. As an intergovernmental organization (IGO), the OAS does not have the autonomy to take bolder steps to aid ailing democracies. Beholden to its members, it acts tepidly because those members do not perceive their own vital interests to be at stake.

Peru

When Peruvian foreign minister Fernando Trazegnies Granda officially granted permission on October 22, 1999, for the OAS to send an electoral observation team to his country to witness the presidential elections scheduled for that spring, he did not foresee the trouble that invitation would cause for his government. While he may have expected some scrutiny in light of past OAS interventions, neither he nor President Alberto Fujimori were prepared for the unusually aggressive and confrontational approach of this electoral mission. The foreign minister and president were no doubt summoning to mind the events of 1992, when Fujimori's April *autogolpe* prompted the OAS to invoke Resolution 1080 and pressure Peru's leader to hold constituent assembly elections in November of that year. The OAS had staved off a complete authoritarian takeover by allowing the legislative branch to survive. But it would not thwart Fujimori's bid to manipulate those elections, future elections (i.e., in 1995), the Congress, and indeed the entire Peruvian state to his advantage. The president would go on to submit the "democracy" to his autocratic will, while avoiding the glare of official scrutiny from the outside. Why then could he not get away with it again? Optimistic about his chances, the president extended an especially warm welcome to the OAS election mission this time around (McClintock 2002, 143).

Of course electoral observation had, during the past decade, become a matter of course for Latin American countries. From 1990 to 2000, the UPD had assembled fifty-two missions to observe elections in eighteen countries—compared to thirteen such missions in the decade before (Unit for the Promotion of Democracy 2004). Foreign monitoring had become a legitimate practice in the region. To have refused its entry would have been to summon all kinds of suspicions about what Fujimori might have in store for the electorate. Of the Latin American presidents, he could least of all afford to sow doubts at this time. He was already treading on thin ice because his bid for a third term was unprecedented and constitutionally illegal. Almost everyone at the time believed he had rigged the political system to allow for his own succession attempt and had earned notoriety for doing so. Still, political leaders do not issue invitations to be scrutinized by foreign observers simply so that they can conform to regional norms or trends; they do so because they see some advantage to be gained. The president probably reasoned that he could once again get an OAS stamp of approval that would dissuade future interventions and allow him to reclaim for his government some of the legitimacy that had been lost. He may have thought that in some subtle if not sophisticated way his trusted and shadowy security adviser, Vladimir Montesinos, could maneuver the election machinery in his favor, even under the watchful eye of the mission, and then rest comfortably with victory in hand once the election was over.

The OAS was quite cognizant of the fact that it had some unfinished business to attend to. Looking back on the events of 1992, and remembering how on December 14 of that year, it had closed the book on Fujimori's *autogolpe*, it now was of the view it had been duped. It was then that the ad hoc committee of foreign ministers resolved that the November 22, 1992, constituent assembly elections had "represented an important phase in process of re-establishing democratic institutional order," and because that was so, the OAS investigation could come to an end.[12] With the benefit of hindsight, it is clear that decision was premature. In closing the book, the OAS had kept in its sights the election itself but had turned a blind eye toward the president's crafty maneuvers leading up to the election and, more important, to the maneuvers that would transpire in the years ahead. The mission had ignored the pre-election measures designed to strengthen Fujimori's party at the expense of the others and to transform what was supposed to be a constituent assembly into an obsequious congress. Instead, the OAS focused just on the election day and whether there was fraud—something Peruvians suspected, but could never prove.[13]

President Fujimori had bet that if he could just get past the constituent elections themselves, he would have won an important victory with the regional community and would be free to pursue his policies with less outside scrutiny and intervention. He was right. The OAS left the scene having bestowed its blessings, but without having established clear guidelines for measuring Peru's observance of democratic rules, without having set up a timetable to assess progress, and without having spelled out consequences should the timetable and goals not be met (Palmer 1996). As a result, Fujimori operated with a free hand and would go on to tamper with and dismantle some basic democratic safeguards of his country.[14] Once the OAS moved from confrontation to collaboration to indifference, the president's "democracy" would become increasingly authoritarian, so much so that by the end of the decade, scholars of Peru were doubting whether it merited the democratic label at all.[15] What had Fujimori done in the interim? What follows is just a partial catalog of the president's malfeasance, and that of those who served under him, especially Vladimir Montesinos:

- Likely fraud in the tally of rural votes in the referendum on the new constitution in October 1993, with a yes vote much higher than polls had indicated in areas under military control
- Questionable vote tallies and violations of civil liberties and freedoms, including the wiretapping of opposition candidate Javier Pérez de Cuéllar in the 1995 presidential elections
- Stripping citizenship and control of his business from a television station owner for having reported that the government had placed some two hundred wiretaps on media and opposition figures
- Arbitrary ouster of three Constitutional Tribunal judges who opposed his bid for a third term
- Persuasion of congressional supporters to reject a referendum initiative that challenged the constitutionality of this third term—despite the initiative's legality and surfeit of required signatures
- Stacking of the National Election Commission with his supporters
- Murder and cover-up by SIN officials of an intelligence officer who had exposed the workings of Grupo Molina, a military hit squad (McClintock 2003; Palmer 2000)

These and many other moves were masterminded by Montesinos, a former cashiered army captain turned drug cartel lawyer who quickly rose to the pinnacles of power in Fujimori's administration. He became the architect of a systematic effort to control the courts, the congress, the electoral commissions, the media, the military, and other vital institutions of democracy. As head of the feared Sistema de Inteligencia Nacional (SIN), he collected intelligence on friends and foes alike, illegally infiltrated all branches of government, and used security forces to harass, and sometimes eliminate, Fujimori's opposition. All this occurred without triggering any significant reactions or reprisals from regional organizations.

Some have argued that without the OAS intervention of 1992 things could have been worse. But what is to be said when the regional organization endorses a process that drives the country further away from democratic norms, not closer to them? Now, in the spring of 2000, the OAS was returning to observe an election in which President Fujimori would never have been allowed to participate, were it not for his own antidemocratic maneuvers. Having suffered an embarrassment once before, the new mission that arrived in Peru in March 2000 seemed intent on regaining some stature by examining in detail the events leading up to the elections, the quality of the elections themselves, the electoral institutions, and more broadly, the democratic context in which all the candidates would be operating. These were ambitious plans; the question would be to what extent it could fulfill those plans and make a difference.

From Mission Arrival to First-Round Elections

The OAS Electoral Observation Mission headed by Eduardo Stein, former Guatemalan foreign minister, arrived in Peru on March 2, 2000, with a new self-described attitude and mandate.[16] Previous missions were, in Stein's words, "mute sentinels," there to silently record observations and then report these findings five or six months later. "Our mission," he said "would behave differently. We wanted to be an activist mission that would report to the public our observations in real time, as we made them," said Stein. "We also intended to become more aggressive once we saw signs of wrongdoing, or when the authorities would not cooperate with us," he added.[17]

With one hundred members from nineteen countries, the mission fanned out into twelve Peruvian provinces, taking stock of the situation. Were conditions propitious for free and fair elections to be held on April 9? It quickly became apparent to the mission that there were serious obstacles and irregularities, and if these persisted without correction, they would prevent such an election from occurring. Confidence in the electoral process had already been shaken just two days before the OAS team's arrival. On February 29, the daily El Comercio revealed that up to 1.2 million signatures needed for qualifying Fujimori's campaign had been falsified. The mission considered as one of its objectives the restoration of that confidence by being able to certify that the process was credible. For the mission, the process had broader connotations than just balloting; it meant the electoral commission and whether it was operating in an impartial manner, as well as the wider political context, including media access, unfair use of state revenues to support the incumbent, and possible state-sanctioned harassment of opposition figures. In this respect, the Stein team intended to test the waters between the narrow, mechanical elements of balloting and the broader elements of how democratic institutions functioned in Peruvian society.

On election day itself, suspicions about the balloting process surfaced quickly, as the mission and other independent monitoring agencies received information regarding a series of irregularities. There were reports that police and military officials were harassing election monitors appointed by opposition parties and that soldiers were slowing up voter lines to cause huge delays, only to deny entrance to those at the end of the cue. Precinct officials detected discrepancies between the numbers of voters and those on the lists, and the OAS noted delays getting ballots and tally sheets to counting centers, and the appearance of premarked ballots for President Fujimori.[18] Transparencia, an independent Peruvian election-monitoring agency, reported a mysterious computer virus, telephone cutoff, and power outage at its headquarters during the elections.[19]

Then the government itself reported difficulties with its computers, which were temporarily shut down. That meant it would have to renege on its promise to tabulate 30 percent of the vote by that election day evening and instead delay releasing results for perhaps as long as forty-eight hours. This lag caused the Stein mission to worry, especially since by four o'clock that afternoon, one independent exit poll by Datum had lead opposition candidate Alejandro Toledo out ahead 48.5 percent to Fujimori's 42.7 percent. At eleven thirty that evening, José Portillo Campbell, head of Peru's electoral commission, the Oficina Nacional de Procesos Electorales (ONPE), announced that the computer system had only tallied 3 percent of the vote, not nearly enough to declare a first-round winner.[20]

But after an evening filled with computer problems and delayed ballot deliveries, the government could suddenly announce by midday on the tenth that 77 percent of the vote had been counted and Fujimori was ahead with 49.85 percent to Toledo's 40.41 percent.[21] Were these results to go unchallenged, Fujimori could possibly top the 50 percent mark, thus eliminating a runoff. The whiff of fraud filled the air. The OAS immediately turned up the heat, throwing doubt on the credibility of these results. Said Eduardo Stein: "A first round victory simply would not be a politically acceptable result for the Peruvian electorate or the international community, and it would have grave repercussions for Peru."[22] The U.S. government chimed in saying it expected a second round of voting in Peru.

The mission's attention to detail, its fast tabulation of votes (along with those done by Transparencia) that could be matched with final tallies, and generally quick reactions to potential wrongdoings were proving effective. It put the Fujimori administration on the spot, forcing it to either push forward despite the entire region knowing it was up to no good, or to back down in order to receive some blessings from the OAS.

On Tuesday, April 12, the government conceded that a runoff would be necessary after all, putting Fujimori's total at 49.8 percent, with 97.7 percent of the votes counted.[23] This concession was the first significant setback for President Fujimori's four-year effort to win a third term. As Catherine Conaghan has said: "The failure of the Fujimori re-election project was profound. Not only had the Fujimori administration been unable to orchestrate a convincing win in the first round, but the manner of its failure generated circumstances that would make the pursuit of the re-election project even more problematic in the second round" (2001a, 14).

Seldom did the Peruvian government publicly take umbrage with the OAS, even though many of its advisements were uncompromising. The mantle of collective legitimacy that the Stein mission wore made it considerably more persuasive than the United States, whose equally blunt messages were often deeply offensive to the Peruvians.[24] Summing up the impact of the OAS mission so far, the New York Times editorialized, "Mr. Stein's unremitting public criticism of unexplained delays in the handling and computing of vote tallies proved to be a decisive element in breaking Mr. Fujimori's international support."[25] Stein's mission continued to receive the full backing of the OAS, whose member states had, amidst the upheaval, contemplated political and economic reprisals against the Fujimori government had it decided not to schedule runoffs. As suggested by our model, when the viability of an election is on the line, it is a high politics affair, and the OAS is prepared to resort to more stringent measures, including the threat of sanction. The OAS, along with other external agencies such as the Carter Center and the National Democratic Institute, had thus intervened in a very significant and positive way. Principal opposition candidate Alejandro Toledo said, "The international community has played a critical role in defense of democracy."[26]

From First-Round to Second-Round Elections

The presidential runoff was set to occur on May 28. Eduardo Stein wasted no time setting down markers for the next phase, saying on April 14, "I want to point out again that if the anomalies detected in the first phase are repeated, this election cannot be endorsed."[27] As more facts surfaced about the first round, it became clearer just how much work lay ahead if Peru was to hold a free and fair election next time around. These problems could be divided into questions of media communications, organization, human skills, and technology.

Much of the media, especially certain television stations, made life difficult for opposition candidates. Candidates were routinely denied equal access, including the right to air paid advertisements.[28] Media coverage of opposition rallies was at times nonexistent. Systematic media bias was not something cooked up in the television studio. It was suspected then, and has come to light since, that Vladimir Montesinos conceived, orchestrated, and financed a scheme to influence media coverage of the elections. Apparently, Montesinos raised some $30 million as payment for giving a shady business group illegal contracts to sell weaponry to the Peruvian military. This money was used to pay off newspapers, magazines, and especially television stations (the principal source of news for Peruvians) to slant coverage in favor of Fujimori while engaging in character assassinations against Toledo and other opposition candidates. The owner of one television station was receiving as much as $1.5 million a month.[29] Bribery was not Montesinos's only weapon. He manipulated tax rates and used the judicial system to pressure the press into conformity, appointing obsequious judges who would render unfavorable rulings toward media outlets that were too independent minded.[30] It is difficult to know how Fujimori would have faired in the campaign without the aid of a biased press. But it must be assumed that he achieved some significant advantage by having powerful news outlets help shape public perceptions in his favor.

The OAS mission found serious deficiencies in the way the ONPE went about organizing national elections. The system seemed to have broken down at nearly every point, from the operation, staffing, and supervision of polling places, to the diffusion of voter information, to the timely delivery of ballot sheets to headquarters, to the tallying of votes themselves. It was not uncommon to find ONPE-appointed election officials who were ill-trained to explain voting procedures to voters, to assess the validity of completed ballots, and even to secure the secrecy of the voting process. The OAS mission worked with the ONPE to coordinate training workshops for polling officials, but within ten days of the second round, only 25 percent of those officials had even bothered to show up. The mission concluded that there was a high level of indifference among ONPE-designated officials who could not see the point of being retrained for elections they had already served (Unidad para la Promoción de la Democracia 2001, 54–55). There were other organizational glitches that were noted, including the failure to communicate electoral results in a timely fashion and lack of vehicles to deliver ballots. The OAS mission concluded that there was a "persistent absence" of sufficient planning and management, especially at logistical and informational levels, that led to the occurrence of perfectly avoidable problems (Unidad para la Promoción de la Democracia 2001, 67–68).

But perhaps the most serious problem was the nation's official computer system. Questions were raised about the tabulation of votes, the integrity and security of the system, and the failure to adequately test that system prior to election day. First-round results indicated that some 1.5 million more ballots had been tabulated than there were registered voters. The OAS, along with the opposition political parties, was expecting the government to make corrections in the system and was thus surprised to hear on May 12 that the ONPE had decided to install new software altogether, designed solely for presidential elections. ONPE had not left enough time to test the new system, which Stein said would require at least three weeks.[31] The runoff was scheduled in two weeks' time. Also, ONPE had kept its new program under wraps, refusing to share information with opposition parties or the OAS. It was not until May 20 that it finally invited the OAS to observe a trial run of the system. There, the OAS observers concluded there were "grave problems with it, including serious glitches to work out, including one that erased voting data from certain districts."[32] To allow for sufficient time to correct the problems, the Stein mission insisted that the elections be postponed till June 11. But ONPE disputed Stein's assessment, saying it was "absolutely certain" that the program was running properly, and then tried to validate its conclusions by the very fact that the OAS observers had been there.[33]

Following a week of intense negotiations with the OAS mission, and U.S. and Latin American diplomats, the National Election Commission by a vote of 3–2 decided to go forward with the election as scheduled on the twenty-eighth. The constitution, they argued, prohibited any flexibility on this because it mandated elections to occur no more than thirty days after the declaration of victors in round one.[34] Stein reacted saying, "we are quite disappointed." A U.S. embassy official weighed in, remarking that his government "deeply regrets this outcome." The very next day, Stein told forty-two of his monitors to pack their bags and leave Peru, rather than stay for an election he contended would be "far from free or fair."[35] Alejandro Toledo had already withdrawn from the contest.[36] On May 28 President Fujimori ran for a third term uncontested, although Toledo's name stayed on the ballot. Fujimori earned 51 percent of total votes cast, to Toledo's 18 percent. At the urging of Toledo, the remaining ballots had been left blank or spoiled. While there were no obvious instances of fraud reported that day, few save Fujimori himself were willing to confer any legitimacy on the results.[37]

In its final report the Stein mission said, "In accord with international standards, the Peruvian electoral process is far from free and just" (Unidad para la Promoción de Democracia 2001, 113). Not confining its critique to the imperfections of the computer system or other mechanical elements of balloting, the mission indicted the Peruvian democracy itself, citing a lack of separation of powers among branches of government. The report said, "It is imperative that the clear autonomy of government branches, especially the Judiciary and Public Ministry, be re-established" (Unidad para la Promoción de Democracia 2001, 121). But in the end, these were just recommendations; political power would determine which reforms, if any, would be embraced. And for now power rested squarely with Fujimori.

From Second-Round Elections to Mesa del Diálogo

Member nations had given the Stein mission a long leash, allowing it to work with great independence, resolve, and dispatch to oversee and attempt to influence the electoral process. Now, with the election results in and the mission having completed its work, the dynamic had changed. Members would be more willing to tilt toward principles of nonintervention and away from democratic defense. They were unsure what more they could do or should do to influence Peruvian democracy in the postelection period. They seemed ready to move back down the ladder from more intrusive to less intrusive actions. On May 31, at a meeting of the OAS Permanent Council, the overwhelming majority of members concluded that the reelection of President Alberto Fujimori should stand, arguing this was an internal affair of Peru. A proposal by the U.S. representative to the OAS, Luis Lauredo, to invoke Resolution 1080 was soundly defeated on grounds of inapplicability.[38] In voting this way, most of the nations agreed with Brazil that the OAS had to balance the defense of democracy with respect for sovereignty. Mexico argued that the OAS cannot and should not substitute for functions that correspond to a sovereign government. The Uruguayan representative added that there was no legal precedent allowing them to annul or refuse to accept the results.[39] After the Permanent Council vote, the Peruvian ambassador to the OAS declared it a "total victory" for her country, boasting that the principle of nonintervention had prevailed at the meeting.[40] The council members did agree, however, to the U.S. request to have the matter of the election brought before the OAS General Assembly scheduled to meet in Windsor, Canada, on June 4–5.[41]

At that meeting, after what the OAS itself described as "hours of tense and difficult negotiations," all the foreign ministers minus Venezuela's agreed on a Canadian-sponsored resolution (1753) to send a high-level mission to Peru to "explore with the Peruvian government and other sectors of the political community, options and recommendations directed to a significant strengthening of democracy in that country, and in particular measures to reform the electoral process, including reform of the constitutional and judicial tribunals and strengthening of the free press."[42] There would be no condemnation or further assessment of the election itself. In fact, the decision to send a high-level delegation down to work with the Peruvians was a tacit admission by the OAS that Fujimori's victory was a fait accompli. The president of the thirtieth General Assembly, Canadian foreign minister Lloyd Axworthy, admitted as such, saying Fujimori's reelection "is a reality."[43]

The Peruvians accepted the proposal believing that not to do so would have backfired on them. In commenting on the decision, Peru's foreign minister, Fernando de Trazegnies, reaffirmed the legitimacy of the elections and then added, "But in the shadow of an unjust doubt, the Fujimori government is committed to strengthening its institutions in the following presidential period."[44] The foreign minister also seemed to acknowledge and accept the imperfections of the Peruvian political system, saying, "not all the countries have the same level of democracy."[45] The implication was clear: so long as countries were in some sense minimally democratic, they should be left alone to create their own version of democracy. There is no doubt that this expression resonated well with the other Latin American countries who themselves were struggling to match practice with principles.[46] Thus, the problem alluded to earlier had emerged full blown:

widespread democratic deficiencies would preclude any one member from pressing the issue of democratic deepening. The United States emerged from the General Assembly meeting itself having drawn closer to the Peruvian position. Undersecretary of State Thomas Pickering said, "There are no perfect democracies," and switched his government's assessment of the second-round elections from "invalid" to "seriously imperfect."[47] With the United States on board, the regional community was now unanimous in its appraisal that there were serious limits to how far nations could coerce other nations to consolidate their democratic systems.[48]

With these meetings concluded, the OAS had both lost and gained an opportunity. A presidential election is always a crucial test of democratic commitment. It is also a clearly defined event that if tainted or fraudulent could more easily trigger a forceful OAS reaction. With the election having come and gone, the OAS no longer had that signal event to focus its energies on. Instead, it was about to enter murkier waters. It would have to deal with threats to democracy that were, in Ambassador Lauredo's words, "more subtle than ever."[49] Its mandate was to find ways to strengthen the full panoply of Peruvian democratic institutions and processes by working with the authorities, not against them. It could move well below the procedural level to deal with matters of substance, and well beyond the limits of elections to confront problems of a systemic nature. It would have to do so by partnering with the Fujimori government. Those were daunting tasks, which if fulfilled would have far-reaching implications for Peru and the region. But what would be the benchmarks for success or failure? How would the OAS decide if Peru had complied with suggestions or not? Would there be strict timetables for fulfilling goals? And most important, could the organization get Peru to comply or sanction Peru for noncompliance?

The high-level mission, led by OAS secretary general César Gaviria and General Assembly chair and Canadian foreign minister Lloyd Axworthy, arrived in Lima on June 27, 2000, under a certain cloud of suspicion. Alejandro Toledo proclaimed that the mission was tainted because the OAS had failed to invalidate the election. Others suspected the mission would be used by Fujimori to legitimize his authoritarian democracy.[50] The mission avoided the bolder alternatives of calling for new elections or endorsing a referendum on Fujimori's third term proposed by national ombudsman Jorge Santistevan.[51] But conscious of the need to at least project an image of resoluteness, the mission stated that the intelligence agencies would have to be overhauled and that Vladimiro Montesinos, the president's infamous security czar, would have to go if genuine reform were to be advanced.[52] And it soon became apparent that the mission also intended to move beyond the procedural minimums of electoral practices to involve itself in broader and more fundamental problems of the democratic system. It would propose an historic agenda for change, setting up a permanent mission office in Lima and appointing former Dominican foreign minister Eduardo LaTorre to head it up. The agenda for change was drafted in the form of twenty-nine points by Canadian representative to the OAS Peter Boehm and presented to the Peruvian authorities at the end of June 2000.[53]

The points ranged from guarantees for judicial independence to promotion of human rights to civilian control of intelligence services and the armed forces. The proposals included many of the hot-button issues that had been raised countless times by human rights groups and the opposition. The OAS mission wanted to place on the table for discussion the problem of provisional judges who had served six-month terms at the pleasure of Fujimori; reinstallation of three judges who had been dismissed by Congress; correction of human rights abuses by establishing an independent human rights commission; reform of the media to guarantee access to all political parties while returning a confiscated television station to its rightful owner; reform of the electoral system, empowering it to investigate, prosecute, and punish wrongdoing; choice of election commissioners to ensure impartiality; restoration of the balance of power between branches of government, civilian control over intelligence agencies, and a more active civilian presence in the national defense council; and restoration of a professional process by which promotions are awarded and retirements are considered.[54]

Just in terms of laying out an agenda for internal democratic change, the OAS's twenty-nine points was one of unprecedented ambition for an outside organization. If indeed the mission was to succeed in compelling the Peruvian government to adopt all or at least most of these changes, it would mark a watershed event in the history of relations between the OAS and a member state.[55] But however impressive the objectives may have been, the means to advance those objectives were not. OAS strategy fits very well with the conceptual framework outlined in figure 4.1. As the OAS moved into areas of democratic quality, the nature of its involvement became more tepid. Lloyd Axworthy himself, in referring to the twenty-nine points, repeatedly stressed these were recommendations, not demands.[56] All involved in the mission saw these as a starting point for dialogue, nothing more. The Canadian-led delegation would facilitate an exchange of views by setting up a Mesa del Diálogo that comprised representatives of the government, civil society, and some from the political opposition.

OAS secretary general Gaviria said he hoped the proposals would be implemented in time for municipal elections in 2002.[57] While the mission said it would not close its Lima office until the goals were fulfilled within that timeframe, it never imposed a schedule of completion with intermediate deadlines, or penalties for noncompliance. Objectives remained vague, as did indicators for verifying fulfillment or nonconformity.[58] In an interview, the author of these points, Peter Boehm, admitted that politically the mission did not feel it had the power to put teeth into its points. Though the mission suggested there would be serious repercussions for Peru should it not comply—by way of being blacklisted from receipt of Inter-American Development Bank (IDB) and World Bank funds, along with foreign investments—it undercut the credibility of these threats by suggesting, not demanding, action. An organization that is recommending, not insisting, upon change is hardly one that will be prepared to impose sanctions for noncompliance. The Peruvian authorities knew full well that the mission would not enforce its will on them after members had already resigned themselves to President Fujimori's new five-year term. Moreover, Fujimori could reasonably predict that international lenders and the United States would prefer doing business with his country so long as he kept Peru on a steady course toward economic liberalization while making some cosmetic political changes.

In fact, once reelected, Fujimori wasted little time before backpeddling on pledges he had made to the mission regarding proposed changes. A month after promising to consider the twenty-nine-point plan, Fujimori reasserted his government's sovereignty over all matters of democratic reform, saying that Peru would remodel its democratic institutions as it saw fit and that the "opinions of other countries are not important to us." Fujimori's version of cleaning up a politically corrupt system was to have his party's congressional investigation find several lower-rung ONPE officials guilty of vote rigging in the case regarding the falsification of signatures to register his candidacy. But ONPE's head, along with the six congressional beneficiaries of the fraud, were cleared of criminal wrongdoing.[59] It seemed as if the Axworthy mission would have its hands full.

The OAS's Mesa del Diálogo first convened on August 21 to discuss timelines and modalities for implementing the twenty-nine points, followed on September 4 by a meeting at which working groups were set up to discuss the inter-American court, media freedom, the intelligence services, and the renewal of the Constitutional Tribunal. If the dialogue succeeded at all it did so by providing a much needed forum for a freewheeling debate that had hitherto been taboo. At the time, it was literally the only venue in Peru in which the political opposition and civil society could sit down with government representatives to voice their perspectives and attempt to hammer out solutions to key problems. Andrew Cooper and Thomas Legler go further, saying that the Mesa "became the locus of real decision-making power during the final days of the Fujimori government and before the Peruvian opposition could win control of congress and for an interim government" (2001, 33). Was that so? What was the singular impact of the mission and its "Mesa"?

Too great an influence should not be ascribed to the Mesa since its deliberations coincided with the unfolding of cataclysmic political events inside Peru. The fall of President Fujimori, Vladimiro Montesinos, and the entire government began just three weeks after the inaugural session of the dialogue and before anything of substance had been achieved. While these events may have helped to push Mesa discussions further along than they might have otherwise gone, at other times they rendered them irrelevant. The signal event of the fall was the September 14 revelation of a videotape showing Montesinos bribing a congressman to become a *transfuga*—to shift allegiance to the government's political party.[60] The video was the smoking gun to the theory that the mysterious defection of several congressmen in June of that year—enough to give Fujimori a majority in the legislature—had been paid for. After the videotape, political change accelerated as President Fujimori called for new elections in which he would not be a candidate, fired Montesino as his senior adviser and National Intelligence head, and finally fled the country on November 13. Nine days later, congressional leader Valentín Paniagua was installed as the interim president of Peru. In between, legislation had been passed to establish a committee to investigate Montesinos's activities, convoke early elections on April 8, 2000, without preconditions, dismantle the SIN, and repeal the law that had allowed for provisional judges. All of these pieces of legislation had been the subject of dialogue discussions.[61] But here, the counterfactual is critical: how much would have been achieved had the scandalous videos not been revealed and had Fujimori not been fatally weakened by it all? It is doubtful much would have been achieved.

The principal reason is that for the Fujimori government to have agreed to most of the twenty-nine points it would have had to thoroughly weaken the base of its own power. For example, working committees were set up by the dialogue to consider the deactivation of SIN, freedom of the press, the return of Peru to the Inter-American Court, and the reconstitution of the Constitutional Tribunal.[62] Significant progress in any of these directions would have struck blows at the very instruments that Montesinos had used to fortify Fujimori's autocratic government. Montesinos operated surreptitiously and illegally via surveillance, repression, bribery, and blackmail. Coercion and criminality were the regime's modus operandi. These methods were operationalized, institutionalized, and centralized within the SIN. To dismantle that agency would be to strip the security czar of his power. To liberate the press would have been to expose his misdeeds. And to resubmit Peru to the rule of law would have been to punish him for his crimes. Once so threatened, Montesinos would have wasted no time implicating Fujimori, thus bringing down the president and his entire government. Consequently, Fujimori could not allow the dialogue to make significant strides without gravely harming himself.

With this in mind, it was no coincidence that the president and his trusted adviser held a press conference on the eve of the Mesa's first meeting at which they exposed an alleged scheme to smuggle arms to the Colombian FARC guerrillas.[63] As it later became apparent, this was done to deflect attention away from Montesinos's own complicity in the illegal arms operation. But it was also undoubtedly done to elevate Montesinos's stature at home and abroad and thus complicate the start of the OAS-led dialogue. It was also in keeping with the president's style, which was to avoid any direct confrontation and feign just enough support for the dialogue to mollify his external critics while attempting to delay and dilute the mission's work. The president welcomed the dialogue and appointed several top officials to represent his interests at the table.

But on more than one occasion, the president's delegation made life difficult for the others, provoking OAS mission chief Eduardo LaTorre to temporarily suspend the dialogue on October 13 after congressional representatives from Cambio 90 (Fujimori's political party) voted to extend the legislative session to October 31, despite a prior agreement at the Mesa not to. Ten days later, an OAS communiqué expressed the high-level mission's "deep concern" about the government's behavior at the meetings.[64] Among its concerns was the government's tabling of discussion of draft legislation to dismantle the SIN. Apparently, the administration had decided to draft its own and send it on to the Congress for approval before advising the Mesa. It had also decided to set up a committee to preside over the SIN's demise, comprised entirely of cabinet members, who in turn would report to the Defense Committee of Congress chaired by a pro-Fujimori representative. The OAS mission was also irked by the government's unveiling of a proposal to the dialogue that would make the holding of early elections contingent on acceptance of a sweeping amnesty for government and military officials, along with the validation of all government actions since the *autogolpe* of April 5, 1992.[65] While the government finally did yield on the amnesty issue, it did so in its waning moments, as the world came crashing in on Fujimori. Such a concession, by a fatally weakened government, can hardly be ascribed to the weight of OAS-proctored discussions (Conaghan 2001b). In the final analysis, the Peruvian regime self-destructed under the weight of its own criminality. That set the stage for the transition to a more valid democracy, which would have occurred with or without the OAS dialogue and its twenty-nine points.

Summing Up

The case study of Peru's 2000 elections and beyond reveals a regional organization testing the waters between high and low politics. States of the region understood that free and fair elections were a centerpiece to democracy. The OAS acted with considerable resolve in its attempt to safeguard the electoral process. Toward that end, it conferred upon the Stein mission all the authority it needed to carry out its work in a vigorous way. But once the mission had packed its bags, the second-round elections had been held, and Fujimori had won a third term, the dynamic changed. The question—at least in the eyes of the OAS members—was no longer the either/or of democracy or the sanctity of elections, but rather the particulars of how the democracy would operate in the future. What would or could be done to improve the quality of Peruvian democratic institutions? With this its agenda, the organization backed away from the more aggressive, at times confrontational, tactics of its electoral observation team to embrace the more friendly and collaborative moves of the Axworthy mission. Recommendations—not demands—were made, threats were withdrawn, timetables never proposed, and penalties for noncompliance not contemplated. The goals of the Mesa were far reaching, but its means were inadequate.

The Peruvian story demonstrates the difficulty foreign states have in drumming up the will to press forcefully for deeper institutional reforms even when the domestic opposition implores them to do so. The OAS's 1992 response to democratic violations in Peru occurred against the backdrop of public enthusiasm for Fujimori's *autogolpe*. OAS officials readily admit the difficulty of taking decisive measures to strengthen democracy when citizens themselves are not supportive.[66] But that excuse was not available eight years later, when demands for democratic deepening had swelled into a mass movement. Political party opponents were now joined by a vast array of organizations from civil society and citizens from different social classes in rejecting Fujimori's regime and pressing for an authentic democracy (Conaghan 2001a, 29). Those organizations knew full well that much of the leverage they enjoyed in their struggle to transform the regime hinged on what empathetic attention they could command from the outside world.

But in the end, they could not rely on consistent support from the OAS. As the Peruvian case makes clear, foreign states do not predicate their response to democratic infringements so much on the strength of the domestic opposition as they do on the contents of the issue. From the vantage point of another Latin American state, too strong an endorsement for deep reform could very well backfire. Should social protests erupt back at home over the dismal state of their own democratic institutions and practices, they would be almost obliged to make painful concessions after having pushed other governments to do the same. The safest strategy is to back off. The disturbing effect of repeatedly doing so region-wide is to acquiesce to a kind of low-level democracy that at times borders on autocracy. Summing up the Peruvian experience, Cynthia McClintock and Fabian Vallas say, "During both crises [1992 and 2000] U.S. and OAS pressure achieved certain results. Ultimately, however, President Fujimori prevailed, and democratic standards for the region were lowered—at least in the short run" (2002, 155).

Ecuador

Six weeks before Eduardo Stein's mission touched down in Peru, Ecuador was convulsed by a constitutional crisis that would briefly draw in regional actors. The coup of January 20–21, 2000, threw into sharp relief just how quickly and effectively the OAS and regional community could respond when the democratic regime was on the line. But the problem of succession that immediately followed the coup revealed the limits to external involvement once calm, stability, and the trappings of democracy had been restored and problems of democratic deepening took over.

Anger over economic disparities induced by IMF-styled economic adjustment measures had been simmering for years among Ecuador's indigenous and working-class populations. But President Jamil Mahuad's last austerity plan to secure external financing, a plan that included the freezing of life savings and the "dollarization" of the currency, were the straws that broke the camel's back. Dollarizing the national currency would have wiped out the savings of Ecuador's working poor.[67] Mahuad's purpose in advancing this controversial plan was to lower inflation and therefore prove to Ecuador's lenders it was worthy of desperately needed credit. It was also an affront to those who saw this as yet another strategy to place the burden of neoliberal reform squarely on the backs of workers, students, and peasants. Swarms of indigenous protesters stormed the congressional building in Quito on January 20 to demand the president's ouster and his replacement by a civil-military junta. Military guards assigned to the building politely stepped aside to let them in. Soon thereafter, some four hundred officers and soldiers joined the occupation themselves, ranging in rank from sublieutenant to colonel. They came from the War Academy, the Army Polytechnic School, and various brigades and battalions, and many were heroes of the 1995 war with Peru.

With the legislative building secured, the rebels next aimed their sights on the presidential palace. When the military and the Indian rebels arrived there, they were met by the military chief of staff, General Carlos Mendoza, army head General Telmo Sandoval, and other members of the top command. Earlier that day, the generals had asked for Mahuad's resignation. The president refused and was then escorted out of the palace after the generals told him they could no longer guarantee his security.[68] While not co-conspirators themselves, the top brass from the army abandoned Mahuad rather quickly, and reports suggest they had prior knowledge of the plot, failed to take measures to foil it, and never warned the president.[69] In fact, accounts now indicate that well prior to January 20, civilian control had broken down within the chain of command and disrespect for the president within the rank and file was rampant.

The military and civilian rebels had formed a civil-military *junta de salvación* comprised of army colonel Lucio Gutiérrez, Indian leader Antonio Vargas, and president of the Confederación de Nacionalidades Indígenas del Ecuador and former Supreme Court president Carlos Solórzano. When they arrived at the presidential palace later in the day on January 20, they asked the military to abandon the building so they could take over. The military refused, and a tense standoff gave way to negotiation, which ended at midnight when the junta agreed to substitute Colonel Gutiérrez for General Mendoza in the triumvirate. The midlevel rebel officers quickly realized that if they took over, at least one hundred higher ranking officers would have to retire. That would have split the military institution wide open. To preserve institutional unity, the agreement to join forces was forged.

But the junta would not last long, and on the twenty-first it was disbanded by General Mendoza himself. The general surmised that a de facto government would face stiff regional and international resistance and would bring dishonor to his armed forces. He was in a good position to know. Throughout that evening and into the early morning he was the subject of a barrage of telephone calls from U.S. State Department officials advising him "A coup in Ecuador will mean being sanctioned and international isolation."[70] Reportedly, the United States vowed to cut economic assistance and discourage investment to Ecuador unless democracy was restored.[71] Meanwhile, the Permanent Council of the OAS vigorously condemned the coup attempt against the Jamil Mahuad government,[72] while OAS secretary general Cesar Gaviria referred to the "enormous international pressure" that would be brought to bear on a coup-led government, including suspension of foreign lending.[73] Individual OAS states added fuel to the fire when the presidents of all the other Andean nations and Chile called President Mahuad while he was being held captive at the air force base, expressing their "firm and energetic support" for his administration.[74] Under the weight of this combined pressure, General Mendoza announced that the junta had stood down to "prevent the international isolation of Ecuador," claiming that it had seized power only to "prevent a bloodbath."[75] Vice President Gustavo Noboa was immediately installed by the military as the next president of Ecuador, a decision ratified by the Ecuadorian Congress in a special session held that same day in Guayaquil.[76]

In one respect, it was truly remarkable how quickly the military had folded. This was, after all, the same institution that had seized and held on to power for lengthy periods of time in the 1960s and 1970s. During their last stewardship, from 1972 to 1979, the armed forces presided over a growing economy and were known to be considerably less repressive than their counterparts in the Southern

Cone. As a result, they earned high marks from most Ecuadorians and transferred authority to civilians with their reputations intact (Isaacs 1993).[77] While the public has a low opinion of civilian democratic institutions, it holds the military in high regard and has even ranked it ahead of the Catholic Church in institutions it trusts (Fitch 1998, 89). Moreover, regionwide, Ecuadorians are among the least supportive of and satisfied with democratic rule, and many would not be averse to a military takeover were economic conditions to deteriorate further.[78] Dissatisfaction with the particular government in power was running very high by late 1999 and early 2000, with approval ratings for Mahuad dipping into single digits. Thus, should the military have chosen to stay in power it is unlikely that it would have triggered public outrage and may very well have met with considerable approval.

Not only is the military popular in Ecuador, it is also powerful. The military does not usually intervene but reserves the right to do so in a country where its subordination to civilian control is conditional. Civilian leaders have, since the transition to democracy in 1979, pursued what J. Samuel Fitch describes as policies of "cautious accommodation with the armed forces" (1998, 79) in order to keep the military at bay. They do so by respecting the military's autonomy over socioeconomic missions, business ventures, and defense policy itself in return for military noninterference in most of the governmental policy decisions outside the defense realm. Fitch concludes, "Although the regime remains nominally democratic, the armed forces have assumed an increasingly active policy voice on matters of concern to senior officers, including the future of the current system . . . the trend in Ecuador has been toward an increasing military role in politics" (Fitch 1998, 89). It is a role the military feels comfortable with and confident about, and one that it has justified to itself. Consequently, if the military had decided to support the *junta de salvación*, it is unlikely it could have been easily discouraged or dislodged by domestic countervailing forces. Of course, it is conceivable that the military never had any real desire to hold onto power from the start. It could have been quite content with playing the role of political arbiters who briefly enter the fray to resolve a crisis and then return to the barracks. Indeed, it is a role it had assumed numerous times in the past. Still, its reluctance to move from arbiters to rulers must be appraised in terms of its calculation of potential costs. And if those costs seemed high to the armed forces, and they did, it was not because of fears of domestic reprisals but rather regional and international ones.

The Ecuadorian case demonstrates quite convincingly how foreign states rally when a democracy within their midst is under siege. As illustrated in figure 4.1, the OAS resorted to more draconian measures because the stakes were higher. The organization threatened the conspirators with sanctions in the form of loan and investment suspensions. These were not idle threats. Reportedly, after Noboa was ratified by the Congress, the World Bank refused to release any funds to Ecuador until it received a green light from the OAS secretary general. Noboa anxiously awaited Gaviria's endorsement, and well into February the secretary general remained the point man between Ecuador and its international creditors. The OAS now enjoyed a kind of economic leverage that was unprecedented for this organization.

The OAS, its secretary general, and individual member states all responded to the takeover with energetic condemnations and warnings. While these external reactions to the coup were commendable and no doubt effective, reactions to the swift succession were not. Once the Ecuadorian Congress had ratified Noboa's ascension to the presidency, and calm, stability, and "democracy" had been restored to this Andean nation, external actors leaped in to endorse the new leader before fully contemplating the implications for democratic strengthening. On January 26, just five days after condemning the coup, the OAS Permanent Council voted its approval of the Noboa government on grounds that not only had the Congress acted but that Mahuad had "publicly asked the people and the National Congress of Ecuador to support President Noboa's administration."[79] The United States changed its tune as well, saying it was "disposed to work with" the government that resulted from the *golpe*. "While we regret the circumstances that led for President Mahuad to call for public support for a Noboa presidency, his magnanimous gesture paves the way for restoring the country to constitutional order," said a National Security Council spokesman.[80]

As magnanimous as Mahuad's gesture may have been, it was not a legal justification for a coup-provoked succession. That succession rested on a slender constitutional reed at best. The Congress asserted that Mahuad had abandoned his post, which under the constitution gives the legislative branch the right to designate the vice president as his replacement.[81] But Mahuad never vacated the presidency on his own volition, nor had he formally resigned—a move that would have added a measure of constitutionality to the process.[82] Instead, he had been illegally and forcefully evicted from office. As Mahuad himself said on the twenty-first in a nationally televised speech, "A deposed president neither resigns nor abandons his post; he is deposed."[83] Four days later, to reiterate the point, he said he was "a president overthrown by a military coup."[84] Gustavo Noboa himself knew full well to whom he owed his presidency. Soon after his appointment, he allegedly paid a visit to the Defense Ministry where he embraced a military colonel saying "without your [military's] support I would not be here" (Lascano 2001, 82).

The OAS and United States had sent the world mixed signals. On the one hand they had condemned actions that violated the democratic and constitutional order. On other hand they had also quickly ratified a new government that came to power because of those violations. This situation was awkward for the OAS, which is prohibited by its own charter from accepting an unconstitutional government. The organization was extremely pleased that Mahuad had provided it some cover but was still somewhat uneasy about its decision. As if to acknowledge the tenuous basis for democratic succession, OAS secretary general Gaviria said, "at least they have been able to conserve the *thread* of democratic regime leadership" (authors' emphasis).[85] The Ecuadorian ambassador to the OAS was candid in saying that the process was "not a strictly constitutional solution, but strictly logical."[86]

As it had done before during presidential crises, the Ecuadorian congress improvised.[87] It skirted with constitutionality in order to achieve a quick fix to a deep problem with roots in Ecuador's presidential-legislative system. The congress is an institutionally weak actor plagued by numerous parties, huge personnel turnover, and thus a lack of accumulated memory and expertise. Without much legislative punch of its own, it tends to act as a gadfly that relishes an opportunity to spoil presidential initiatives. The president in turn often retaliates with unilateral decree measures that only cause greater congressional irritation. The result is deadlock. Not surprisingly, many interest groups and social movements in Ecuador see little advantage in working through legislative channels, and all but the most powerful are blocked from direct access to the presidency (Burbano de Lara 1998). Hence, they often take to the streets in organized, sometimes violent protests or rebellions, which precipitate crises of the sort witnessed in January 2000. At bottom, these are institutional problems—separation of powers, checks and balances, representation, accountability, and efficiency— that Ecuador must come to grips with. While it does, the regional community keeps its distance. Relieved that the accouterments of democratic rule had been restored with Noboa's inauguration, the OAS and Washington left as quickly as they had entered, leaving it to others to work out the nasty dilemmas of democratic deepening.

The Limits to Defending Democracy

The Peruvian and Ecuadorian cases confirm the notion that regional actors, including the OAS, are still torn between aggressive and tepid responses to democratic dilemmas. The regional community has acted with unprecedented resolve during moments of sudden, systemic crisis—when a democracy itself is clearly threatened with extinction. And it has fine-tuned its ability to oversee electoral processes to keep them honest and on track. In these instances, foreign states show little hesitation to influence the internal affairs of another state. Increasingly, democratic defense has become a high politics affair, as governments associate the protection of another democracy with their own survival.

But once a coup has been suppressed, or an election completed, and a new incumbent is installed in office, the dynamic changes. Despite the persistence of very serious irregularities with the democratic order following the inauguration of a new president, external actors will either disengage or scale back their involvement. They do so because democracies are sometimes altered in incremental, subtle, or insidious ways that once detected do not serve as effective rallying points for international outrage. Stacking a national election commission or high court with obsequious followers of the regime is unquestionably damaging to a democracy's integrity. But it can never measure up to the drama of a cancelled election or a closed judicial branch. Governments in Latin America have increasingly been able to get away with preserving the form of democratic institutions while debasing, sometimes gutting, their essence.

Meanwhile sovereignty reemerges as a force to be reckoned with, as the newly legitimized head of state and his government assert their rights to conduct policy free from external intervention. Foreign states will be reluctant to butt heads with a member of their own community by challenging their sovereign claims, unless they perceive sizeable stakes for themselves.

And therein lies the inherent difficulty with getting outsiders to care enough about deep-seated dilemmas within a troubled democratic state. The principal reason external actors retreat is because they do not associate these dilemmas with their own vital interests but do fear that too much persistent intrusion on their part will come back to haunt them. Regional states will not intrude, and the OAS as an intergovernmental organization lacks sufficient autonomy to take matters into its own hands, leaving it to domestic actors to grapple with their own predicaments. Thus, problems of democratic deepening and consolidation in Latin America remain in the province of low politics. Because the region will not intrude on democratic quality issues but will resolutely protect competitive systems from the threat of extinction, the Western Hemisphere now embraces a system that shores up "low quality democracies" of decreasing legitimacy to their own populations. This is a new kind of unsettling equilibrium that does not bode well for democratic consolidation.

An OAS member state does not mind adhering to norms pertaining to all in the region when those norms can also work to its own advantage. The problem arises when a norm sets a standard of behavior that a member state finds too difficult to fulfill. As an ideal, democratic consolidation has unquestionably earned greater currency in Latin America over the last two decades. States of the region easily endorse the principle of strengthening democratic processes and institutions. But the power of that ideal cannot override the peril of commitment to a rule of actually waging a collective struggle in its defense. The regional community is likely to continue limiting the duration and depth of its involvement in democratic affairs, as principles of sovereignty and nonintervention resurface and the self-interest of member states—coping with their own flawed democracies—dictates that they not throw stones while living in glass houses.

5. Human Rights and the Chilean Courts

Chile's human rights past is well known. The abuses committed by military personnel during the 1970s were extensive, shocking, and a matter of record. In human rights terms Chile was the quintessential pariah state and its military leader, General Augusto Pinochet, perhaps the world's most notorious right-wing dictator of the time. The negative attention Chile attracted from the press and the public was enormous. Nearly every year, the United Nations General Assembly would pass resolutions condemning the regime. Human rights organizations honed their skills on the Chilean case, developing new strategies to expose misdeeds and win the release of political prisoners. Entire movements dedicated to the defeat of the Pinochet regime cropped up in Europe and the United States. The collective outrage expressed abroad against this particular tyranny was unequalled.

But if the world often spoke loudly against the Chilean dictatorship, it also carried a small stick. States would vocalize concern about human rights transgressions but were very reluctant to punish Chile for its crimes. For example, Western European states repeatedly condemned Chile inside and outside the United Nations and did much to help opposition parties, human rights organizations, and intellectual centers stay afloat in Chile during difficult times.[1] Yet these same governments maintained commercial relations with the regime, never threatening to withhold economic assistance should human rights not improve. Western European arms sales to Pinochet actually increased from 1982 to 1986, and with one or two exceptions governments there refused to vote against World Bank loans to the Chilean government (Portales 1995, 261). The stakes were simply not high enough for foreign powers to cut Chile's economic lifelines. Nonstate actors inside and outside Chile exhorted foreign governments to do more, usually with only limited results. These are the patterns we might expect in the realm of low politics, where Chile's internal human rights dilemmas did not generate enough troubling externalities for foreign states to pay much attention. The result was that during its seventeen-year reign, the Pinochet regime was never in danger of being destabilized by outsiders.

Nonetheless, the regime was not invulnerable to foreign influences. Concerned about its international image, it would make occasional gestures on behalf of human rights to ward off its international critics. U.S. administrations let it be known to Chile that commercial military relations would not be fully normalized until there was a resolution to the Letelier case.[2] Undoubtedly, pressures from Washington created the climate in which the Chilean Supreme Court finally upheld the appealed convictions of the two DINA (secret police) agents responsible for that crime.[3] Under the weight of diplomatic pressure from states in the region, the dictatorship fulfilled its commitment to carry out the 1988 plebiscite that would determine whether Pinochet would enjoy another eight years at the helm. When the regime lost the referendum, the United States kept its feet to the fire so that it would honor those results and then transfer power peacefully to a democratic successor a year and a half later (Portales 1995). A transition to democratic rule is itself a major step toward improving human rights, and it is hard to imagine this having occurred so smoothly and according to timetable without the input of foreign states.

It is, as we will discover, a key feature of low politics that while the domestic tends to dominate, the foreign has its moments—those occasions when it can make its presence known inside a state. Foreign influence played a role under Pinochet's reign, but even more so in the post-Pinochet era when Chile and its courts had to come to grips with what to do about the human rights transgressions of years past. What began as an internal matter pitting families seeking justice against courts bent on intransigence ended up being a multinational affair that engaged politicians, judges, lawyers, and human rights activists from three countries across two continents. The result was the arrest of General Pinochet, followed by a set of stunning verdicts in British courts that would catalyze judicial change back in Chile.[4] It is our task here to assess why and how the international encroached on a contentious issue that historically had been fought over inside the confines of nations, but our task is also to understand the limits to that encroachment.

For centuries, sovereignty has stood as a formidable barrier against interference from the outside. When it comes to a low politics phenomenon like human rights violations, foreign states would rather not meddle in what are deemed to be the internal affairs of others. They tend to respect the sovereign claims of other states either because their own national interests are not adversely affected or because the costs to humanitarian intervention are too high (Rothenberg 2002). It takes great prodding on the part of activists to get state leaders and institutions to occasionally concern themselves with the human rights tragedies of other states. Chilean and European activists did just that with the Pinochet case.

On those rare occasions when foreign leaders are prompted to intervene, the targeted states—whether authoritarian or democratic—take umbrage, which is especially so of small Third World nations that resent efforts by more powerful states to impose their will or their standards on them. At the same time, small, weaker states are in a quandary. They recognize that the world around them has changed. It is one in which absolute sovereignty is under siege and where respect for the universality of human rights norms has grown and become more codified (Lutz and Sikkink 2000). Some refer to the new international order as a human rights regime (Donnelly 1986; Moravscik 2000).[5] Accordingly, their own reputations within the global community hinge in part on their adherence to norms that are now more widely shared and embedded, not only into international treaties to which they are signatories, but often into their own national laws and constitutions. States and state institutions that are sensitive about their international stature would, it seems, find it in their self-interest to avert international condemnation by remedying human rights injustices occurring within their borders. In adjusting their behavior so that they fit in more comfortably with contemporary global standards, they may be giving up some measure of sovereignty if they reform their human rights practices in response to the demands of outsiders and not of their own free will.

Chile found itself in exactly this situation. It is a small but proud Third World country that was caught between a desire to defend its sovereignty and a need to repair its human rights reputation, one damaged by courts that had been profoundly servile to military interests. But who would force Chile to make amends? No one, really, because there is no enforcement mechanism within the global human rights regime. Moreover, for reasons already given, powerful states are unwilling to leverage Chile's compliance by threatening to cut off economic or military assistance. But according to Margaret Keck and Kathryn Sikkink, states can be occasionally shamed into compliance when their conduct is held up to intense international scrutiny (1998, 23–24). They are especially vulnerable to this kind of moral pressure when others expose the gap between their professed principles and failed practices (1998, 24). States that affirm their commitment to justice must either close the gap or be subject to global humiliation.

With the arrest, indictment, and rulings against Pinochet in England in 1998–1999, Chile was so challenged. Offended by what they perceived as foreign meddling in their judicial affairs, yet determined to prove that theirs was a country that could finally administer justice fairly, Chile's political leaders repeatedly asserted they had the sovereign right to bring the general and others to trial on their own soil. Ironically, by pressing the issue of national judicial sovereignty and eventually winning the release and return of General Pinochet to Chile, they made themselves more vulnerable than ever to external pressures, ones that undoubtedly influenced—however indirectly—deliberations in the courts. They would now either have to make good on their promise to see justice done or be exposed to moral shaming by an international community now fixated on the Chilean case.

The notion of shaming is quite useful and begins to unravel the puzzle of judicial change in Chile. But more specification is needed. Who within the Chilean state felt the moral pressure? Who was concerned about its international stature? It was the Chilean administration that felt compelled to square professed principles with practices, not the courts. It was the Eduardo Frei government (1994–1999) that put the gloss on its judicial system by professing that not only did Chile have the sovereign right to try its own but that it had the sovereign will to do so as well. If Pinochet were to be returned home only to be exonerated by the courts, the international humiliation experienced by the government would be extraordinary. But Pinochet's legal fate did not rest with the executive branch. To avoid international shame, the government had to put pressure on the courts to come through for them. It becomes important then to explore the relation between the executive and judicial branches to see just how international shaming might have had an indirect effect on the courts.

The actions of Spanish and British jurists interceded as catalytic agents to give greater impetus to changes that were underway inside Chile. There had been discernible progress in Chile, whose democratic leaders and institutions were slowly coming to terms with the need to administer justice and to distance themselves from disreputable legacies of the past. Even political figures on the right were coming to this realization, and they would join others in pushing for judicial reforms. The European verdicts set Chile on a steeper and swifter trajectory toward change than would have otherwise been possible. Yet the European impact was fleeting. A window of opportunity opened up with Pinochet's travel to London, one that families, advocates, lawyers, and judges seized advantage of. But once the burden shifted back to Chile, the solution to the human rights problem became distinctly Chilean, and the European window closed. Ironically, the European assaults on Chilean sovereignty prompted a more vigorous and nationalistic defense on the part of its government and courts. That was fine with the Spanish and English governments who were anxious to be rid of the Pinochet affair once and for all.

The Chilean Courts and Human Rights Obstruction

The transition from authoritarian to democratic rule during 1989–1990 raised initial expectations that justice for the victims of the dictatorship would finally be served. But those expectations were dashed once the nature of this transition became apparent to the public. The military had engineered a transition aimed at securing prerogatives and protections for itself while curbing the powers of the incoming democratic administration.[6] The newly elected president, Patricio Aylwin, faced constitutional provisions that afforded the military an imposing presence within the democratic order. Nowhere was that more apparent than in the judicial branch. Anxious to ease the final passage to democratic rule, the opposition did not quarrel with the military's demands that its officers be left untouched by the hands of justice.

The ideological orientations of the Supreme Court judges, holdovers from the Pinochet years, precluded them from taking human rights cases seriously. The court had been profoundly servile to the military regime. Its justices refused to believe that human rights violations had occurred and castigated those who thought otherwise.[7] The court routinely failed to take standard measures to protect the rights of those who were most vulnerable: the detained (*Report of the Chilean National Commission* 1993; Human Rights Watch 1994, 1999; Hilbink 1999). Human rights groups had been filing affidavits in courts for years with little success. According to the Rettig Commission's exhaustive inquiry into human rights abuses under military rule, "Habeas Corpus appeals made on behalf of people arrested for political reasons were rejected invariably well into the 1980s" (*Report of the Chilean National Commission* 1993, 119). The high courts repeatedly tolerated arrests made without warrant, refused to investigate unlawful detention centers, accepted the military's official version of events, and upheld the government's amnesty law as a means of halting court inquiries (*Report of the Chilean National Commission* 1993, 121–125).

When the democratic transition occurred, the high court's subservience to military interests persisted. The Supreme Court ruled in August 1990 that the controversial 1978 amnesty decree, which freed military offenders from criminal wrongdoing, was constitutional.[8] Believing that the amnesty forbade investigations of any sort, the court continued to have cases transferred to military tribunals where they were abruptly suspended. The court's interpretation of the amnesty was a matter of dispute. Legal experts have pointed out that the Chilean Code of Criminal Procedure (article 413) states that proceedings cannot be suspended until an investigation has exhausted all leads in determining the facts of the case and the perpetrator's identity.[9] Some maverick judges had kept inquiries open on these procedural grounds until the Supreme Court or the military courts themselves stepped in to close them.

On March 6, 1991, President Patricio Aylwin asserted in a letter to the justices that the amnesty should never be applied in advance of a criminal investigation, but only after. By 1993, some lower court judges were following Aylwin's lead by reopening some thirty cases previously closed by the amnesty's application.[10] But this did not set into motion a pattern of consistent court action in defense of victims' rights, and during the Aylwin period the high court justices showed little sensitivity toward the human rights issue. Commenting on these first few years after the transition, Lisa Hilbink says: "The judiciary upheld and legitimated the entire corpus of laws inherited from the authoritarian regime, including the hotly contested amnesty law" (1999, 445).

Indeed, well into 1997, the prognosis was not good for families of the victims seeking justice in the courtroom. Most judges still clung to the military's notion that an amnesty nullified the crime rather than the penalty. If so, then once it was determined that a crime had occurred, the judges felt justified in closing the case. Had they held to the latter interpretation, they would have permitted investigations to be kept alive so that those culpable could be identified and indicted. Even there, culpability would not have necessarily led to conviction since the perpetrator could then be exonerated.

Thus, in the first few years following President Aylwin's departure from office and the coming to power of President Eduardo Frei, the judiciary remained a largely inhospitable place for those families seeking truth and justice. One 1996 case in particular seemed to epitomize the frustrations of that time and would ignite an effort to seek justice abroad.

The Case of Carmelo Soria

Married to a Chilean, Carmelo Soria was a Spaniard who had been working for the UN Economic Commission for Latin America in Chile at the time of the coup. On July 14, 1976, he was seized from his auto by DINA operators, detained, tortured, and murdered. After a superficial review, the military court had the case closed, but following the transition to democracy, the Spanish government petitioned the Supreme Court to reopen it, which it did, in 1996. It seemed that if any human rights conviction could be won, it would be won there. As a diplomat of the United Nations, Soria was granted special protection under the provisions of an international convention signed by Chile (United Nations 1997). The convention considers an attack on such an individual a "grave concern to the international community" and demands the state in question make those attacks punishable crimes with penalties that "take into account their grave nature (United Nations 1997, art. 2, no. 2). Furthermore, many at the time thought the court would not want to offend the sensibilities of Spain, which was after all an important political ally and trading partner of Chile.

But in June of that year, a Supreme Court judge applied the military's amnesty law, exonerating officers of any wrongdoing. The Soria family appealed this decision back to the penal chamber of the high court, which sustained the judge's ruling shortly thereafter. In doing so, the court denied that Soria's UN employment constituted diplomatic status and said that even if it had, the international treaty would not pertain because it was ratified by Chile *after* the military's amnesty law had gone into effect .

The Spanish government expressed disappointment at the outcome. The daughter of the slain diplomat was more blunt, saying, "this country [Chile] is shameful," and the "legislators ought to apply enough pressure . . . to change the constitution," adding, "in a country where justice is not applied, there will never be social or national peace."[11] The families of Chilean victims tended to agree. More than dismaying to them, this verdict was the straw that broke the camel's back. It reinforced, like no other case before it, the belief that in Chile a conviction could not be won against military human rights offenders. Impunity reigned supreme, and justice would have to be sought elsewhere. But where, and how?

Seeking Justice in Spain

By no coincidence, the very next month (July 1996) lawyers were in Spain's National Court (Audiencia Nacional), filing charges against Pinochet and his subordinates for the disappearance and death of some three thousand people, Carmelo Soria among them.[12] These legal efforts, which would be sustained over the next two years and culminate with General Pinochet's arrest in London in October 1998, were part of an orchestrated transnational campaign to shift legal action outside Chile to a country where due process could be found.

In many respects, Spain was a natural place for this campaign to gravitate toward. First, a number of Spanish citizens had lost their lives at the hands of the Pinochet regime, and the first lawsuits filed were on behalf of them. Also, a few left-leaning Spaniards had personally witnessed the overthrow of Chilean democracy in September 1973 along with the death of friends and colleagues, and they had scores to settle with Pinochet. These individuals would prove instrumental in helping to advance the legal case. For example, among the attorneys present in the Audiencia Nacional that July was Joan Garcés.[13] Garcés was of Spanish descent but had been a close collaborator of Salvador Allende and had been in La Moneda the day of the coup. In court he entered charges on behalf of the Salvador Allende Foundation, a group that coordinated the legal cases, co-founded by Garcés two years before with Victor Pey. Through his foundation Pey helped provide the court with documentation on human rights abuses in Chile.[14]

And finally, Spain provided an excellent legal forum with which to pursue charges against Chilean human rights abusers. Prosecutors could rely on a multilayered body of law that justified trials against foreign offenders. Garcés filed a class action suit on behalf of literally thousands of Chilean victims, using a procedural mechanism known as *acción popular* (Wilson 1999, 935).[15] This law allows any Spanish citizen to lodge a complaint in court whether a crime victim or not.

Furthermore, Spain recognized the principle of universal jurisdiction (Joyner 1996; Amnesty International 1999; García Arán and López Garrido 2000; Kamminga 2001). Once used to prosecute international crimes such as piracy, universal jurisdiction has in contemporary times been used to adjudicate crimes committed abroad by citizens of other lands. The theory at work in both instances is essentially the same. Genocide, torture, and forced disappearance are of sufficient gravity to be considered crimes against humanity. They are an affront to the international community, and their perpetrators become enemies of that community. It follows that all states (and the judicial powers within) are within their rights to bring those perpetrators to justice if they can.

In theory, a judge need not demonstrate that an offender violated any laws of the prosecuting state to bring him into custody.[16] In practice, judges are on firmer grounds when they can point to domestic legislation that embodies international conventions or customary laws that prohibit such human rights abuses. Article 96 of Spain's constitution makes signed treaties part of the country's internal law. Since it had ratified various conventions on crimes against humanity (i.e., the four Geneva War Conventions, the Convention against Torture, Convention on the Prevention and Punishment of the Crime of Genocide), Spain obligated itself to criminalize those offenses domestically and to prosecute as well.[17]

Spanish law goes further to specify court powers in this regard. Article 23.4 of its 1985 Organic Law of Judicial Power, which governs the functioning of courts, authorized the National Court to engage in extraterritorial prosecution of those crimes—whether they be committed by Spaniards or not—that disregard national boundaries, including genocide, terrorism, drug trafficking, or "any other that according to international conventions or treaties, ought to be pursued in Spain" (García Arán and López Garrido 2000, 101). That clause permitted Spain to prosecute cases of torture, since it had signed that convention on November 9, 1987. So too had Chile.

It is important to note that these legal principles and laws did not translate into effective enforcement. There is no international agency charged with ensuring that nations abide by universal principles or adhere to treaties. While economic organizations like the WTO do have a system of sanctions they can use against offending nations, that is not the case for international human rights organizations. Consequently, although the number of legal obligations for compliance within the international human rights order has grown, so too has practical noncompliance.

Thus, none of these legal instruments meant that Chileans would one day win a conviction against Pinochet and his generals, let alone ever see them in Spanish court or behind bars. Spanish law did not allow for trials in absentia (Rothenberg 2002, 928),[18] and it was inconceivable that the culprits would voluntarily turn themselves over to the Spanish authorities. Although Chile and Spain did share an extradition treaty, it would soon become evident that the Chilean government had absolutely no intention of honoring that treaty or cooperating on any level with Judge Manuel García-Castellón who presided over the Chilean trials. But the families of victims also knew that they would get a fair hearing, that their cause could be publicized, and that perhaps, just perhaps, the trials could set in motion events back in their own country (Wilson 1999, 933). Human rights activists in Chile were convinced that just as the economy had become increasingly globalized, so too could justice. An international effort could possibly boomerang back to Chile to spark positive change.[19]

With that in mind, a host of Chilean organizations cooperated with the Spanish lawyers, turning over valuable documents and powers of attorney to them.[20] Soon, an entire network of Chilean and Spanish organizations had crystallized, devoted to building a legal case.[21] On the Chilean side there was the Association of Families of the Chilean Detained and Disappeared, the Committee for the Defense of Human Rights, and the Peace and Justice Service in Chile. In Spain there was the Allende Foundation as well as the Union of Progressive Prosecutors who first laid the legal groundwork for the actions that followed. The Chilean organizations were key because they not only turned over evidence of criminal wrongdoing along with the names of perpetrators but also helped to prove that legal channels had been blocked in Chile by submitting into evidence thousands of unanswered letters of inquiry and writs of habeas corpus sent to Pinochet, the Supreme Court, and the Ministry of Justice.[22] The evidence allowed Spanish lawyers to argue that pursuit of these cases in Spain had not and would not duplicate any similar efforts in Chile since there were none.[23]

By the following year, 1997, Chileans were traveling to Madrid to offer testimony.[24] As a result of their testimony, Judge García-Castellón was able to build a credible human rights case against General Pinochet, other junta members, and top military commanders of the period. That case would be handed over to Judge Baltasar Garzón in the fall of 1998 and set the stage for the indictment against Pinochet once he was detained in London.

The Impact of Spanish Proceedings on Chile

Chileans were both surprised and offended by the Spanish proceedings. How could crimes committed in Chile be prosecuted in Spain? many asked. Individuals across the political spectrum, from left to right, had much the same reaction.[25] So too did former President Patricio Aylwin, who went to Lisbon to receive a human rights award and decided to stop over in Madrid in May 1997 to visit relatives. Upon his arrival at the airport, he was stunned to discover that Judge García-Castellón had subpoenaed him to testify in the Pinochet case. Instead of going to his hotel where the citation had been delivered, Aylwin rushed straight to the Chilean embassy so that his government could cloak him with diplomatic protection under the guise of being on a special mission.[26]

There was another reaction however that was building within the Chilean government and the military: worry. In June 1997, U.S. attorney general Janet Reno, at the urging of a group of congressional Democrats, agreed to turn over to Judge Garzón hitherto confidential information from FBI and CIA files regarding human rights abuses committed by Chilean officials and others during Operation Condor. Condor was a systematized effort by South American military regimes to gather intelligence data on, and ultimately eliminate, left-wing opponents. Washington's willingness to cooperate with the Spanish investigation was an embarrassment to the Chilean government, which just four weeks before had turned down a similar request from the Spanish judge.[27]

Moreover, developments in Argentina were beginning to concern the Chileans. A former navy captain, Francisco Scilingo, stunned his country in 1995 when he publicly confessed to his role in a Dirty War operation that pushed political dissidents out of airplanes over the Atlantic. After making his confession, Scilingo faced continual harassment and at one point was abducted and told by his captors to cease the revelations or suffer the fate of disappearance himself. Frustrated with his inability to find justice in Argentina, Scilingo departed for Spain in the fall of 1997 with a briefcase full of documentation for Judge Garzón who had been investigating Argentine disappearances. Scilingo testified about what he knew and then unexpectedly found himself under detention at the judge's orders. But based on Scilingo's testimony regarding the navy's death flights, Garzón soon issued an international arrest warrant for former navy head Emilio Massera. Chilean military officials fretted that the same judge might seize upon Pinochet's retirement from the military in March 1998 as the occasion to slap an arrest order on the old Chilean general himself. There was a growing sense in Chile that the Spanish trial was getting out of hand, that with the help of the United States renegade judges like Baltasar Garzón were pushing the envelope by testing the limits of international human rights law. There was no telling where such actions would lead.

Perhaps in an effort to cut their losses or even to bring an end to the proceedings, the Chilean armed forces sent a close associate of Pinochet and former auditor general for the army, General Fernando Torres Silva, to Spain to pay an undisclosed visit to Judge García-Castellón on October 6, 1997. The purpose of his court appearance was to deliver legal documents he hoped would exonerate the general.[28] Since the Spanish trials had begun the year before, both the Chilean military and government had repeatedly refused to acknowledge their legitimacy on grounds that Spain had no legal jurisdiction. But now, the mere fact that Torres Silva appeared in García-Castellón's court—a fact that he first denied to the press and then later had to admit—gave credence to the court's actions.

Chile's justice minister, Mariá Soledad Alvear, and foreign affairs minister, José Miguel Insulza, were also troubled by the trials, arguing that Spain had illegitimately violated Chile's jurisdiction and that these matters ought to and could be resolved in Chilean courts (Paz Rojas 1998, 21, 23). In November 1997, Insulza said he could not understand why Chileans were not filing charges against Pinochet inside Chile; there was nothing to prevent them from doing so, he claimed. Unwittingly, Insulza provoked what was to be an interminable stream of lawsuits. Gladys Marín, president of the Chilean communist party, took him up on his offer and in January became the first Chilean to file criminal charges against Pinochet, for the murder of her husband. Some two hundred lawsuits against the former dictator would follow over the next two and a half years.[29]

Thus, a year before Pinochet's arrest in London, events in Spain were already having an effect on Chilean government officials, soldiers, civilians, and courts. Chileans were increasingly defensive about a judicial process that had become internationalized and that had clearly slipped from their grasp. The military was plotting strategies to cut its losses should the Spanish proceedings get out of hand. The government was defending Chilean sovereignty against what they believed were unwarranted interferences from abroad. And some Chilean activists were, as a result of Spanish trials, beginning to overcome whatever qualms they had had about going after Pinochet in court.

In sum, the Spanish investigations into Chilean human rights abuses, culminating in Judge Garzón's arrest order and indictment of Pinochet, represented the first "foreign moment" in this phase of Chile's domestic human rights drama. A transnational advocacy network (TAN) of Chilean and Spanish human rights organizations and individuals had succeeded in energizing the Spanish court to take their cases. Back in Chile, the Spanish judicial investigations provoked various reactions, from concern to defensiveness to assertiveness. But Spain's real effect on Chile would not be felt until later and indirectly, through its impact on events in England. With Judge Garzón's arrest order of Pinochet, the ball was now in the British court.

The British Rulings and Their Impact on Chile

In October 1998 while visiting Great Britain, General Pinochet was placed under arrest. On October 16, at the request of Judge Garzón, British authorities detained the general while he was recuperating from back surgery. As he had with the Argentine generals, Garzón sought Pinochet's extradition to Spain to stand trial on grounds that he had committed crimes against humanity (genocide, torture, and terrorism). In a formal indictment issued two months later, he charged the general with designing and implementing a scheme to eliminate a sector of the Chilean population, coordinated and planned down to the smallest details. The general, he alleged, also plotted with military friends in the region to illegally detain, kidnap, torture, disappear, and murder thousands of political dissidents during Operation Condor. The objective of this conspiracy was to destroy organizations and eliminate individuals ideologically opposed to the military regimes in power in Chile, Argentina, Uruguay, Paraguay, and Brazil.

The conspiracy gave rise to Garzón's charge of genocide against Pinochet, depending on a looser definition of the term that would include persecution against groups for other than ethnic, racial, and religious reasons.[30] Crimes of this sort are outlawed by international treaties, and countries, like Spain, are within their rights to pursue the perpetrators regardless of their national origin, Garzón alleged. The penal chamber of Spain's National Court agreed, saying, "Spain is competent to judge the events [Pinochet case] by virtue of the principle of universal prosecution for certain crimes—a category of international law established by our internal legislation" (Woodhouse 2000, 117).

Pinochet had contended that he enjoyed immunity from arrest and prosecution, as a former head of state. The British high court, which first took on the case, concurred, ruling all charges brought against him by British prosecutors representing Spain be dropped. But the Law Lords in the House of Lords, the final appellate court for criminal matters in England, overturned the ruling in November and stripped the general of his diplomatic immunity, stating, "International Law has made plain that certain types of conduct, including torture and hostage taking, are not acceptable conduct on the part of anyone. This applies as much to heads of state, or even more so, as it does to everyone else."[31]

That November decision was set aside in December when one of the judges, Lord Hoffman, was found to have a conflict of interest by virtue of his affiliation with Amnesty International. The case was revisited by a newly formed appellate panel of the Law Lords who issued their ruling on March 24, 1999. In a six to one vote, they essentially sustained but constrained the prior decision, arguing Pinochet could be extradited only for the crime of torture (and conspiracy to commit) and only for those acts committed after Britain had signed the Convention against Torture (December 8, 1988) thus incorporating the international treaty into its own Criminal Act of Justice (*Regina v. Bartle* 1999).[32] While this vastly reduced the list of actionable offenses, a key principle was upheld: British courts had every right to try a foreigner for acts of this nature even if perpetrated in Chile, or anywhere else for that matter. Since this was now considered a punishable crime under British and Spanish law, Britain could commence with extradition proceedings to Spain should Home Secretary Jack Straw give the go-ahead. This he did on April 15, 1999.[33]

These developments were historic—never before had human rights principles been placed on such a high plane. A court had simultaneously defeated the doctrine of state immunity based on international human rights law and upheld the notion of extraterritorial jurisdiction, thus allowing an arrest and extradition request against a foreign dictator to stand (Human Rights Watch 1999, 17–23). A lawyer representing Amnesty International and families of victims said the decision was the most important case in human rights law in the twentieth century (Human Rights Watch 1999, 17–23).

But for the next year, lawyers for Pinochet and the Chilean government would engage in legal maneuvers to prevent his extradition to Spain. Finally they succeeded, and on March 3, 2000, Jack Straw sent Pinochet back to Chile.[34] What impact, if any, did the entire episode—from Pinochet's arrest to his indictment, to his trial and eventual release—have on Chile? During this time, from 1999 to 2000 in particular, the Chilean high courts rendered a number of verdicts that gave a significant boost to the human rights cause. What were these rulings? How significant were they? And were they motivated by the actions of Spanish and British courts, or were they the natural consequence of changes already underway in Chile?

Historic Human Rights Verdicts in Chile, 1999–2000

In 1999 and 2000, there were several dramatic court decisions that together represented a significant departure from judicial practices and thinking of the past. The first occurred on June 8, 1999, just three months after the second historic ruling by the British lord judges. Judge Juan Guzmán, the appellate court judge assigned to handle cases against army officers, contrived a new and controversial legal strategy. He would refuse to apply the amnesty law to top military officials who had disappeared prisoners, defining that as an act of aggravated kidnapping. On that basis he indicted General Sergio Arellano Stark and four other senior army officers implicated in the disappearance of some nineteen political prisoners shortly after the coup of 1973—a military operation known as the Caravan of Death.[35] Guzmán argued when an individual disappears into thin air, with no proof of his death, then for all intents and purposes, he has been kidnapped. Unless or until it could be proven that he had been killed within the time frame of the amnesty (September 1973 to March 1978), the presumption must be that he is alive, that the crime committed against him is still in progress, and that it should be investigated and prosecuted.[36]

The military's self-amnesty would receive a second and third blow that summer when the Santiago Appellate Court and then the Supreme Court sustained Guzmán's ruling. The more dramatic moment occurred on July 20 when by a 5–0 vote the criminal chamber of the Supreme Court upheld the indictments issued by Guzmán in the Caravan of Death case against the five former army officers.[37] The judges ruled that the case remain open for further investigation and that the accused could not be amnestied for an ongoing crime. Should the case be solved, the amnesty, if appropriate, could only be applied at sentencing, not before.[38]

This decision was a watershed event that in the words of the government's secretary general "marks a substantial advance in human rights matters."[39]

Hugo Gutiérrez, a plaintiff lawyer who represented numerous families of victims, went further, saying, "I believe this Supreme Court decision is the true beginning of the transition in Chile because there cannot be change without justice and it is impossible to construct a true democracy if those responsible for human rights violations go unpunished."[40] Many referred to this decision as a "new doctrine" in the evolution of judicial thought on the amnesty law, one that could permit the reopening of hundreds of cases previously closed by military and civilian courts.[41] It also raised the theoretical possibility that General Pinochet himself could be indicted, since presumably he had, as commander of all forces and head of military tribunals in times of war, condoned the Caravan of Death executions of political prisoners, if not ordered them himself.[42]

But could Pinochet ever be indicted for these crimes *inside* Chile? In August 1999, that still seemed unlikely but not impossible. Upon his return in March of the following year, he was not immediately vulnerable to court action since as senator for life he was shielded from prosecution. Hence, Judge Guzmán filed a petition with the court of appeals to lift Pinochet's immunity so that he could stand trial. Three months later, the appeals court would render its verdict: by a vote of 13–9, the court stripped Pinochet of his immunity, laying him open to judicial action.[43] The general's lawyers appealed the decision to the Supreme Court. A month later, by a 14–6 decision, the Supreme Court upheld the appeals court ruling, thus paving the way for an indictment against the former dictator (Desafuero del senador Augusto Pinochet Ugarte 2000).

The judges argued there was a well-founded suspicion of Pinochet's connivance in human rights crimes committed during the Caravan of Death of October 1973, as author, accomplice, or accessory to the fact. As head of the military junta ruling the nation at the time, Pinochet was held responsible for their deaths because he not only named General Sergio Arellano Stark to lead the military expedition but gave him extraordinary powers (beyond those normally conferred on regional commanders) to countermand the authority of local military officials who were prepared to place the prisoners on trial.[44] The decision also ratified the new judicial doctrine regarding amnesties and disappearances. Drawing on the original meaning found in article 93 of the nation's penal code, the judges said that amnesties nullify individual penalties, not crimes. Thus, investigations into any and all human rights abuses cannot be suspended until the perpetrators have been identified, so it could be known to whom such a reprieve would be granted.

From the point of view of those outside the courtroom, this was another land-mark judicial decision, representing the first time that a former Chilean presi-dent had lost his immunity from prosecution. Guzmán remarked, "This is an historic leap for Chile. The Supreme Court which long sheltered General Pino-chet has finally ruled against him."[45] Based on the court's ruling, Guzmán would prepare a formal indictment against the general that was delivered in January 2001. Human rights leaders, not normally prone to accolades when it came to a judiciary they had long held in contempt, could not contain their enthusiasm. Eduardo Contreras, the attorney who filed the first lawsuit against Pinochet in January 1998, said, "This is a very emotional moment. We dedicate it to the many victims of repression under Pinochet."[46] Viviana Diaz, head of the Association for Chilean Families of the Disappeared, said, "Today, the course of history has begun to change."[47] And internationally it was hailed as a "breakthrough for hu-man rights law and another indication that former dictators are no longer safe even in their own countries."[48]

Naturally, we wanted to know how Chile's high court judges themselves viewed the decisions. In interviews conducted with six judges who had served on the appellate court or the Supreme Court at the time the amnesty and immunity rulings were handed down, one thing was clear. These magistrates believed the rulings were decisively important, characterizing them as "milestones in the de-velopment of Chilean democracy," and as a "landmark in jurisprudence." Judges disagreed as to whether these changes represented a radical break with the past. Some saw it as so, while others viewed the change in evolutionary terms. When asked whether these verdicts represented a permanent or ephemeral change in the judiciary, all the judges concurred that the changes were bound to be long lasting.[49]

So far, they have been proven correct. Taken together, the rulings of 1999–2000 have had a sustained impact on cases pending or resolved in the courts. Dozens of military officers continue to be charged for human rights crimes, and a number of convictions have been handed down. Most significant have been those trials involving crimes committed during the period covered by the amnesty. In April 2003, a Chilean court waived the amnesty law and found sev-eral former members of the Chilean secret police guilty of 1975 kidnappings. DINA's head, Manuel Contreras, was sentenced to fifteen years in prison.[50] Trials against other perpetrators continue.

What Caused Judicial Change?

The timing of the verdicts in 1999 and 2000, and the urgency with which they were rendered, strongly suggests a connection with events in Europe. Though hundreds of lawsuits against Pinochet had piled up on Judge Guzmán's desk beginning in January 1998, it was not until June 1999, a year and a half later, that the judge made his first ruling. Curiously, that ruling came less than three months after the final British verdict. Then, literally, the day of Pinochet's arrival back into Chile after his long stay in London, Judge Guzmán filed the petition with the court of appeals to lift the former dictator's immunity so that he could stand trial. Three months later, the appeals court would strip Pinochet of his immunity, a decision upheld only a month later by the Supreme Court (Desafuero del senador Augusto Pinochet Ugarte 2000). What brought on this sudden sense of urgency, this flurry of legal action, in sharp contrast to the interminable delays and setbacks of years past? It all seems too oddly coincidental. But timing itself only hints at the causal connections. If Europe mattered, precisely how? How was influence transmitted from the British courts to Chilean courts?

What first must be considered is whether the British verdicts had any *direct, legal* influence on Chilean judges. The British judgments were stunning, were widely disseminated, and became the immediate object of reflection and debate by legal scholars worldwide. Chilean judges could not have helped but notice. But it is debatable whether they had allowed foreign verdicts to influence their judgments. All of those judges interviewed by this author were emphatic in insisting that the British verdicts had no legal bearing on them whatsoever. With or without the British verdicts, they would have made the historic judgments on their own.[51] Three main reasons were given for this.

The first is nationalism. Chilean judges were prideful of their own legal tools, institutions, heritage, and homeland. To a man, the judges believed they had always been well qualified to deliberate such a case, without guidance or prodding from anyone abroad. They were offended that a foreign court would interfere in a Chilean matter, as if to patronize the nation for not fulfilling its obligations. Their state, as well as their courts, are sovereign; beyond its borders no nation or court can claim jurisdiction over its affairs, the judges typically argued. One appellate judge went so far as to say that the British verdicts were counterproductive because they caused a backlash. From that point forward, judges who may have been previously inclined to incorporate international human rights treaties in their judgments refused to do so, he said, so offended were they by the presumptuous attitudes of European courts.[52] Interestingly, one judge spoke of the London verdicts as if they were just another form of public opinion. Magistrates such as ourselves would never permit our judgments to be shaped by *public views* from abroad, he argued (authors' emphasis).[53] In short, the Chilean judges were confident that external judgments and opinions had no influence on them at all. National sovereignty and pride seemed to have reigned supreme.

Moreover, the judges maintained that the legal process had begun to unfold prior to Pinochet's arrest and it was just a matter of time before rulings would be made. Investigations had begun, evidence had accumulated, and charges had been filed before the British courts got their hands on Pinochet. In particular, the judges had a thick dossier on the Caravan of Death—the episode on which the high courts had pinned their case against Pinochet and his subordinates.

Besides having the facts on their side, they also had Chilean law. Thus, the final argument was that possible criminal guilt could be established comfortably within the confines of Chilean statutes, without any need to consult international treaties, norms, or laws.[54] For example, to justify ongoing investigations despite the existence of the amnesty, Judge Guzmán and others could refer back to article 413 of the Code of Criminal Proceedings, which stipulates that a stay of proceedings cannot be invoked until a thorough investigation has established the facts of the crime (República de Chile 1997, 184). To weaken the amnesty itself, the justices could point to its original meaning as detailed in article 93, no. 3, of the penal code. According to that provision, an amnesty nullifies the individualized penalty not the crime, thus justifying an investigation to determine who the guilty party is so that he could be potentially absolved (República de Chile 2001, 57).

In removing Pinochet's senatorial immunity, all the judges had to prove was that a crime had been committed and that they had a "well-founded suspicion" that the general was either an author of or accomplice to the crime, or had concealed it after the fact. The criminal nature of Pinochet's behavior is defined in article 141 of the penal code, and the justification for the court proceedings can be found in article 255 of the Chilean Code of Criminal Procedure.[55] To then indict Pinochet, as Judge Guzmán did in January 2001, he needed to interrogate the suspect and be able to prove his wrongdoing, under article 274 of the same code (República de Chile 1997, 135). In short, Chilean judges had in their view a legal arsenal with which to go after Pinochet and his subordinates. They had no need to rely on foreign court decisions, or even international treaties for that matter.

For example, no mention was ever made of the British verdicts in any of the Chilean high court rulings of 2000 that pertained to Pinochet. The London decisions that denied the general diplomatic immunity for the grave crimes he was accused of could have been made relevant to the Chilean *desafuero* (denial of immunity) case, were the justices so inclined.[56] Also, with one exception,[57] no reference was ever made in the 1999–2000 high court verdicts to any of the international human rights conventions that Chile had signed.[58]

The judges may have been technically right in asserting that the British verdicts had no *legal* influence on them. But it is also highly doubtful that the Chilean high courts had been prepared all along to use Chilean law to serve justice on Pinochet. If they were so inclined, why did they not request that their government extradite Pinochet from London to stand trial? The Chilean government went to great lengths to insist that as a sovereign nation, Chile could bring its own perpetrators to justice. What better way to demonstrate its resolve to the British than to officially request that the general be extradited back to Chile? No such request was ever made. Thus, it must be asked whether the verdicts set in motion a chain of events that *indirectly and politically* affected the judges. For an answer to this question, we turn to other interpretations.

It is plausible that Chile had been shamed into delivering some justice to the families of Pinochet's victims. After all, the British verdicts against Pinochet were historic and grabbed international headlines. They were also delivered with stunning speed, in sharp contrast to the failure of the Chilean judiciary to mete out any justice after so many years. Now that Pinochet was back, the spotlight was thrown on Chile. Could Chilean judges pick up where the Law Lords had left off? The world was anxiously awaiting. Perhaps, then, the judges wanted to avoid the embarrassment of being judged negatively in the court of world opinion.

The problem is that the Chilean judges, like judges everywhere, routinely deny that they are ever swayed by public opinion. They make decisions based on their understanding of the law and the facts before them. What would cause them humiliation if indeed they were relatively desensitized to world views? One theory is that while the courts may not pay much attention to international opinion, they do pay careful attention to the views espoused by their own government. As numerous human rights attorneys stated in interviews, the Chilean judges always render sensitive decisions with one eye trained on La Moneda, the presidential palace.[59] The justices are, with a few historical exceptions, reluctant to adapt positions on critical issues that place them at odds with the administration in power. To the contrary, the Chilean high courts have throughout history shown extraordinary deference to executive preferences on the most controversial issues. If this is so, then the courts may have taken cues from the Frei administration, which had staked its reputation on the idea that Chilean magistrates could pursue justice on their own.[60]

In their presentation before the Law Lords, the Chilean government lawyers argued that returning Pinochet was a matter of sovereignty and capacity.[61] It was within Chile's right as a sovereign nation to bring Chilean subjects to justice for crimes committed on its own soil, free from interference from abroad. If Spain and Britain took their own sovereignty seriously, they were obligated to respect Chile's rightful claim. Any suggestion that a foreign court was entitled, let alone better able, to bring a Chilean national to justice for crimes committed in Chile was an affront to the aforementioned principles.[62]

Moreover, Chilean courts were more than capable of handling the Pinochet case. It was untrue, they said, that the amnesty law prevented justice from being served because the amnesty was a question to be settled case by case, not a sweeping exclusion. After the Law Lords had ruled a second time in March 1999, the Chilean government noted that their own courts had an advantage over Spain's: they were not subject to the restrictions imposed by the Law Lords and could instead extend their review to cover alleged crimes over a much longer period. In conclusion, the Chilean government asked the home secretary to return Pinochet "not with the goal of protecting him from justice, but to acknowledge the right of the Chilean Republic to deal with matters that are inherently within its jurisdiction as a sovereign state," and added, "Chilean Tribunals will take on his case in conformance with Chilean Law" (authors' emphasis).[63]

In essence, the administration had made a daring bet and in doing so considerably upped the ante on itself and the courts. If the British home secretary were to eventually rule in Chile's favor by returning Pinochet home, then all those (including Chilean justice minister Soledad Alvear and foreign affairs minister José Miguel Insulza) who had chafed at the violation of Chilean jurisdiction at the hands of Spain and Britain would now have to make good on their outrage by supporting legal actions against him, or otherwise be humiliated internationally. In other words, to avoid great harm to its international reputation the Chilean government would have to prove that it was not disingenuous in its legal assertions to win the general's release. But it could not do so without cooperation from the high courts in whose hands the Pinochet case would fall.

As if on cue, the day that British home secretary Jack Straw sent Pinochet home, March 3, 2000, outgoing president Eduardo Frei said:

All our efforts towards ensuring Senator Pinochet's return have been aimed at a single goal; that is, that the Chilean courts, not any foreign court, should be the ones enforcing the law. . . . No Chilean may rise above the rule of law and justice in our country. It will be incumbent upon the Chilean courts, without any interference, to decide whether Senator Pinochet is responsible for the crimes attributed to him. I am particularly confident that our judges will discharge their duties without any consideration other than applying the law.[64]

President Frei was stating unequivocally that his government had fought for Pinochet's release not so a frail and aging general could be spared the ordeal of a trial in Spain while enjoying a quiet retirement, but so he could be exposed to judicial action at home. Frei's successor, president-elect Ricardo Lagos, said that same day that he felt obligated to help create the political conditions to allow for Pinochet's prosecution, because if not, "we will be a false democracy" (Facultad Latino Americana 2000, 76). Just how those conditions were to be created is another matter, and one that cannot be easily discerned. After all, in a democracy with separation of powers, there is an explicit expectation that one branch of government not interfere in the affairs of another. Few in government would be so crass as to publicly threaten the magistrates into a decision. Those who have done so have been quickly rebuked.[65] But politics is often an indirect art form, and the statements made by government officials, both before and after Pinochet's return, left little doubt as to what their expectations were and in whose court the ball was now resting. It is highly unlikely that the high courts could have been tone deaf to the political signals issued by the administration during the course of Pinochet's London confinement and release to Chile.

In fact, the judges who were interviewed did candidly acknowledge that the European courts had a nonjuridical, political influence on them. Some argued that Pinochet's supporters inside and out of the military had been properly immunized by the barrage of hostile legal assaults from Europe. By the time of Pinochet's return to Chile, they were no longer shocked by anything the Chilean courts were prepared to do.[66] To the contrary, many military officers and friends fully expected legal actions to be taken against the general and his subordinates. Accordingly, they had already begun to shift their strategy from one of outright denial about human rights crimes to some admission of wrongdoing in order to cut their losses. Knowing that the military were not prepared to put up an institutional fight against the trials provided judges with a great measure of comfort.[67] They could render sensitive decisions without having to look nervously over their shoulders at the armed forces, wondering what they may do next. And yes, some justices admitted that the British verdicts imposed a burden on the Chilean political authorities to follow through after claiming that justice could be served inside Chile.[68]

In short, the British verdicts, followed by the British government's decision to send Pinochet home, mattered to the conduct of Chilean judicial affairs, but indirectly so. The British trial against Pinochet had in the eyes of the Chilean government challenged Chile's sovereignty, its right to mete out justice to its own citizens charged with crimes committed on its own soil. In winning Pinochet's release, the Chilean government risked being shamed by international opinion were Pinochet to be granted complete immunity. To avoid that shame, it placed political pressure on its courts to pursue legal action against the former dictator.

Europe as a Catalyst, Not a Cause

While Europe mattered, it was not the only agent of change. As our theory suggests, human rights remains largely a domestic politics issue, with the international encroaching only at rare moments. Europe certainly had its moment, but developments were brewing inside Chile as well. Personnel changes and the passage of new laws governing the Supreme Court's functions and its relation to other branches of government had combined to produce a somewhat new judicial environment that undoubtedly helped set the stage for the dramatic verdicts of 1999–2000. Also contributing were attitudinal changes, both inside Chile's high courts and within Chilean media and society. And yet, it is unlikely that in the absence of external prodding, these changes alone would have sufficed. It would be more accurate, then, to characterize the European actions as a catalyst than a cause. The Spanish and British courts set Chile on a surer and swifter path toward reform than would otherwise have been the case.

What was occurring inside Chile? The first domestic change of note is the restoration of the democracy itself that permitted elected presidents to select their own justices from a list of five nominees. In theory, those appointees would have a freer hand since they did not owe their career advancement to Pinochet, nor were they operating in the intimidating environment of a de facto regime. Presidents Aylwin and Frei would go on to appoint seventeen of the twenty justices who served on the high court at the time of the *desafuero* ruling. Fourteen of those seventeen would vote to strip Pinochet of his immunity (see table 5.1). Yet, at least through 1997, most of the judges promoted during the early phase of democratic restoration (between 1991 and 1994) joined their older, more conservative, and more numerous brethren on the bench in resisting efforts to investigate human rights crimes or to reinterpret the amnesty law. They would not demonstrate any empathy for human rights arguments until 1998, and in a vigorous way only after the British court ruling against Pinochet. If, prior to 1998, these appointees held progressive convictions that stood them apart from their colleagues, they certainly kept those views to themselves. Nothing about their behavior during the first seven years after the transition to democratic rule indicates that their inclusion on the high court marked a discernible ideological shift in favor of human rights.

These justices were not only greatly outnumbered by Pinochet's men but were ascending to the high court when a climate of caution and fear still pervaded the political system. It would take the passage of time and transformations of a more fundamental structural nature to occur before a new pattern would emerge, which brings us to the next domestic factor.

In 1997, a sequence of legislative actions would culminate in a constitutional amendment that would alter the Supreme Court in an unprecedented way, ushering in personnel changes that would have an impact on future court decisions. The law made retirement of justices mandatory at age seventy-five, allowed for senate confirmations of all presidential nominees to the court, widened the president's choices from five to ten individuals, expanded the size of the court to twenty-one members, and stipulated that five of those must be chosen from outside the judicial hierarchy.[69]

In essence, the law exposed the court to greater outside influences and scrutiny, breaking down some of its historic insularity. It also effectively brought the Pinochet-dominated court era to a close for two reasons. First, it forced the retirement of most of the judges who had been appointed by Pinochet and who had faithfully served him. Also, it marked something of a rupture in relations between the Supreme Court and the political parties of the right. Members of the Unión Demócrata Independiente (UDI)—the party most closely associated with

5.1. Supreme Court Judges and Their *Desafuero* Votes (August 9, 2000)

Supreme Court Judges Appointed by:	Voted "Yes" on *Desafuero*	Voted "No" on *Desafuero*
President Augusto Pinochet	0	3
President Patricio Aylwin	5	0
President Eduardo Frei	9	3
Appointed before 1997 Reforms	6	3
Appointed after 1997 Reforms	8	3

Source: Appointment data provided to authors by Ingrid Wittebroodt, based on research done at the Supreme Court. Data on votes from "El Impacto del desafuero a Pinochet," *La Tercera*, August 9, 2001, http://www .tercera.cl/diarp.

the military point of view—along with the conservative Renovación Nacional, collaborated with the Concertación parties to write and pass the legislation. Initially, right-wing legislators from these parties were more interested in winning support for an impeachment motion against then Supreme Court President Servando Jordan on charges of serious judicial corruption and malpractice.[70] President Frei and his Concertación legislative allies seized the opportunity to offer their support for the impeachment in exchange for votes in favor of judicial reform. The right-wing parties took the deal.

This agreement was a real breakthrough. Since 1990, the Concertación governments of Patricio Aylwin and Eduardo Frei had tried unsuccessfully to push through legislation and constitutional reforms designed to make the courts less insular, less self-promoting, more accountable to the other branches, and more responsive to citizen needs. Each time, efforts were beaten back by the conservative political parties. Now, the Concertación was able to transform outrage over judicial wrongdoing into a large enough coalition to get judicial reform through the Congress. In their collaboration in the crafting and passage of this historic legislation, Renovación Nacional and UDI were also distancing themselves from the high court. Unable to rely on its traditional legislative allies, and with General Pinochet scheduled to step down from his military command in a few short months, the old Supreme Court was now more politically isolated and out of step than ever. It would either adapt to the new realities or suffer the consequences.

President Frei wasted no time in taking advantage of this new legal and political context by appointing nine justices to the high court in December 1997 and January 1998, and another two later in 1998. As shown in table 5.1, eight of these eleven appointees would vote in favor of the *desafuero*. They were joined by six Aylwin and Frei appointees who had joined the bench prior to the reforms to comprise the solid majority in favor of *desafuero*. The post-reform personnel changes were more numerous and more decisive, however, because they shifted the high court's balance of power away from Pinochet's stalwart supporters.

These changes, it should be pointed out, were no guarantee that justice would prevail. After all, the new members of the high court were not ideological progressives anxious to settle scores with military criminals. To the contrary, four of the new justices chosen by President Frei and confirmed by the senate in the first week of January 1998 were affiliated with conservative or centrist parties, had rendered pro-military decisions before, or had served under Pinochet in lower courts.[71] Few Chileans expected that any of these appointees would join the assault against the protections devised by the old regime to permit a reopening of the human rights cases, yet some did.[72] Why did they? Many of the new jurists seemed to understand the historic role they had been thrust into. They had ascended to the high court as a result of landmark legislation supported by parties across the spectrum. They were now members of a new cohort, serving on a new court situated within a transformed domestic and international context. There was no turning back the clock.[73]

Not only had the high court changed, so too had Chilean society. The political parties of the right were positioning themselves for future presidential elections. To improve their chances of gaining the presidency they knew they would have to somehow appeal to a broader cross section of Chileans. One way of doing that would be to disassociate themselves from disreputable figures and institutions of the past and demonstrate that they too could be on the side of change. Thus, in the eyes of the political right, the old general was no longer entitled to special privileges or protections. Joaquín Lavín, the then and now presidential candidate of the conservative alliance, remarked that Pinochet ought to confront charges in court just like any other Chilean (Facultad Latino Americana 2000, 72).

The military itself was undergoing change. General Pinochet stepped down as head of the army in March 1998, in accordance with his own constitution. Once removed from a position of official military authority, Pinochet would no longer exert quite the same influence on the rest of the officer corps. His departure would allow a new generation of officers to ascend the ranks who did not owe their career advancement to him, nor were as closely associated with the worst human rights abuses of the past. In 1999, these officers would join in a dialog with Chilean human rights activists and government representatives on how to locate the remains of the disappeared.[74] It was there that for the first time the military admitted they held responsibility for those disappearances.[75]

All of this occurred prior to Pinochet's arrest and trial in London. But the European actions and particularly the British arrest and trial had a way of catalyzing change in Chile. They did so by deflating Pinochet's stature among Chileans of all persuasions and walks of life. Before his arrest in England, Pinochet had been considered by Chileans to be untouchable. No longer. Before, Chileans had placed little faith in the judiciary to resolve human rights problems afflicting their society. Now, they looked toward the courts to rectify grave injustices. This change marked a kind of cultural shift in Chile toward an awakened sense that the legal arena mattered and that if human rights could be legally defended abroad they could be defended at home.[76]

Perhaps the most telling reflection of this shift in Chilean opinion was to be found in the conservative mass media. Papers like El Mercurio that previously had refused to even acknowledge the legal proceedings in Europe now admitted it was time to strip Pinochet of his parliamentary immunity so that he could stand trial. The equally conservative daily La Tercera editorialized that the desafuero will be "the price to pay" if Pinochet is to retire in dignity and peace. Only when trials for Pinochet and other members of the armed forces are held "will it be said that Chile had entered a new era," it added.[77] Of course, the other side of the coin from prosecution of offenders was relief for the victims' survivors. Here too the press showed a greater empathy. Two days after Pinochet's return to Chile, La Tercera opined that Chile "ought to redouble its efforts to pay the debt it has with the families of the detained-disappeared and with its hackneyed international image."[78]

What about the public in general? Certainly the judges had to be cognizant of the public's changing view toward Pinochet and justice. Were they influenced by it? Justices do not exist in splendid isolation. Scholars of the U.S. Supreme Court have found that judges are influenced by the shifting tide of public opinion and often want to align themselves with views that command strong majorities within society (Baum 2001, 173).

If that also holds true for the Chilean high justices, it is worth noting a few trends in public opinion regarding the Pinochet case. In December 1998, just a month after the Law Lords handed down their first verdict, the London-based Market Opinion Research International (MORI) found that 63 percent of

Chileans believed Pinochet was guilty of the crimes of which he was charged, 57 percent thought he should be tried, and 29 percent thought he should be set free.[79] Just a month after the third British ruling (March 1999), which again established Pinochet's guilt, Chileans were asked what was best for their nation's future: that General Pinochet remain in London so he could be extradited to Spain, that he return to Chile to stand trial, or that he return to Chile and not be tried? The poll showed that 31 percent said he should remain in London, 41 percent said he should return to Chile for trial, 17 percent said he should return without trial, and 11 percent did not respond or had no opinion. Hence, a year before his actual return, 72 percent of Chileans wanted Pinochet to see his day in court, whether that be in Spain or in Chile.[80]

After his return, another poll found that 52 percent were in favor of stripping him of his immunity and 35 percent were opposed, with the remainder voicing no opinion. A month after the verdict, 61 percent expressed their support for the *desafuero*, while 29 percent opposed.[81] In short, most Chileans were anxious to see justice done. It remains a matter of speculation as to whether or to what degree these opinions influenced the high courts.

Europe Mattered, but Only Momentarily

Pinochet's arrest in England created a window of opportunity for families, human rights activists, NGOs, and attorneys to press for change in Chile, one they took advantage of. The courts in Spain and Britain opened up avenues of ingress for them, taking evidence, hearing testimony, issuing indictments, and handing down verdicts. Once the legal processes were set in motion, they could not be easily reversed or stalled. Executive leaders from Spain and Britain seemed to be willing, *at first*, to let the process run its course and were certainly unwilling to tamper with judicial autonomy. When, for example, the trial judges of Spain's Audiencia Nacional upheld the right of Spanish courts to hear the Pinochet case, and when Judge Garzón issued an arrest order followed by an indictment against Pinochet, there was little that the José María Aznar government could do to block those efforts short of violating the separation of powers governing his state. Nor could British prime minister Tony Blair directly intercede in the proceedings of the British high courts without incurring serious charges against himself.

Yet the British, Spanish, and Chilean national leaders had every incentive to find a legal means to close the window of opportunity, derail the process, and end the ordeal. And they did so. Their efforts offer compelling proof of the thesis that in the realm of low politics, foreign states are ultimately more concerned with furthering their economic and military interests than they are in proving their moral virtuosity by coming to the defense of human rights victims abroad. The Spanish and British prime ministers, along with the Chilean president, were anxious and determined to find a political solution to a problem that had already threatened to harm the much valued ties between their nations. What was at stake was not just diplomatic friendship, but important economic and military interests.

By 1999, Spain had become the single largest foreign investor in Chile, accounting for 50 percent of the total. It was the lead investor in construction (64 percent), electricity, gas, and water (70 percent), and services (59 percent). That same year, Chile was Spain's fourth most important trading partner in Latin America (behind Mexico, Brazil, and Argentina) with $380 million in exports and $366 million in imports (International Monetary Fund 2001). Britain invested and traded less with Chile, but not insignificantly. Britain accounted for all foreign investment in the fishing industry and was third largest in mining.

Britain's interest in restoring amicable relations with Chile can best be understood in military terms. During the Malvinas War of 1982, the Chilean government offered Britain valuable warfare intelligence on Argentina and use of bases in exchange for military hardware. Great Britain wasted no time in taking up the offer. Within weeks of the war's commencement, British Canberra and Hawker Hunter aircraft were already en route to Chile in payment for use of an airbase near Punto Arenas and Chilean naval intercepts of Argentine military signals (Phythian 2000, 116–17). From that point forward, Anglo-Chilean military and political relations remained close, as Chile sought other armaments, including naval vessels, armored vehicles, and rocket launchers, and Britain seemed only too pleased to oblige.[82] While other nations, including the United States, had blocked arms sales to Chile on human rights grounds, Britain's arms bazaar was always open to Chilean procurers, during and after the Pinochet era.

It is these commercial relations that were at risk with a prolongation of Pinochet's arrest and potential trial. In the summer of 1999, Chile began to turn up the diplomatic heat on Spain, saying it was prepared to review all facets of its relationship and withdrawing its ambassador. Britain too had feared that its relations with Chile had been strained almost to the breaking point. And while Chile was engaged in diplomatic brinkmanship, it too was worried about a fracture in its relations with both countries.

With these vital interests in mind, it is little wonder, then, that evidence surfaced in 2001 of a secret plan hatched between the three leaders to find a political solution to the Pinochet problem. The idea was to get Pinochet back to Chile on humanitarian grounds. The British home secretary, Jack Straw, who served Tony Blair and had ample discretion when it came to decisions on whether to extradite a defendant, would be at the center of this plan. The British would suggest to the Chileans that they have Pinochet submit to medical exams and then have the home secretary use the results of those exams to make a case for blocking extradition on grounds that the aging general was in no condition to withstand or understand a trial in Spain. The Spanish government would then agree to go along. The foreign ministers of these three nations had a series of meetings during the second half of 1999 to work out the details of this arrangement.[83]

The efforts to secure this political solution accelerated after October 8, 1999, when British high court judge Ronald Bartle gave the green light for Pinochet's extradition to Spain.[84] Naturally, Pinochet's lawyers appealed the decision. But even if Chile were to prevail in the appeal, the legal process could have taken up to two years. Time was of the essence for these three countries, not to mention for Pinochet himself. Thus, Chile's embassy immediately sent new medical reports on Pinochet to the British suggesting there had been a significant, recent deterioration in his health, followed shortly thereafter by a request that Pinochet be freed on health grounds.[85] Not coincidentally, on November 5, 1999, Jack Straw invited Chile to submit Pinochet to official medical tests, a necessary first step toward a humanitarian release. Straw was prepared to use all his legal discretion as home secretary by permitting the tests to go forward *well before* the appeal process had exhausted itself.

Straw's decision to deny the extradition and send Pinochet home was made on March 1, 2000. The Spanish government immediately announced it would not appeal that decision. In doing so, Spanish foreign minister Abel Matutes refused to transmit Garzón's instructions to his legal representatives in London to try to block Pinochet's release, saying that the Foreign Affairs Ministry "would no longer serve as Garzón's conduit to the British government."[86] The British and Spanish governments had finally put the Pinochet ordeal behind them and in doing so had patched things up with Chile as well. Foreign state economic and military interests had trumped human rights, pushing the Pinochet case back to the domestic, Chilean arena where it would remain.

Returning the Pinochet Case to Chile

In the low politics realm of human rights, external actors are not expected to exert much influence over the internal affairs of an offending state. Foreign states are not sufficiently motivated to do so, and foreign nonstate activists are not sufficiently empowered to do so. Long stretches of contemporary Chilean history by and large bear this out. The dictatorship could not escape rhetorical condemnation for its human rights abuses yet did escape harsh economic and military reprisals. And for almost a decade, the successor democratic regime could not or would not serve justice on the generals nor was it under pressure from abroad to do so.

But we have hypothesized that there are international moments in the realm of low politics when nonstate activists can capture the attention of state leaders just long enough to set in motion a chain of events that will reverberate abroad. Hugely motivated and well informed, these activists seize an opportunity to press their appeal with foreign state officials. And those officials discover—albeit briefly—some motivation to listen to those appeals and act on them. This convergence of activists and state actors sets the stage for a low politics issue like human rights to fall under the weight of international influence. When it does, foreigners demonstrate greater interest and resolve to do something about human rights dilemmas within the targeted state.

The Chilean case confirms this hypothesis. The European moment—as captured by stunning judicial investigations, indictments, and verdicts meted out by Spanish and then British courts—tore at the sovereign walls separating the Chilean courts and Chile itself from the external world. High court judges were influenced by events in Europe, but indirectly and politically so. They seemed to have little regard for the legal views of the Spanish and British magistrates, yet they could not ignore the political views and predicament of their own government, brought on by the Pinochet case. The government transferred part of their burden onto the courts by imposing pressure on them to move against Pinochet.

On matters of human rights, sovereignty has been and will continue to be a force to be reckoned with, throwing up great obstacles to transnational actors wishing to cultivate change. But paradoxically, the Chilean high courts became vulnerable to international opinion on this issue precisely because they had been so closed off for so long to the pleas of families seeking justice. The contrast between their obstruction on the one hand and the bold decisions taken by Spanish and British magistrates on the other hand was inescapable. The Pinochet case was able to focus attention on Chile in a way that few other cases have. The verdict from Europe was in: Pinochet was guilty of crimes against humanity, and no amount of immunity or state sovereignty could conceal that fact.

Still, and as our theory suggests, the gravitational pull is always toward the domestic when it comes to low politics issues, notwithstanding the fact that the international has its moments. The Spanish and British administrations became preoccupied with preserving their vital economic and military ties to Chile and could only do so by unloading the Pinochet case. Once the case shifted back to Santiago, the solution to the human rights problem became distinctly Chilean. While the high courts did take some decisive actions against Pinochet, they have to date not been able to convict him of any crimes. His lawyers argued that he should not be forced to withstand the rigors of a trial due to his failing health. In July 2001, the appellate court agreed and issued a temporary stay to the proceedings. That decision was appealed to the Supreme Court, which on July 1, 2002, upheld the appellate ruling, declaring Pinochet mentally unfit to stand trial.[87] It is now likely that Pinochet will never see a day in court, let alone find himself behind bars in Chile.[88]

Speak to Chilean human rights lawyers and they will describe the *desafuero* ruling of August 2000 as Chile's version of punishment, the closest one could expect the nation to get to a conviction of the former military president.[89] What has been accomplished? The general remains under suspicion, he has failed to clear his name, and he can no longer serve in the Senate or any other public office. And yet, he has to date not served any time. Most outside human rights activists would have wished for a lot more but cannot simply reexert leverage on a sovereign state. The window of opportunity pried open by the Spanish and British courts has already closed. It remains to be seen what Chile will accomplish on its own to deliver to those victims of the dictatorship the justice they have long sought.

6. Regional Security in Central America

I t is difficult to discuss security issues in Central America without reference to external actors. The United States long ago marked out the region as part of its backyard, and its involvement only intensified with the onset of the Cold War as the country scoured the region for the slightest hint of Soviet expansionism. When civil wars raged across the isthmus at the twilight of the Cold War and beyond, the scope of foreign intervention widened as neighboring Latin American states and international organizations entered to propose and support resolutions. At the dawn of the twenty-first century, the region no longer represents a hub of superpower conflict, and international organizations have turned their attention elsewhere. Nonetheless, the United States now hovers over the area with little competition, prepared to intervene when it sees fit, expressing a form of "episodic hegemony."

Given the magnitude of foreign influence, many might be surprised to learn that Central America constructed its own regional security institutions in the 1990s, a domestic moment in the high politics of security. Washington's grip on the region relaxed in the post–Cold War era, just long enough for Central America to assemble the civilian Central American Security Commission (Comisión de Seguridad Centroamericana—CSC), which unites all the countries on the isthmus, and the Conference of Central American Armed Forces (Conferencia de las Fuerzas Armadas Centroamericanas—CFAC), a military-based organization that bands those states with militaries—El Salvador, Guatemala, Honduras, and Nicaragua (the CA-4). How was it that such highly dependent, vulnerable countries found room to express and act upon their own interests in high politics? Can these regional institutions retain any measure of significance when hegemony returns? And where will this significance be felt?

It was, of course, ebbing hegemony and the political space this opened for Central America that allowed these developments to occur. But this does not mean that the United States vacated the scene altogether. U.S. policy did play a role. Hegemons can linger even as hegemony recedes. The more important point is that the U.S. role became subsidiary; the dynamic behind regional security developments during this time came to rest in the domestic arenas of Central American states. Rather than simply identifying this period as aberrant or peculiar, the discussion locates it as a domestic moment—an observable and explicable occurrence made plain by the high-low politics framework.

But what of these regional security arrangements that now rest under the umbrella of hegemony? These institutions stand with one foot in the international, and the other in the domestic. For the region, a security organization permits more effective responses to cross-country threats and concerns (e.g., drug trafficking and hurricanes), stimulates confidence-building measures, and provides an agenda-setting mechanism to counter, or at least respond to, hegemonic bids to control security policy. The benefits are real and difficult to deny. But the story grows more complex in the domestic arena. Security defines the corporate identity of the armed forces, and the management of security policy is the yardstick of civilian control. Because a regional organization opens new questions regarding missions, duties, military prerogatives, and expenditures, it inevitably reverberates in the civil-military relations of each member country.

Hence, the dynamics of regional security and civil-military relations intersect in Central America. The domestic moment opened an opportunity for domestic expression in regional security, but the trials and tribulations of civilian supremacy in each country color this expression and ultimately determine the domestic moment's final impact. Indeed, Central American civil-military relations have played themselves out within the very institutions of regional security. CFAC and the CSC have emerged to address many of the same issues, and CFAC has scored more progress. Why is this important?

Current impediments to greater civilian control in the region largely rest in the lack of security-related expertise held by civilians and tensions emerging from the historic mistrust, misunderstanding, and dearth of interactions between politicians and soldiers. For a country with sufficient civilian control, CFAC is likely to provide rewards as relations with neighbors improve, common threats are more successfully countered, and professional duties defined by civilians occupy the military forces. For a country struggling with questions of civilian control, the organization could further harm civil-military relations, depending on how it evolves. Its current status as a nonadvisory, operative organization will only present problems insofar as CFAC continues to demonstrate greater relative success than its regional counterparts in the civilian field and thereby contributes to the perception that the military succeeds where politicians fail. It will also facilitate the retention by the military of nonmilitary duties that would be better served by civilian agencies. Under these conditions, the organization will buttress the status quo and restrict civilian empowerment. If the organization assumes consultative and even policy-making duties, it could serve as a springboard for greater military influence and more gravely undermine democratic rule.

CFAC therefore represents an intriguing window on the dynamics of the foreign and domestic in Central American security affairs. The birth of the organization depended on a hegemonic retreat, and its impact will vary in tandem with the domestic civil-military relations of each country. Moreover, as we shall see, the closing of the domestic moment is unlikely to halt this process. Washington has moved to end the moment in response to renewed security concerns, but the hegemon remains less motivated to immerse itself in civil-military relations. CFAC will therefore weigh more heavily upon the domestic even as it is crowded out of the international arena by U.S. prerogatives.

Regional Cooperation and Security in the Post–Cold War Era

Central American regional security should be placed in the context of the post–Cold War era, an exciting period in world history that opened new hopes and challenges for developing countries. Before this time, the superpower rivalry of the Cold War all but extinguished independent foreign policy making. States felt compelled to choose one side and adjust their interstate relations to the interests of their respective patron (Clawson 1986). But the collapse of the Soviet Union in 1989 recast world politics in a new mold. Recoiling Soviet hegemony led to a similar move by the United States, which lost the Cold War rationale to police developments in the Third World. Moreover, while the passing of Soviet authority opened new regions to U.S. influence, the United States simply lacked the capacity to regulate world politics and faced domestic pressures to reduce excessive expenditures associated with this role. Well over $6 billion in aid had flowed to El Salvador alone from 1979 to 1989 (Molineu 1990, 217). Lacking a communist adversary to confront and unable to point to any real socioeconomic gains in the aftermath, U.S. policy makers would be hard pressed to justify anything close to a repeat in the 1990s.

The retraction of superpower politics unlatched new opportunities for developing countries to assess and respond to their own regional concerns. Scholars have begun to write of a "new regionalism," different from the failed regionalist projects of the 1950s and 1960s in that, among other aspects, countries are integrating not only economically but also politically and socially (Hettne and Inotai 1994; Fawcett and Hurrell 1995). In the realm of security concerns, regional arrangements have emerged to buttress UN efforts toward peacekeeping and dispute settlement. Success stories in the developing world include ECOWAS in West Africa and the ASEAN in Cambodia. Ultimately, the United Nations and regional organizations complement each other. Regional groups can employ historical, cultural, and individual connections to encourage the pacific settlement of disputes, and the United Nations can provide financial resources and expertise. And each carries distinct sources of legitimacy—regional arrangements typically hold more profound understandings of the conflict, while the United Nations stands above the fray as a neutral arbiter (Barnett 1995).

Aside from the new regionalist push, the conceptual expansion of security beyond traditional interstate military affairs marks a second fundamental change in security matters (Williams and Krause 1996). The impoverishing effects of the 1980s debt crisis, numerous experiences with brutal authoritarian rule, and dramatic increases in crime levels encouraged the study of human, as opposed to state, security. Resource depletion and other forms of environmental degradation, as well as the mounting costs of natural disasters in terms of both human life and economic development, drew security studies to the environmental realm. The rise of nonstate actors such as terrorist groups, organized criminal networks, and drug traffickers challenged the interstate focus of security studies. Finally, tighter levels of interdependence in areas such as economic relations and migration patterns led states to view many domestic events as matters of international security. Central America witnessed all these troubles intensifying in the 1990s.

The province of security matters and their guiding norms has thus become debatable (Freedman 1998). For many issues, the road to high politics runs through security, with significant political implications. The security link legitimizes the use of extraordinary means to address the issue and can even justify breaking the rules of the political game, for example, through secrecy and restrictions on civil liberties (Wæver 1995). In much of Latin America during the 1960s and 1970s, when national security doctrine led military governments to subsume economic development under the security umbrella, military officers directed state businesses, repressed labor rights, and purged bureaucracies on the basis of political affiliation. More recently in the region, as drug production, transport, and related activities have been pushed from criminal to national security issues, the military has supported or even replaced local police enforcement, search and seizure regulations have been relaxed, and habeas corpus protections have been weakened. The terrorist attacks on the United States in September 2001 have also opened new questions of security issue linkages in Latin America.[1]

The prospect of security issue linkages makes the newly energized regional arrangements of the post–Cold War world all the more important. These organizations allow developing states to pool their resources and possibly counteract or at least influence persistent great power efforts to frame security issues. One need look no further than Central America during the Cold War to illustrate the costs incurred when an outside actor monopolizes security issues. During this time, U.S. efforts to neutralize any challenges (communist or otherwise) to its hegemonic position, or to the local status quo as it enforced its own security norms, worked against the political and ultimately economic development of Central American countries.[2]

On the other hand, the Central American peace processes exemplify the benefits to be gained through independent regional action. Faced with U.S. attempts to impose a solution on the various conflicts through military means, Mexico, Venezuela, Colombia, and Panama organized the Contadora Group in 1983 to advocate a negotiated settlement. The countries placed local socioeconomic inequities rather than international communist subversion at the root of the conflicts and encouraged respect for the principle of nonintervention. In 1987, Oscar Arias of Costa Rica further refashioned security norms when he led an expressly Central American effort to achieve peace. This effort culminated in the Esquipulas II agreement, which incorporated much of the Contadora proposals and also called for greater involvement by the international community and intense efforts at national reconciliation within each country. The agreement spurned U.S. security ideas and represents a success story for Central America (Moreno 1994).

Regional security organizations thus have value, but what of their potential? Scholars have identified regional security systems as "open systems"—vulnerable to influences from the global system, other regional systems, and outside states (Lake and Morgan 1997, 9–10). When they rest in the heart of a superpower's historic sphere of influence, they are all the more assailable. This vulnerability is clearly the case for Central America, where we should expect the United States to maintain its sway over security norms and decisions (Stein and Lobell 1997). However, the precise expression of U.S. influence has differed from that of the Cold War. In particular, the intrusion of an external power can take one of two forms. In a situation of *overlay*, "one or more external powers moves directly into the regional complex with the effect of suppressing the indigenous security dynamic." The other form of intrusion is *intervention*, whereby local security dynamics are determined regionally but remain permeable to manipulation by an external power. The indigenous security arrangements remain intact and are reinforced from the outside, albeit with an outcome largely influenced by the foreign power (Buzan, Wæver, and de Wilde 1998, 12–14).

While overlay characterized Cold War dynamics in Central America, the 1990s revealed a movement toward intervention, and this trend is likely to continue. Indeed, the dramatic decline in U.S. economic and military aid to the region would make the continuation of overlay difficult (Fitch 1993).[3] In the absence of the hypersecurity environment of the Cold War, some argue that the United States is growing indifferent to the region (Zeledón Torres 1998, 223; Hennelly 1993). A theoretical explanation for the movement is provided by Michael Desch (1998), who argues that economic and ideological considerations rise to the fore in the absence of unifying threats such as communism. Unlike the immediate, tangible security threats that galvanize political elites under the common banner of defense, economic and ideological issues generate greater debate and introduce more diverse actors, and thereby undermine coherent, rational policy making. While the "war on terrorism" has increased U.S. security interests worldwide, regions other than Central America stand at the forefront, and tightening budgets have forced policy makers to reassess existing and proposed programs in this region (Shifter 2002).

Nonetheless, the United States retains a tremendous capacity to express its interests in the region, and security concerns, perhaps even those related to terrorism, might very well lead it to replay its Cold War role. This very capacity also grants it the ability to maneuver in *and out* of the region with some fluidity. The fact that it has few real rivals attenuates its desire to be continuously involved. Hence, we can say that the United States has the capacity to intervene, but only a potential will to intervene, one that it expresses at its own discretion.

Indeed, episodic hegemony is not new to Latin America. While current U.S. participation in the region falls below that found in the 1960s and 1970s, its interest during the 1980s clearly outpaced those two decades, as did its involvement in the days of "dollar diplomacy." Periods of relaxed U.S. influence open domestic moments when both regional and domestic political arrangements are able to change such that when the hegemon returns it finds a different reception.

The Growth of Regional Security Institutions in Central America

The Central American conflicts of the 1980s were complex. Civil wars raged in Guatemala and El Salvador; U.S.-supported *contras* stationed themselves in Costa Rica and Honduras for invasions into Nicaragua; the Salvadoran insurgency group, the FMLN, was suspected of receiving support from refugee camps in Honduras and arms transfers from the Sandinista government; and military buildups created a tense atmosphere throughout the region. The peace processes emerging from the conflicts were similarly complex, addressing issues such as truth commissions, refugee assistance, free elections, economic development, amnesty, disarmament, cease-fires, interstate confidence-building measures, and the balance of forces in the region. Although the Esquipulas II accord, signed on August 7, 1987, is widely recognized as the centerpiece of the peace plan, a series of Central American presidential summits would produce additional agreements and modifications. Moreover, the civil wars in El Salvador and Guatemala lingered to 1992 and 1995, respectively, and the peace agreements in these countries added to the evolution of the Central American peace process more generally.

It was within this mélange of peace agreements that the current Central American regional security system unfolded. If there is a prevailing pattern in the development of the regional security institutions, it is one in which the scope of involved actors gradually narrowed over time. Although contemporary regional security cooperation emerged as part of a larger scheme of Central American integration and involved the close participation of the international community, the agenda increasingly fell into the hands of military officers in the CA-4 countries, and out of the hands of those Central American countries lacking military establishments (Costa Rica and Panama), civilians more generally, and the international community. This dynamic corresponds to the opening of a domestic moment. External actors took a step back, allowing internal actors to take the lead. The move also meant that the struggles among these internal actors would play out more autonomously.

The impetus for regional security cooperation in Central America can be traced to the 1987 Esquipulas agreement, but real independent movement in this issue area would have to wait for hegemony to recede. That would begin just after the 1990 electoral defeat of the Sandinista government in Nicaragua. With the United States no longer looking over their shoulders, Central American presidents fed off their successes in the peace agreements and gained confidence to challenge the historic monopoly of the armed forces over security affairs. Their efforts culminated with the Framework Treaty on Democratic Security in 1995. But in this very same year the militaries began to reassert control over security issues, a move that manifested itself most visibly in the creation of an expressly military regional security arrangement, the Conference of Central American Armed Forces (CFAC), in 1997. A hegemonic withdrawal enabled these civil-military dynamics to come center stage and unfold with greater autonomy than in the past.

From Esquipulas to the Treaty on Democratic Security

The Esquipulas II peace agreement, signed by the CA-4 and Costa Rica in 1987, set the groundwork for contemporary Central American security institutions. This document established the International Verification and Follow-Up Commission (Comisión Internacional de Verificación y Seguimiento—CIVS) and invited participants from outside the region to ensure compliance.[4] The signatories institutionalized their own participation by organizing the Central American Security Commission (Comisión de Seguridad Centroamericana— CSC) in October 1987. In January 1988, the five Central American presidents, convened as the Executive Commission of the Esquipulas II agreement, declared the work of the CIVS to be completed and announced that further verification would be the responsibility of the CSC acting under the authority of the Executive Commission.[5] But, the move for greater autonomy proved to be premature.

Despite the elevated status of the CSC, the institution fell into a state of dormancy due to both international organizations that crowded out the CSC as they assured compliance with the Esquipulas II agreement, and to continued conflict in the region. Qualms about the Sandinista government presented the first hurdles to greater interstate cooperation. Efforts by the Reagan administration to undermine negotiations between the Sandinistas and its opposition raised regional tensions through 1988. The Nicaraguan government cracked down on its opponents to demonstrate its resolve, and *contra* encampments in Honduras remained a problem. Relations progressed somewhat through 1989 when the more flexible Bush administration entered the White House and after Nicaragua invited missions from the United Nations to observe political reforms leading to the February 1990 elections. In this improved environment, a new mission emerged to oversee compliance with Esquipulas II, this one organized by the United Nations (UN Observer Group in Central America—ONUCA), and a joint OAS-UN mission was created to oversee the demobilization of the *contras*.

Interstate security anxieties receded after the 1990 Sandinista electoral defeat, and ONUCA's mandate was allowed to expire on June 29, 1990. The domestic moment had arrived, and the onus to address security issues came to rest on the shoulders of domestic actors. But now they had their own problems to resolve. Early moves to address other pressing concerns congested the agenda, and policy differences on how to approach security frustrated debate. The presidential summits in Montelimar, Nicaragua, April 1990, and Antigua, Guatemala, June 1990, shifted focus toward common economic problems and away from security (Moreno 1994, 128–29). The CSC was still charged with devising arms reduction measures, negotiating a balance of forces in the region, discussing the role of foreign bases, and studying common security dilemmas, but ongoing civil wars in Guatemala and El Salvador hindered its work. These countries were wary of opening their armament inventories, let alone conceding arms and personnel reductions, in the midst of an armed struggle. Hence, it was largely a political statement when the presidents called for a new model of regional security in their Declaration of Puntarenas (December 1990).[6]

But the call was not without consequence. The growing realization that the Central American conflicts could only be effectively addressed regionally had significant effects on civil-military relations within each country. The presidents were empowered by the fact that they were tackling the regional crises and had solid backing from the international community. Military approaches had not resolved the crises, and this denied the armed forces an opportunity to champion their role as the conflicts were brought to a close.[7] Consequentially, a new political space opened, this one within the domestic arena, for the Central American presidents to address regional security on their own, outside the traditional military framework (Aguilera Peralta 1994, 123–24). Through fits and starts, they would eventually make progress.

It is not surprising that Honduras provided the impetus to redefine regional security. El Salvador, Guatemala, and Nicaragua had issues of national reconciliation to confront and could not concentrate pointedly on civil-military relations (although this remained a significant component in national reconciliation). Costa Rica, and later Panama, could not be expected to lead discussions on regional military security through their participation in the CSC because they lacked militaries. But Honduras was different. The decline in Cold War and regional security preoccupations led the United States to reduce military aid to the country and greatly toned down the security-related rhetoric that had heightened the political behavior of the armed forces. No longer considered untouchable, and in the midst of a revival of civil society, the military had its reputation sullied by revelations of human rights abuses, corruption, and criminal activity. Finally, it was in Honduras that the United States first and most forcefully applied pressure to demilitarize in the 1990s (Ruhl 1996).

Honduras presented its proposal for a regional security scheme at the San Salvador presidential summit in July 1991. The proposal called for confidence-building measures and the reduction of armaments and personnel, as well as verification and control thereof, and addressed human rights concerns and the Esquipulas agreements (e.g., prohibitions on support for irregular forces fighting neighboring countries or the lending of territory to these forces, cooperation on refugee issues, democratization, and cooperative calls for international economic aid). Guatemala and El Salvador gave the document a cold reception, and Nicaragua criticized the absence of any references to foreign military bases and installations. The document was ferried to the CSC, where it would remain under review and study for the next four years.[8] At subsequent summit meetings, the presidents would pronounce celebratory support for the CSC, but disagreements over how to define a "reasonable balance of forces," and precisely how to count armaments and military personnel, continued to stifle progress of any significance.[9] For a time, it seemed that the domestic moment would be remembered only as a lost opportunity.

Compromise and concession began to take their toll. Over time, the Honduran proposal would be tempered into a more political document that proposed a new philosophy of national security, and less an explicitly military document that mandated precise changes in defense matters. The 1992 draft that emerged from the CSC backtracked as it eliminated the time limits for the execution of some of the agreements, as well as the numerical restrictions on foreign advisers (Solís Rivera and Rojas Aravena 1994, 19–26). At the August 1995 CSC meeting in Managua, the content of the document was diluted when it incorporated a Nicaraguan proposal to redefine security beyond military matters.[10] The proposal dovetailed with Costa Rican efforts to tie security to democratic consolidation and the safety of citizens against crime.[11] The proposals held merit, but they masked a more important reality—contention over security matters was creating a drag on cooperative efforts and leading negotiators to avoid the thorny issues that demanded confrontation with military interests. At the completion of the August meeting, a draft treaty was submitted for approval by the Central American presidents at their upcoming December summit in San Pedro Sula, Honduras.

The four months leading up to the San Pedro Sula summit were critical and illustrated the lack of civilian expertise in military matters as well as the political resurgence of the armed forces in the region. After its own meeting, the CSC offered to organize a conference to publicize the treaty and collect input from civil society, but the meeting never transpired. Instead, the militaries of the region organized their own conference in October to suggest revisions. It is assumed that the meeting significantly altered the content of the treaty, especially the parts that covered military reductions and foreign bases (Isaacson 1998). It was at this time that the militaries, at the initiative of Guatemala, began a series of meetings of their ministers of defense (for Guatemala and El Salvador, both of which had a military officer in this position) and army commanders (for Nicaragua and Honduras) to discuss the creation of CFAC.[12] They did so without the participation of or input from the Pentagon, U.S. military attachés, or the Southern Command. It is telling that the proposal to create CFAC came from Guatemala, the country with the greatest level of military influence at the time. Enough time had passed for the armed forces to recuperate, and officers sensed a civilian push into security affairs that threatened to become a shove.

Still, civilian leaders were their own worst enemy—factionalism eased the resurgence of military influence. When the presidents met in December, the differences in military policy were difficult to hide. Costa Rica and Panama pushed for more extensive reductions and controls on military institutions, and the CA-4 countries proved reluctant to move too swiftly against the interests of their military institutions (Bull 1999, 966).[13] It is thus little surprise that the countries focused their efforts on redefining security along the lines of the Nicaraguan and prior Costa Rican proposals—a regional security arrangement geared toward military reductions would have involved contentious details and ultimately would have failed in the heat of debate. But the oversights would leave room for CFAC to stake its own claims in the security field.

The final product, the Framework Treaty on Democratic Security, is an important document, despite Costa Rica's legitimate reservations.[14] As a contribution to security theory, the treaty marks a significant break from traditional approaches with its emphasis on human, rather than state, security. Respect for human rights, efforts to combat poverty, and the promotion of sustainable development, economic freedom, cultural heritage, political pluralism, and even consumer protection are all incorporated as matters of security. The emphasis on cooperative interstate efforts to address these concerns marks a further step away from traditional security approaches, which presume mistrust to be an inexorable force. The document is clearly designed to further the process of democratic consolidation in the CA-4 through the empowerment of civilian authorities and the circumspection of independent military action. Article 1 begins, "The Central American Democratic Security Model is based on democracy," and article 4 states, "Each of the Parties shall establish and maintain at all times effective control over their military and public security forces by their constitutionally established civil authorities."

Beyond its contribution to security doctrine, the treaty details a number of confidence-building measures and establishes a hierarchical framework for regional security policy making that runs from the presidential summits, to a Council of Ministers of Foreign Relations, to the CSC, which is to comprise the vice ministers of foreign relations and defense (or their equivalent in the area of public security). The CSC is explicitly charged with implementing decisions made by the presidents or Council of Ministers of Foreign Relations, acting as a body of mediation for interstate disputes, studying security dilemmas, and strengthening mechanisms of interstate security cooperation, maintaining a registry of armaments and transferences thereof, and communicating security concerns to the System of Central American Integration (SICA—Sistema de la

Integración Centroamericana), an umbrella organization that has as its goal the integration of Central America as a region of peace, freedom, democracy, and development.[15] The Framework Treaty thus stands as a significant milestone for civil-military relations and democratic consolidation in the region. Nonetheless, it is ultimately a goal-oriented document that can live up to its promise only if backed by the political will to implement it. If its brief history is a prelude of what is to come, one finds it difficult not to be skeptical about its future.

CFAC and the Eclipse of the CSC

Officially, CFAC justified its existence on the need to replace the Consejo de Defensa Centroamericana (CONDECA), created in 1963 but defunct since the 1969 border war between Honduras and El Salvador. CONDECA, a relic of U.S. designs under the Cold War, was oriented toward an external attack and had become outdated. It was not designed to deal with more contemporary problems of development, poverty, and natural disasters, nor the arrangement of confidence building (CFAC 2000a). Of course, the CSC had emerged to cope with this newly defined range of security issues, but the armed forces openly questioned its expertise. A news report from the period, citing a military source, noted "the militaries consider the Security Commission currently functioning to be insufficient for the coordination of new activities by the armed forces."[16] That these military efforts might undermine the civilian work of the CSC was not lost on analysts of the area.[17] In general, the need to replace CONDECA dovetailed with military desires to revitalize regional approaches to security in line with movements by the CSC.

The CA-4 military meetings begun in 1995 to address these concerns finally bore fruit in 1997 with the creation of CFAC. Final touches to the proposal were completed March 6–8, 1997, at Roatán, Honduras, and June 11, in Guatemala, in meetings with the defense ministers of El Salvador and Guatemala, and the army commanders in chief from Nicaragua and Honduras (Bonilla Martinez 2000). When the CA-4 presidents convened in Nicaragua on September 4, 1997, to mark the eighteenth anniversary of the Nicaraguan army, the military officials took the opportunity to present their proposal.[18] A decree by the CA-4 presidents then gave CFAC legal standing on November 12, 1997. A ceremony to deactivate CONDECA and inaugurate CFAC was held December 17, 1997.

CFAC is an explicitly military organization. The foundational document of

CFAC gave to the highest ranking military officer in each country the responsibility to design the organization and draft its regulations. They established as the
principal organ of CFAC the Consejo Superior, with representation to come from
either the defense minister or chief military officer in each country, and a (largely
ceremonial) presidential seat to be rotated among the representatives biennially.
The representational option probably reflects tensions that transpired in some
countries as pressures grew to civilianize the ministries of defense.[19]

Beneath the Consejo Superior, there is no chance for civilian input. The second body of importance, the Comité Ejecutivo, is composed of the chiefs of staff
(or their equivalent) of member countries. It has some advisory duties but is primarily responsible for implementing decisions made by the Consejo Superior.
The third body, the Secretaría General Pro-Tempore, has administrative and sec-
retarial duties. It consists of military representatives from member countries and
is led by an officer with the rank of colonel. Lines of authority to the national militaries are drawn directly from the Comité Ejecutivo.

Since inception, CFAC has gradually encroached upon and assumed many of
the functions previously set aside for the CSC. Indeed, the foundational documents of CFAC make confrontation almost inevitable, and only the inability of
CFAC to realize all of its listed objectives has prevented a more intense clash. The
stated mission of CFAC is "to promote confidence building and a permanent and
systematic effort of cooperation, coordination, and mutual support from the
armed forces of the isthmus, in order to contribute to security, development, and
military integration in the region." Under this mission, six objectives are to be
pursued: (1) to recommend substantive actions against threats to democracy,
peace, and liberty, to furnish an optimal level of defense; (2) to exchange information and experiences in all aspects of cooperation, and to execute mechanisms of mutual confidence among the member countries; (3) to participate in
political, economic, psychosocial, and military conferences of interest to the integration of defense, and to democratic security, peace, and liberty in the region;
(4) to use specialized activities to promote study, discussion, and reflection on
military affairs and other common interests; (5) to extend mutual assistance toward studies that contribute to regional development, and to reduce the impact
of natural disasters in the region; and (6) to establish permanent communication with the secretary-general of the System of Central American Integration
(SICA) (CFAC 2000b).

Of these objectives, CFAC's greatest success has undoubtedly been in the area of confidence building through operational and educational exchange programs, and through periodic meetings that allow senior officers to discuss any issues at hand.[20] Also, the organization has convened an impressive number of activities. It completed drills against forest fires and for ecosystem preservation, and more general naval and air force maneuvers, as well as intelligence exercises. It organized specialized meetings that covered de-mining efforts, health services extension programs, civilian affairs, and intelligence coordination; sponsored regional conferences for the UNESCO Culture of Peace and Nonviolence program; and has attempted to establish an educational liaison with the Inter-American Institute of Human Rights. CFAC also created a special humanitarian rescue unit (UHR-CFAC—Unidad Humanitaria de Rescate-CFAC) to be used during natural disasters and has worked on a similar specialized unit for ecosystem preservation.

True to its stated goal of integrating the armed forces of Central America, CFAC has acted as a medium for institutionalizing cooperation. For example, the region's air forces designed a system of command and control for combined aerial confidence-building exercises, cooperation on the prevention of illegal flights (most often associated with narco-trafficking), and coordinating humanitarian efforts in the event of natural disasters.[21] CFAC addressed three recent crises in the region: Hurricane Mitch (1998); the earthquake in El Salvador (2001); and the dengue epidemics that have plagued El Salvador and Honduras (2000–present). The CSC, while geared toward regional security, has never seriously coordinated military activities, despite its mandate. But CFAC has done just that.[22]

But CFAC has had less success in its goal to become a policy consultant and to establish communications with SICA. Nonetheless, the reason for these difficulties rests just as much outside the armed forces as inside. Economic integration in the region, promoted with great fanfare through the 1990s, has not lived up to expectations. Costa Rica approaches unification with its relatively less developed neighbors apprehensively, and the region as a whole faces problems that typically stifle integration efforts in developing countries (economies that lack diversity, greater trade and investment relations with outside countries, independent commitments to international financial institutions, etc.). The flagship regional political institution, the Central American Parliament (PARLACEN), wracked by scandals and charges of ineffectiveness, saw its budget cut and popular appeal fall, and was even threatened with closure. SICA and SIECA (Secretaría de Integración Económica de Centroamérica) have both been criticized as increasingly bureaucratic institutions that "create new institutions as a 'solution' to the inadequate functioning of existing ones" (Bulmer-Thomas 1996, 45).[23]

Hence, when CFAC looks to civilian regional institutions, it finds counterparts that have failed to keep pace. The consequences are captured in the following commentary from a senior CFAC officer: "Well, the problem is that CFAC, at the regional instance, has no regional influence at the political level. They can't make policies and they can't push for policies in security issues because they can't—who can they deal with? It could be a very interesting organization when we become a union in Central America. But the problem is, who would we deal with? There's nobody. That's the problem."[24]

The result is that CFAC remains an operative organization, with no standing advisory functions. This truncated role may very well please the armed forces, because it shelters them from politics. Many officers would likely agree with the statement: "the positive characteristic of CFAC and its success is that at this moment it has not been politically infected."[25] Moreover, avoiding advisory functions shields the armed forces from an international environment that is increasingly vigilant in its scrutiny of military influence. As indicated by one senior officer, "in these times we are living now, CFAC will not make policy, will not be an advisor, and will stay at the operative level. You can't expect more than that in the region now."[26] But this raises a question: Is this enough for the armed forces?

To appreciate the value of CFAC to the militaries, even in this curtailed role, one must recognize the institutional crisis facing the armed forces since the end of the Cold War. Regionalism has challenged nationalist military traditions, economic crisis has prompted severe downsizing, and the legacy of human rights abuses under military dictatorships has opened the armed forces to criticism. In this environment, and with Costa Rica and Panama as functioning models, militaries are compelled to take seriously and rebut not only demands for reduction but also calls for elimination. One senior Central American military officer, under condition of anonymity, and with the claim that every other officer would say the same, stated that the only reason the militaries of the region have turned to CFAC is to justify their own survival.[27]

The motivation behind participation in CFAC is important because it indicates that involvement does not necessarily indicate devotion to new norms of democratic security, human development, or other concepts devised to replace traditional security obsessions within military doctrine—norms that place the state and security above democracy, the individual, and personal well-being. Whether a military has actually adopted such doctrinal changes as it works with CFAC, or remains committed simply for instrumental reasons, is an open question. Indeed, many military activities carried out under the rubric of human security can just as easily be squared with traditional national security precepts. A recent Guatemalan contribution to a CFAC effort against a growing dengue epidemic in Honduras—a justifiable move under the doctrine of human security—was instead described by the minister of health as an operation to secure a "health corridor" along the borders of Honduras and El Salvador for the security of Guatemala.[28] Mark Peceny and William Stanley (2001) have argued the significance of genuine, as opposed to instrumental, commitments to liberal democratic norms in the Central American transitions to democracy, and the difference is no less important to military reform.

Can the CSC Respond to CFAC?

The swelling reach of CFAC has not gone unnoticed by those members of the CSC lacking CFAC membership. At the April 2001 CSC meeting, Costa Rica pushed efforts to revisit the Framework Treaty and renew conversations on human security, the role of the armed forces, and regional answers to crisis resolution—all issues marked as fundamental to the CSC since its founding but increasingly taken up by CFAC. The country found support from Panama and Belize.[29] Costa Rica later used its time as interim president of SICA in 2003 to convene an international conference to reinvigorate civilian thinking on regional security. In a clear effort to counteract military initiatives and the stimulant they received after the September 11, 2001, terrorist attacks, the conference called for greater involvement by NGOs in discussions over regional security matters.[30]

Indeed, CFAC's placement in Central American integration more broadly remains a point of contention. For the CA-4 militaries, the 1991 Protocol of Tegucigalpa, which created SICA and called for comprehensive integration, is where CFAC finds its "legal support."[31] And the Framework Treaty on Democratic Security signals an important change in doctrine that is considered to be part of CFAC's cooperative focus.[32] Finally, as noted, the vision of a supportive relationship, with the CSC as a policy making and advisory body and CFAC as an operative body, is promoted. All this stands in contradistinction to comments from a member of the Ministry of Foreign Affairs in Costa Rica assigned to the Security

Commission, who notes, "officially, there is no relationship [between the two organizations]" and "Costa Rica does not recognize CFAC as an integration institution, since it is not contemplated in the Tegucigalpa Treaty or the Democratic Security Treaty."[33]

But if the CSC is to more fully envelop regional security matters, it now must contend with an organization in CFAC that has clearly outpaced it. Yes, the CSC does have its own string of achievements. Beyond its contribution to the Framework Treaty on Democratic Security, the organ has coordinated other mechanisms of regional cooperation and integration such as the Central American Treaty on the Recuperation and Return of Stolen, Appropriated, or Illicitly Retained Vehicles; the Central American Agreement for the Prevention and Repression of Money and Asset Laundering Crimes Related to Drug Trafficking; the Central American Institute of Higher Police Studies; a draft of a plan of action for the protection of visitors; a basis of communication between the CSC and the Center of Coordination for the Prevention of Natural Disasters in Central America (CCPDNC); input into the Treaty for Mutual Assistance in Penal Matters; agreements for annual military confidence-building activities; and a registry of criminal activities.

While each of these activities represents a significant contribution to regional cooperation and integration, it is telling that most of them deal with issues of common crime rather than traditional security or defense. And though common crime currently does pose the greatest security threat to individuals in Central America, the CSC was created to deal with all security affairs. Moreover, even where the CSC has been successful, these victories are shared or even undermined by military accomplishments. For instance, while the CSC has established communications with the CCPDNC, CFAC has created the UHR-CFAC and coordinated exercises to combat forest fires. The Institute of Higher Police Studies must contend with police forces that remain under the influence of the armed forces (especially in Guatemala and El Salvador), and its efforts to address regional criminal activity is paralleled by CFAC moves to integrate military intelligence agencies, many of which retain domestic functions. Finally, the regional forum for confidence-building activities is lodged within CFAC—a function that is only enhanced by the organization's personnel overlap with the Defense Ministerial of the Americas, which coordinates confidence building on a hemispheric basis.[34] This group and the Organization of American States have officially commended CFAC activities in this area. Further endorsements from the international arena come from the Conference of American Armies, which has accepted CFAC membership, and the observer status in CFAC first accepted by France and Germany and, later in 2004, by Spain and the United States.

CFAC's advantage over the CSC is in part organizational. Overall, CFAC has been able to place itself in a superior position to address regional security. CFAC works at a higher level in that it has more direct access to the individual presidents than does the CSC, which by contrast must weave through the Council of Ministers of Foreign Relations and the SICA secretariat.[35] Another advantage for the armed forces is that CFAC has fewer voices to contend with than does the civilian organization. With the entrance of Belize to SICA, this umbrella organization now counts its membership at seven to CFAC's four. And while both military and civilian organizations find themselves saddled with the Nicaraguan-Honduran dispute (as well as disputes between these two countries and El Salvador), the civilian organizations must also contend with the Guatemala-Belize border quarrel, and tensions between Costa Rica and Nicaragua arising from immigration and other frontier-crossing issues. And clearly, as the number of members rises, so too does the number of distinct national security perspectives. For example, for Panama, the safety of the canal, its role as a major trans-shipment point, and protective measures regarding containerized freight orient its security relations more toward actors outside the region.[36] Finally, the fact that Panama and Costa Rica lack armed forces makes it difficult for the civilian organizations to speak in a united voice on military affairs.

The continuing maritime dispute between Nicaragua and Honduras illustrates the general weakness of civilian regional security institutions in Central America.[37] The dispute most recently reemerged in November 1999 after Honduras ratified a treaty with Colombia that defined their Pacific maritime boundary near the 15th parallel and thus accepted the Colombian claim of sovereignty over the San Andres Islands, a claim disputed by Nicaragua. Also, the treaty established shared control by Colombia and Honduras to the Seranilla and Rosalinda banks, which are rich in fishing resources also thought to hold vast oil deposits. Nicaragua has claims on these banks as well. In response to the treaty, the Nicaraguan Congress placed a 35 percent "sovereignty tariff" on all Honduran and Colombian goods, in spite of the free trade agreements signed under SICA. One can also link the treaty ratification to Nicaraguan-Honduran tensions in the Gulf of Fonseca early the following year. While the two countries (along with El Salvador) agreed to the demarcation in the Gulf of Fonseca decided by the International Court of Justice in 1992, the lack of marker buoys led to a number of confrontations between Honduran fishing boats and Nicaraguan naval patrols. The Honduran navy responded with more vigilant patrols of its own, and in the Atlantic, Nicaragua called attention to the placement of Honduran troops on Cayo Sur, an islet north of the 15th parallel but south of the 17th parallel and thus held in dispute by the two countries.

The dispute seemed to be tailor-made for the recently designed regional institutions in Central America. The Framework Treaty on Democratic Security calls for the ministers of foreign affairs of countries in disagreement to immediately establish communications and allows any of the parties to a dispute to convene a meeting of the CSC or Council of Foreign Ministers.[38] But neither Honduras nor Nicaragua decided to work through this system. Rather, the dispute spilled over into the legislative branch (in Nicaragua) and the armed forces (through both pronouncements by high-ranking officers and military force movements). The CSC was not heard from. The SICA secretariat did offer its good offices, but it was U.S. diplomat Luigi Einaudi, acting as an OAS-appointed mediator, who brokered an agreement for joint patrols by the two countries in the Gulf of Fonseca, and the OAS emerged as the primary coordinator for confidence building in regard to the dispute.[39] And when tensions rose over the Cayo Sur, military attachés from the United States, Venezuela, Taiwan, Chile, and El Salvador acted as observers. Later, Spanish prime minister José Maria Aznar entered the picture to remind the countries that donor nations might grow less sympathetic to their needs if the dispute should boil over.[40]

The only regional institution to play a significant role was in fact CFAC. Its meetings served as an instrument of communication for the military leaders of Nicaragua and Honduras as the countries grappled with the implementation of joint patrols, and combined operations encouraged a cooperative military spirit.[41] The two countries struck a further blow to regional civilian institutions when they both decided to ignore decisions by the Central American Court of Justice on the dispute and instead appeal to the International Court of Justice.

From Regional Security to Civil-Military Relations

It may be too late for the CSC to find its niche in regional security. The domestic moment in Central American regional security was but a temporary reprieve from the regional reality—that of a lurking U.S. hegemony that vigilantly patrols the region to protect and advance U.S. prerogatives. That reality recently reappeared rather abruptly. As late as 2002, the United States saw no need to establish special relations with CFAC; its bilateral ties to the militaries of the region and the periodic multilateral meetings convened under U.S. auspices were deemed sufficient.[42] But by early 2003, the U.S. Southern Command was contemplating observer status within the organization.[43] General James T. Hill, army commander at the U.S. Southern Command, clearly articulated this emergent interest in a March 2003 statement before the Senate Armed Services Committee: "Central America is . . . key to our counter-drug and counter-terrorist efforts, which include regional operations to strengthen capabilities and foster cooperation within nations of the region. We are working more closely with the Organization of Central American Armed Forces (CFAC) to promote military integration and cooperation in maintaining regional security."[44]

Unsurprisingly, the United States sent an observer to the Eleventh Meeting of the Consejo Superior in May 2003, and at that meeting CFAC prioritized narco-trafficking and counter-terrorism missions, at the clear expense of issues more pressing to Central America, such as disaster relief, humanitarian exercises, and confidence-building measures.[45] Hegemony has returned, and for Central American regional security the domestic moment has come to a close.

But what does this mean for the security organizations forged in the interlude? Are they like finely crafted sandcastles, gleaming in the midday sun and so engrossing in their presence one almost forgets they will be but a memory by the evening's tide? If the hegemonic tide were this simple in its effects, it would wash away whatever Latin America had created on its own. Indeed, the analogy belies the very premise of the high-low politics framework—that foreign influences are shaped and constrained by the issues at hand.

CFAC involves itself in both regional security and civil-military affairs, and though the United States may be drawn to regional security in Central America, it prefers to remain one step removed from the more complex world of civil-military relations. The termination of the domestic moment will thus hinder CFAC's influence in the regional security arena, but it will have less effect on how CFAC impacts civil-military affairs inside each country. Thus, diversity continues to exist alongside the forces of conformity in Central America, and Latin America more generally. To explain the consequences of CFAC after the domestic moment, we first reach back to theory one more time.

How Regional Security and Civil-Military Relations Interact

Ideally, regional arrangements would benefit each Central American country by handling interstate problems more adroitly. But a regional security organization does not simply materialize out of nowhere—there is a process involved in the emergence of the organization, one with clear path-dependent characteristics. A path-dependent approach argues that "history matters."[46] History matters because that which happens at one time constrains or opens the range of outcomes likely to transpire at a later time (Sewell 1996, 262–63). Sequencing is integral to path-dependent approaches. As noted by Paul Pierson (2000a, 79), "when a path dependent process is at work, early developments get deeply embedded in a particular political environment, modifying the incentive structures and hence behaviors of social actors, and thereby changing the social significance or pattern of unfolding of events or processes occurring later in the sequence." Hence, identifying a and b as causes of x is insufficient. The sequence of causal factors also has an impact on the manifestation of x. One might find that only a then b leads to x, while b then a leads to something very different.

These elements hold relevance to the Central American case. Specifically, a regional security arrangement will furnish benefits only if it is constructed in tandem with or after improvements in the level of civilian control over the military.[47] Lacking increases in civilian control, a regional security organization, if dominated by the military, is likely to leave a country worse off, democratically. In this sense, the impact of such an organization cannot be judged in isolation; it must be judged in concert with the evolution of domestic civil-military relations.

Figure 6.1 charts the sequential dynamics associated with the development of a regional security organization. Beginning with both weak civilian control and weak regional institutional development—a situation that typified each of the CA-4 countries in the early 1990s—the move to construct a regional security organization can yield four distinct scenarios. Path 1 leads to the best scenario. Here, civilian control and the regional organization develop at near equal rates. The country enjoys the democratic empowerment that comes from greater civilian oversight, sees confidence-building measures reduce regional suspicions, and benefits from cooperation with its neighbors against common threats. Civilian control is emboldened as political leaders supervise regional security policy making and manage the professionalizing benefits that derive from institutionalized, cross-national military ties.

Figure 6.1. *Four Paths toward the Development of a Regional Security Organization*

Starting Point	Path	Development of		Assessment
		Civilian Control	Regional Organization	
Weak Civilian Control	(1)	+	+	best
	(2)	+	o	second best
Weak Regional Organization	(3)	o	+	worst
	(4)	o	o	second worst

("+" signifies increasing levels; "o" signifies little or no movement)

Path 2 represents the second best scenario. Greater civilian control could only benefit political development in the region. Nonetheless, without a multi-nation security institution, the region would be left more vulnerable to U.S. designs, would miss professionalizing activities, and could suffer from the lack of confidence-building measures. Path 3 is the least desirable route. As noted by Felipe Agüero (1995, 19), civilian control is in essence a matter of policy control. Without civilians calling the shots, the organization could serve as a springboard for greater military influence in other policy-making areas such as migration, disaster preparation, environmental degradation, police affairs, and economic development. Finally, a regional security organization, unsupervised by civilians, could also hinder the efforts of international organizations to support democratization. Under the peace processes, international organizations have played a substantial role in police reform, peacekeeping and peacemaking, de-mining, disarmament and demobilization, border demarcation and surveillance, the repatriation of refugees, and electoral supervision (Eguizábal 1999). For each of these activities, the international organizations also monitor observance of human rights. But this oversight would diminish as the CA-4 militaries pool their resources and replace those institutions.

Path 4 indicates little movement from the early 1990s. While each country has seen some improvement in civilian control and a regional security organization has emerged, reversals remain a real possibility. In this scenario, civilian control stays weak, but at least one avenue of negative military empowerment is foreclosed. Within the realm of interstate relations, some foreign actors may enter to coordinate confidence-building measures while others monitor human rights progress.

Though each path is theoretically plausible, the region is more likely to pursue paths 1 and 3—the best and worst scenarios—since it has vested itself in these regional security organizations. Depending on their respective advances in civilian control, the four Central American countries may follow one or the other path simultaneously. It is important to keep in mind that path 1 does not mean civilian supremacy and stable democracy and path 3 does not mean military coup. Path dependency is not a deterministic process. It simply exposes the forces that make it more difficult for a country to veer off in another direction. These are the "feedback loops" or "mechanisms of reproduction" that keep countries on a steady course (Thelen 1999; Pierson 2000a). Path 3 persists due to civilian lack of familiarity with security policy; the unwillingness of political leaders to challenge military positions on security matters; and U.S. responses that favor the armed forces over civilians in policy questions. The mechanisms of reproduction for path 1 are the reverse: civilian expertise, political will, and U.S. support for civilian preponderance.

But does it make sense to expect the United States to support military control of security policy in one country, and civilian control in a neighboring country? Once civil-military relations are identified as a low politics issue, U.S. actions no longer appear inconsistent. Washington would certainly like to help prevent military coups but is less interested in immersing itself in the complexities of civil-military affairs. Civil-military relations go well beyond coup prevention to encompass such intricate matters as education, training, doctrine, procurement, budgetary control, promotions and assignments, and so on. It is little wonder that the United States embraced the idea of a civilian minister of defense as the central strategy for the promotion of civilian supremacy in the 1990s.[48] That strategy takes a complex issue and reduces it to a single, cabinet-level appointment, while allowing the hegemon to earn credit for having been on the right side of the issue. The strategy may also allow problems to fester: even if a country has a civilian minister, officers can retain their seats in CFAC's Consejo Superior; the civilian defense minister can still be left out of the chain of command, as in Nicaragua; and finally, though civilians may staff a ministry, they may be ill trained to do so. Promoting a civilian minister is a step in the right direction, but it is a step on the pathway to low politics, a destination that the United States would rather not visit.

Consequently, on the issue of civil-military relations, the United States is likely to support the status quo whatever it may be, so long as it is stable, poses no immediate threat to U.S. security interests, and does not fall below a minimal threshold of civilian control. The United States stands on the outside, dispensing resources to bolster civilians and applaud their advances, but ultimately backs whatever arrangement is made on a country-by-country basis. Within the framework of our model, what this suggests is that the key forces that sustain a given path are domestic in nature: civilian expertise and political will.

Prospects for Regional Security Cooperation and Implications for Civil-Military Relations

Path dependency highlights the impact of a regional security institution on civil-military relations in Central America. Should such an institution mature, the stage would be set for dramatically different outcomes—propitious for those states with adequate civilian control (path 1), and inauspicious for those lacking such arrangements (path 3). But because the truncated development of CFAC makes it unable (or unwilling) to move beyond the operative level, one might conclude that the Central American states are in reality on paths 2 and 4. So long as it lacks consultative status and mechanisms of policy assessment or even formulation, CFAC will not live up to its potential as a means to professionalize the military on the one hand, nor as an especially threatening springboard for military influence on the other.

But CFAC is a young organization and still desires to earn itself an advisory berth. In one interview, a senior officer optimistically mused over the possibility of CFAC's devising regional security plans, although it should be noted that another officer expressed grave doubts on the same subject due to continued political differences among the countries.[49] Indeed, current concerns over terrorism may validate a strengthened policy role for CFAC. After the September 11 attacks in the United States, Nicaraguan defense officials were quoted as stating, "We seek to reactivate agencies of intelligence under the framework of Central American integration," and the Declaration of the Tenth Meeting of the Consejo Superior in Tegucigalpa, December 2002, initiated a move toward a regional antiterrorist plan, a goal that was echoed at the following meeting and accomplished in 2004.[50] Past CFAC sponsorship of workshops and exercises on intelligence cooperation will no doubt place it in a strong position for this mission.

Whatever the future of CFAC, we can be most confident that its effects will be greatest in the domestic arena, despite its status as a regional apparatus. As an operative agency, it is likely in the short term to wield a demonstrative impact on civil-military relations. This should not be underestimated. The disappointments of civilian regional institutions and the extent to which the armed forces claim success in their integration efforts are important. As noted by Samuel Fitch, "the imbalance between civilian and military institutions contributes to military perceptions that they are better organized, better trained, more cohesive, and more patriotic than civilian political leaders" (1998, 159). The history of civil-military relations in Central America (and in Latin America more generally) is in large part one of military encroachments justified by the argument that civilians are incompetent and the armed forces can get the job done. Indeed, such perceptions have often been shared by civilian constituencies who then support—even instigate—these encroachments.

Again, the point must be made that a military-staffed regional security institution is not necessarily malign. It only becomes so when civilian control is found wanting. The CA-4 countries face severe hurdles in economic development and the extension of basic services, hurdles that have historically drawn the military inward through civic action programs, infrastructure development, police functions, search and rescue missions, and the like. Military involvement in such operations can promote political and economic development so long as three conditions are upheld:

1. There exists no other capable civilian organization to fulfill the operation.

2. Military officials are willing to relinquish control when a civilian organization arises.

3. The government takes effective measures to foster an alternative civilian organization for future needs (Pion-Berlin and Arceneaux 2000, 433).

Involvement in a regional military organization such as CFAC, unsupported by civilian control, makes it very difficult to fulfill these conditions even when the organization formally restrains itself to an operative role. Given the lack of traditional external threats to the CA-4 as a group (and the geopolitical position of the countries within the U.S. security umbrella), military integration activities tend to draw the armed forces toward nontraditional military affairs (ecosystem preservation, civic action, health extension, humanitarian operations, etc.), and these moves can be justified under the emerging doctrine of democratic security.

The concern is that with the current existential crisis surrounding the CA-4 militaries and only instrumental commitments to democratic security norms, the armed forces may embrace these operations as their own—as if they were vital to their professional identity. That would frustrate the development of civilian substitutes. In countries lacking adequate levels of civilian control, the military is likely to succeed in these endeavors.

As noted, a path-dependent approach is useful due to the "mechanisms of reproduction" it exposes. Two domestic mechanisms, civilian expertise in security policy and political will to challenge security policy, will most significantly shape civil-military relations and the impact of CFAC. A third, U.S. involvement, will do more to support than determine outcomes. How will these forces play themselves out in Central America? Mounting levels of civilian control in Honduras and El Salvador will allow CFAC to lend a hand in improving civil-military relations. For these countries, path 1 is achievable. With lower levels of civilian supremacy in Guatemala, CFAC could play a more deleterious role and the country could be headed down path 3. And Nicaraguan civil-military relations stand at a midpoint, although the lack of initiative by civilians points the country toward path 3.

Civilian control has advanced in Honduras, but it rests on the tenuous scaffolding of military enfeeblement. During the *contra* war, massive budgetary supplements from the United States buttressed the armed forces (more precisely, the air force), and this did substantially increase the military presence in Honduran politics. But the well went dry with the passing of the Cold War. The Honduran armed forces, which saw their authority rise so prominently in the 1980s, have now witnessed an equally prominent and precipitous downfall. The ironic result is that Honduran politicians are not under the same pressure as their counterparts in the CA-4 to "justify" their assertion of control over security matters. Militaries flouting proficiency in security matters compel political leaders in neighboring countries to shore up their expertise to legitimate movements into military affairs. But the job has in fact been easier in Honduras.

Political will spurred by electoral incentives, human rights abuses, budgetary constraints, and economic crises did lead Honduran politicians to exert greater control over the armed forces in the early 1990s. There were memorable achievements, including human rights inquiries, termination of obligatory military service, reductions in military expenditures, and the demilitarization of the police. And yet civilians soon found disorder in their own houses. Corruption scandals, political party clientelism, and impunity for the political elites fed public disenchantment with democracy and eroded the credibility of civilian leaders (Ruhl 2000). The political will to pursue further civilian control has dampened, though modest advances have been registered.

But even with legitimacy undermined, Honduran civil-military relations are moderately stable due to the general weakness of the armed forces. This weakness engendered a truce that has contained military encroachment yet precluded deeper reforms in civil-military relations. By contrast, the more conflict-ridden route followed by El Salvador actually makes for a more optimistic future there. The considerable civil-military tensions of the 1990s in effect marked dramatic changes underfoot. The peace accords forced politicians, civil society, and the military to confront their differences. Significant challenges remain, but for the military the result has been important doctrinal change and a role more in tune with long-term advances in civilian control (Peceny and Stanley 2001). Of the four militaries, the El Salvadoran armed forces' involvement in CFAC is driven most by genuine norms of security cooperation than by instrumental calculations.

Civilian control enhancements in Honduras and El Salvador have prepared these countries to take advantage of the professionalizing benefits of CFAC. For example, because Honduran politicians successfully wrested control of the Defense Ministry from military officers, the country is able to send a civilian representative to the Consejo Superior in CFAC, which sends a powerful symbolic message to the armed forces. The benefit to civilian control in El Salvador is underscored by the Salvadoran military's welcome reception of the UNESCO Culture of Peace program in Central America, organized in partnership with CFAC to diffuse new approaches to human security and conflict resolution.[51]

For Guatemala, CFAC is most likely to widen the gulf between civilians and soldiers. Resistance to reforms promised under the peace accords places civilian control in this country under greater stress compared to the other CA-4 countries (Schirmer 2001). As CFAC counts its achievements, military officials will be able to more easily deflect demands for stronger civilian oversight by insisting that further advances in civilian expertise occur first. Whereas educational studies by civilians at the Center for Hemispheric Defense Studies in the United States may spur the development of civilian control in El Salvador, in Guatemala these same institutions can be used as barriers, as the bar for "sufficient expertise" is raised, with the onus on civilians to prove themselves suitable overseers.[52]

In Nicaragua, the United States devoted considerable resources to the development of civilian expertise to counter a military still tightly linked to the San-dinista regime. A three-year program begun in 1993 by the National Institute for Democracy aided the development of a ministry of defense, military reforms, and a civilian think tank, the Centro de Estadios Estratégicos de Nicaragua (CEEN). Unfortunately, and in contrast to the Honduran case, the cultivation of civilian expertise has not been matched by political will. As Sandinista influence in the military was reined in (epitomized by the retirement of General Humberto Ortega as army commander in February 1995), civilian interest in military affairs declined dramatically. In fact, most of the military reforms enacted in the first half of the 1990s were actually inaugurated by the military itself, with a view to-ward professionalization and promises of modernization. While civilians have a ways to go before achieving some level of proficiency on military affairs (most noticeably in the legislature) and while the country is resource deficient now that U.S. interest in the country has waned (obviously tied to the decline of Sandinista influence in the military), Nicaragua does have a respectable foundation upon which to build civilian control. In the end, success will depend on the determina-tion of civilian policy makers themselves (Cajina 1998, 1999).

The United States will ultimately constrain CFAC's impact due to its ongoing security preoccupations in its backyard. While Washington played no role in CFAC's creation, it will continue to support it out of a belief that the organiza-tion's confidence-building mission and its status as a professional forum in which officers and soldiers can mix have had a stabilizing influence on the re-gion.[53] But there is no evidence that the United States is eager to see the organi-zation evolve from a functional to an advisory organization. As it stands, CFAC fosters interstate confidence and could aid U.S. efforts against drug trafficking, terrorism, contraband, migration, money laundering, or other regional afflic-tions. Were the organization to take on an advisory role, it would inevitably invite regional security perspectives that were perhaps at odds with those fostered by the United States.

How the United States will retain its influence is not difficult to explain. CFAC's endeavors to coordinate confidence-building exercises and crisis re-sponse actions (e.g., the UHR-CFAC) require resources—something that the CA-4 armed forces have seen diminish in recent years as budgets have been slashed. The pressure to look toward Washington for aid is overwhelming. Hence, CFAC's natural impetus to demonstrate its value as a regional security apparatus opens the door to United States influence. And with the door now propped open, there arises the very real possibility that the organization may be transformed into a mere conduit of U.S. security policy.

U.S. Hegemony and the New Regional Security Environment

Security issues rest in the core of high politics. For a hegemon, the motivation and capacity to intervene in such affairs is almost beyond question. But even hegemons may periodically recede from an arena, for reasons of resource constraints, threats elsewhere that capture its attention, or costs of involvement that seem to outweigh the benefits. This episodic hegemony creates opportunities for agents in the domestic arena to assert their own prerogatives and pursue new objectives. Without the hegemon to referee, subdue, or decide issues, political outcomes fall squarely into the hands of domestic actors. And although the hegemon is bound to return, its influence will be reconfigured by the changes wrought in its absence, such as new institutions or rearrangements in power relations.

The relaxation of U.S. influence in the 1990s opened space for the Central American countries to act more independently in the security realm. The regional civil-military divide expressed itself with the development of the CSC and CFAC. The military response to the CSC, and this organization's promotion of democratic and human security doctrines, was necessarily guarded in a time of dwindling resources and international worries over military influence. Thus far, CFAC has sought shelter from these storms by avoiding consultative functions and restricting itself to operational activities. But even if CFAC decided to test the waters and expand its reach, it would eventually collide with the long-term desires of the United States to control regional security policy. Thus, over time we should expect CFAC to hold much more relevance to civil-military relations in the domestic arena than to regional security policy in the international realm.

At the regional level, one might lament the lost opportunity for the CA-4 to wrestle security initiatives from the United States. But a more focused analysis illustrates that the impact is more complex than this. For countries with budding civilian control, such as El Salvador and Honduras, CFAC could indeed complement advances in military professionalization under democratic auspices. But in countries such as Guatemala and Nicaragua, where civilian control remains a more distant goal, CFAC could serve as a springboard for military influence, or at least the retention of military prerogatives. Ironically, given its disreputable history of meddling in the region, the reentry of the United States into Central American security issues may at this time have positive effects for some countries (Guatemala and Nicaragua) as CFAC is pushed aside—though at the expense of denying other countries (Honduras and El Salvador) fruitful outcomes, as Washington's own security priorities intrude on and distort Central American security realities.

Nonetheless, even a CFAC that is operationally stunted may stir up trouble. While this will hinder more egregious military encroachments into the political sphere in those countries struggling with civilian control, the ability of CFAC to succeed, even at this level, will substantiate perceptions of military superiority and vex civil-military relations so long as civilian integration projects founder. It will also create a barrier to the promotion of civilian alternatives to military activities in areas beyond traditional security functions. Insofar as changes in civil-military relations raise new security issues for the United States down the road, these seemingly inconsequential security organizations will hold relevance for high politics.

That CFAC potentially augurs unfavorable results for some countries is not to indict the armed forces, nor accuse them of thirsting for power. Civilian failures to further their own political and economic integration efforts in tandem with the military increases the prospects that CFAC will emerge as an isolated institution that further divides civilians and soldiers. Moreover, though their lack of expertise impedes civilians from participating in security affairs, their lack of will to assert greater civilian control is also all too evident. And while the United States is another easy target of condemnation, civilian security integration failures magnify the attraction of CFAC, rather than the CSC, to the United States. Just as regional security in Central America is more complex than the hegemonic status held by the United States would imply, so too is the allotment of culpability surrounding the potential consequences of CFAC.

7. Environmental Degradation, Drug Trafficking, and Immigration

A
s diverse a set of themes and case studies as we have chosen for this volume, it could still be argued that we have been too selective. Among the numerous issues affecting political change in Latin America, we have chosen only four: economics, democracy, human rights, and security. In the eyes of some, these combined may be insufficiently illustrative. Why not investigate other issues? We have chosen to do just that, and for one other reason. The devil's advocate might argue that security and economics lend themselves easily to high politics classification, while human rights fits too perfectly within the low politics category. Predictably, then, the foreign (except for moments) does prevail in security and economics, and, predictably, the domestic (except for moments) prevails in human rights. Have we stacked the deck too deeply in our favor? After all, no one can argue that security and economic well-being are not at the center of national interest. If these can be or must be enhanced via greater immersion in the internal affairs of another state, then why wouldn't a powerful country like the United States do just that? Conversely, unless human rights are so grossly violated that charges of genocide are made, awaking the world's moral conscience, then why would foreign states ever pay attention? They almost never do.

What follows are capsule-like case studies involving three additional and more difficult issues: environmental degradation, immigration, and drug trafficking. While a strong argument can be made that all three fit within the sphere of low politics, none do so perfectly. These are certainly issues that can be easily sourced to specific countries mired in specific difficulties. But they all generate rather huge externalities. In each instance, the problem has a way of spilling over borders to affect other nations. When it does, it may invite greater foreign state and NGO immersion in the affairs of the perpetrating state. But the spillover effect by itself does not automatically trigger foreign influence and intervention, and certainly not in any sustained fashion.

Foreign influence is likely to be a function of two intervening factors. One is the nature of the costs inflicted on the receiving nation. Are these costs security or economics related? If not, then can a reasonable link be made? As powerful as a spillover effect may be, it may not generate a problem that directly harms the vital interests of a receiving nation or that can be construed as vital. How national are these costs? Do they directly impact the country as a whole, or are they more localized? Problems may very well be severely felt at state (provincial) levels, stirring up passionate debate and conflict. But if they do not make the national agenda, they will not be candidates for high politics responses. And how immediately felt are the costs? Politicians can easily discount a serious problem that may manifest itself only in the distant future. In that case, it will be left to NGOs and other issue-sensitive groups to demand a response, but national leaders may not be ready to listen. In sum, for the international to really matter, a low politics issue that generates externalities must be viewed by foreign national political leaders as vital, and its impact must be national in scope and produce immediate, short-term costs.

The other intervening variable is sovereignty. How strongly will the perpetuating country defend its right to be left alone to solve its own problems? Can it ward off foreign intrusion, and does it want to? As we have suggested, Latin American states are unlikely to be able to fend off foreign intervention and influence if the externalities they generate seriously impact the vital national interests of others. But the other possibility is that they may not want to resist and may even solicit help from outside. Problems that so clearly and repeatedly spill over borders are precisely the ones frustrated governments first prefer to solve alone and then invite international cooperation. States can cooperate without one becoming interventionist, and without any loss of sovereignty. However, cooperation, especially between two countries of unequal power, is not always a harmonious affair. A Latin American state may invite the United States to partner with it in order to solve a problem. That partnership may involve joint actions but may also generate dependencies on the stronger nation, which is called upon to assume the primary burden of providing everything from material and technological aid to border, air, and sea patrols. In exchange, the stronger nation may want greater say-so over policy decisions that inevitably trigger questions about national autonomy and sovereignty. Even when prompted by invitation, foreign influence can still erode a nation's ability to make autonomous policy choices.

Brazilian Rain Forest Depletion and International Involvement

The environment is a good example of an ostensibly low politics issue that can occasionally trigger international attention and intervention. It is also an issue that differs from human rights or democratic deepening because of its much greater potential for generating externalities that affect other nations. Environmental degradation is a serious problem afflicting many Latin American nations. When rivers or air are polluted, contaminants cannot be stopped at the border's edge. And the depletion of the Brazilian rain forest will, scientists tell us, aggravate the global warming problem and has already led to the extinction of numerous plant species that may be valuable sources of medicine. The spillover effects should generate much more powerful incentives for foreign countries to want to immerse themselves in the domestic politics of the source nation. And yet, that does not occur as frequently or as intensively as one might think.

Rain forest depletion in Brazil is not entirely a public goods issue. While the effect of deforestation has been and will be felt abroad, the resource itself is territorially confined (Hurrell and Kingsbury 1992). Unlike open oceans and atmosphere, forests lie squarely within the borders of a country or countries. Brazil, Peru, and Ecuador can lay claim to parts of the Amazon, but not nations afar that may nonetheless be affected by the forest's degradation. Hence, Brazil can and does assert its sovereign right to manage, develop, exploit, and care for the Amazon as it sees fit, and to deny others that opportunity. Certainly international treaties and norms acknowledge that environmental problems have global implications, demanding that states cooperate to protect the Earth's ecosystem. That notwithstanding, sovereignty remains a powerful force and an inhibitor of international encroachment. The second principle of the Rio Declaration on Environment and Development states that nations have "the sovereign right to exploit their own resources pursuant to their own environmental and developmental policies" (U.S. Department of State 1992, 17).

But the international had its "moment," which arrived in the late 1980s and early 1990s. At that time, external concern over the Amazonian rain forest widened with NGO efforts to publicize its depletion and the risks that depletion posed to indigenous communities and the world at large. Foreign influence over Brazil's domestic forest policies was conjunctural, very much a function of unique events coming together at a particular period of time: meetings of environmental activists to map out strategies of linkage between international loans and environmental compliance; the coming on line of World Bank and IDB projects for Amazonian development that coincided with these meetings and that had potentially destructive consequences for the rain forests; and the joining of Brazilian rubber tappers with North American environmentalists (Kolk 1998; Keck 1995).

Environmentalists could now humanize the rain forest, associating its destruction with the victimization of those whose livelihoods and survival depended on those woodlands. Rubber tappers meanwhile could strengthen and internationalize their cause for justice by linking it to the broader issue of environmental destruction. And combined, these groups could more effectively pressure the international lenders at one end and the Brazilian government at the other. Most scholars concur that it was the linkup between Amazonian victims and international environmental activists that proved decisive in sensitizing the Brazilian government to foreign views (Hurrell and Kingsbury 1992; Keck 1995; Kolk 1998)[1] and leveraging its forest policies, however briefly.

With global revelations of rain forest destruction at their peak, the Brazilian president, Fernando Collor, decided to host the United Nations Conference on Environment and Development (UNCED) meeting scheduled for June 1992. Collor calculated that by doing so, he might be able to not only improve Brazil's image but also entice developed nations to commit resources to the task of preserving the Amazon. The conference along with the parallel NGO forum helped to further galvanize international attention on the Amazon, and cement and enlarge the network of Brazilian and international activists concerned with environment, labor, and indigenous issues.[2] The accords, which 172 nations joined to sign, featured some 2,500 recommendations on improving environmental protection. The conference did have an impact. At least for a while, Brazilian sovereignty seemed to have been compromised as decisions on what to do with the Amazon were now subject to foreign leveraging. For example, financing was suspended on some World Bank and IDB road, dam, and settlement projects in the Amazon.[3] And Brazil discovered that negotiations in multilateral and bilateral settings had become more difficult as the advanced industrial states of the

Northern Hemisphere linked economic and other kinds of concessions to progress on the environment (Kolk 1998).

But this issue linkage would not endure, as foreign states would soon lose interest in the rain forest and return to business as usual. In fact, the conference and the whole effort to internationalize the rain forest problem succeeded more at the rhetorical level than it did at the material or political level. While activists had succeeded in getting states to make verbal commitments to help finance the cost of Amazonian preservation, few states actually followed through on those commitments. A year after the Rio Summit, a spokesman for the World Wide Fund for Nature said that, save for three Scandinavian countries, no money had been provided to protect the forests, despite firm pledges to do so. The organizer of the Rio Summit, Maurice Strong, noted in September 1993 that the rich industrial countries were already pulling back from commitments to increase technological transfers and foreign aid. And as a leading congressional environmentalist said in 1994, "The symbolic talk of the 1980s hasn't been followed up with concrete practical alternatives. The destruction is bound to get worse."[4]

Indeed it would. Deforestation not only continued unabated but increased. The initial decline in deforestation in the late 1980s and early 1990s is attributed more to a sagging Brazilian economy and logging industry than to fortification and enforcement of environmental laws. Deforestation, according to Brazil's own government, rose 34 percent from 4,296 square miles in 1990–1991 to 5,750 square miles by 1994.[5] Other estimates say that by 1995, the rate of deforestation had doubled since the Rio Summit.[6] The most recent survey indicates that deforestation increased by 40 percent in 2002 over the year before, covering an area almost the size of the state of Massachusetts. To date, about 16 percent of Brazil's rain forest has been destroyed.[7]

Why does deforestation proceed apace despite the international furor over the Amazon destruction? The reason is that the furor was never self-sustaining; it died down once foreign state leaders turned to more pressing and immediate concerns at home. As dangerous as rain forest depletion may be to life in the United States, it is not a peril that lurks around the corner, but rather one that is off in the future. For that reason, it is easier for national politicians to discount the future costs of current inaction. Once they do, then the issue returns to being a largely domestic dispute pitting a consortium of Brazilian environmental human rights and labor groups at one end, and ranchers and loggers at the other, with the government caught somewhere in the middle. In recent years, the political balance seems to have shifted in favor of the loggers and ranchers, with each new stretch of highway that is carved out of the jungle and with each new human settlement in the hinterlands. A newly constructed road, ranch, or community in some remote area means the establishment of economic interests, which in turn alters the political landscape in favor of denuding the forests, which in turn makes the enforcement of antilogging, antifire laws increasingly less effective. The Brazilian government will periodically boast of its get-tough position on the forests, as it announces the latest measures to crackdown on illegal logging. But it usually fails to enforce these measures. For example, by 1996, only eighty inspectors had been hired to monitor logging in an area of two million square miles.

To conclude, the proper framing of a domestic environmental issue followed by transnational organization and coordination can go a long ways toward inviting international attention and reaction. This circumstance occurs at opportunistic moments, when there is a confluence of problems, policy practitioners, and solutions. At these moments, channels of influence can be opened up to those with political power. But while activists can grab the attention of state policy makers long enough to effect some change, seldom can they sustain it. As Margaret Keck says in reference to the environment, "the international attention span, after all, is short" (1995, 421). Foreign influence over the fate of the Amazon faded quickly, as Brazilian politics took over. When it did, the Amazon fell prey to powerful economic forces that have compelled the Brazilian government to become complicit in efforts to further tame the jungle on behalf of soybeans, cattle, and wood-exporting interests, while fortifying their nation's sovereign walls to keep foreign states and activists at arm's length. Thus, this case, like that of human rights, illustrates the point that international influence over a low politics issue is momentary and soon eclipsed by the domestic.

Mexican Immigration and the U.S. Response

Immigration, by its very nature, interfaces the domestic politics of states. Mexican immigration represents a foreign encroachment on U.S. society, and the U.S. policy response—be it to relax or tighten the flow of individuals, to reassess their treatment, to adjust the ease of remittances, or to redefine residency requirements—holds clear consequences for Mexican society. Several studies recognize how Mexican domestic policies—such as urban growth, incomes, and regional development policies (Roberts and Escobar Latapi 1997), agricultural policy (Martin 1997), or population policy (Alba 1989)—are linked to emigration. Likewise, it is also clear that U.S. immigration policy changes produce new predicaments in these areas for Mexico. For example, the recent trend to increase border surveillance has expanded the black market movement of labor and created incentives for permanent rather than seasonal migration (Massey, Durand, and Malone 2002). Also, the move by the United States to reinforce patrols along its peripheral urban areas has pushed migrants toward the deadlier desert areas of the border (Andreas 1999). Clearly, U.S. efforts to open or close the spigot of migration create pressures in Mexican domestic policies.

Migration, then, can be evaluated as a foreign intrusion from either side. Nonetheless, from the perspective of government policy, it is the United States that holds greater sway—U.S. immigration policy weighs far more heavily upon the movement of people than do the various Mexican policies that touch upon migration. More often than not, Mexican policy is a reaction to U.S. policy. And as U.S. officials devise policy, they do so with a marked eye toward U.S. labor needs, social service burdens, security concerns, or electoral stakes, with little regard for the significant impact such changes hold for the Mexican economy and society. In this sense, U.S. immigration policy can be viewed as a foreign influence upon Mexican politics.

The location of immigration on the high-low politics divide is ultimately a political question—one that is decided as U.S. and Mexican interests collide and costs emerge on both sides. For Mexico, the issue is high politics—cross-border remittances and the relief afforded to the labor market significantly shape national economic developments. Keep in mind that some 10 percent of the Mexican labor force works in the United States (and the relative wages earned by this group far outstrip its relative size). But for the United States, immigration is typically low politics—outside the field of national interests. It works its way up from the bottom of the U.S. political system—through the educational system, the local labor market, housing issues, social services, police affairs, and U.S. culture more broadly. Mexico's impact is felt not so much in the corridors of Washington as on the streets of Los Angeles, Houston, and Phoenix. Though concerns over tax burden and job dislocation are economic anxieties felt by many U.S. citizens, these are largely confined to the U.S. Southwest. The upshot is that while Mexico would like to prioritize immigration policy in bilateral talks, the United States downplays negotiation and refocuses discussion on issues more attuned to its national interests, such as trade and investment.

But immigration issues do capture the attention of Washington at certain times. After all, immigration is a foreign policy responsibility of national policy makers. Those policy makers treat immigration as if it were a high politics issue only when it is recast in simplified form as an economic or security matter, or when national leaders sense that it holds electoral stakes. Though these linkages to high politics may not endure, they often elicit dramatic changes in U.S. immigration policy that upend the current flow or character of migration and thus force Mexican officials to adjust. These moments have occurred periodically throughout the long history of U.S.-Mexico relations. A brief survey of this history illustrates the necessity of linkages and the inability of immigration to sustain itself on the plane of high politics.

Periods of localized violence wracked the U.S.-Mexico border through the second half of the nineteenth century as U.S. ranchers and farmers consolidated their property rights, often to the disadvantage of holdovers from the U.S.-Mexico War or more recent migrants (Barrera 1979, 7–57). Tensions flared in the midst of the California gold rush as filibustering prospectors set their sights on anticipated riches in the Sonoran Desert and fomented regional rebellions. The tide would reverse in the early-twentieth century, when the Mexican Revolution saw cross-border raids by Mexican bands seeking financial resources or supporting local grievances against large ranchers. But throughout this time, much of the responsibility for security was handed over to militants at the state level, such as the notorious Texas Rangers (Rosenbaum 1981). It would take a shocking event in the form of the raid by Pancho Villa's forces on Columbus, New Mexico, leaving eighteen U.S. citizens dead, to instigate a stronger U.S. national presence on the border and an expeditionary force to pursue Villa's group.

Though security concerns survived the Mexican Revolution, national attention to the border quickly waned. The 1920–1922 U.S. recession revived the stature of immigration in economic terms, as Mexican laborers gained notice for their purported role in growing unemployment rates (Dunn 1996, 11). The anxiety provided an impetus for the creation of the Border Patrol in 1924, but better economic times dulled the concern. The United States soon settled into a "revolving door" policy, by which Mexican migrants were welcomed and deported in tandem with economic good times and downturns (Cockroft 1986). The Great

Depression offered a clear economic decline and resulted in massive deportation sweeps (Barrera 1979, 104–9).

World War II presented another opportunity for Mexican immigration to be linked to national interests. The war drained the U.S. labor supply, and Mexican workers stood as a ready alternative. To fill the gap, the United States and Mexico negotiated a guest worker program under the Bracero Agreements beginning in 1942. Its link to World War II made it justifiable not only on economic grounds, but on security grounds as well (Cockroft 1986, 67–75).[8] The steady stream of labor provided a boon for U.S. agricultural interests, and immigration issues soon moved to the backburner once again. Continuing movement across the border, aided in part by renewals of the Bracero program, raised tensions in the 1950s. The year 1954 saw "the first large-scale, systematic implementation of military strategy and tactics by the INS against Mexican immigrant workers" (Dunn 1996, 14–17) in a program callously termed "Operation Wetback." The climate of McCarthyism added a security-related tinge to the program. With World War II labor shortages a distant memory, and the costs and benefits of immigration growing increasingly complex, the Bracero Agreements were simply left to expire in 1964.

Policy makers rekindled the security rationale through the 1980s, as immigration issues were tied to the war on drugs and the border grew increasingly militarized (Dunn 1996). But this simply latched immigration on to an issue that is equally ill defined and difficult to sustain on the national agenda.

And over time national policy makers reconsidered the effort as they recognized the important role immigration played for the political and economic stability of Mexico, and the security implications this held for the United States. Finally, the renewed focus roused the lobbying efforts of businessmen dependent on Mexican labor who preferred that government look the other way. The handling of the landmark 1986 Immigration Reform and Control Act illustrated the predicament faced by U.S. policy makers. The act offered two strategies: amnesty for workers and penalties for businesses that hire illegal residents. But because the latter also drew powerful economic interests into the picture, it was really not pursued, and ultimately the reform actually triggered an increase in immigration (Domínguez and Fernández de Castro 2001, 153).

What immigration really meant remained contentious and imprecise; hence, it was no surprise when immigration again fell to the local and state level. Here, the costs and benefits play out more visibly, and the agenda is freed from the national interests of security or of Mexican stability. But can immigration be addressed effectively at this level? Having fallen into recession in the early 1990s, California was primed to confront the issue. The state may share a Mexican population similar in size to that of Texas, but California contains more Mexicans born outside the state (3:4, compared to the Texas ratio of 1:2), lower English fluency rates, and a less politically engaged Mexican population. Also, California's more diverse trade relations lowered Mexico's stature as an economic partner (Domínguez and Fernández de Castro 2001, 143–44). In the early 1990s, these conditions fed into the presidential aspirations of a California governor. Pete Wilson thus embraced immigration as an issue of "cultural security" to rally partisan adherents. English-only bills, attacks on bilingual education, limitations on social services for illegal residents, and demands for tighter border security agitated California politics. But through the 1990s, an improving economic climate and economic ties reinforced by the effects of NAFTA mellowed the uneasiness of the early 1990s. Moreover, Latinos were making their way into (if not becoming) the mainstream, as evidenced by the 1996 benchmark election of Democratic representative Loretta Sanchez in conservative Orange County. Immigration, even at the local level, makes for a difficult electoral issue.

But by the time the Bush administration took office in 2001, immigration returned to make its mark on presidential politics in a way that few national policy makers could ignore. The Latino vote was now of incredible significance to electoral outcomes in the Southwest, with the heavily populated states of California and Texas as well as the less partisan-aligned states of New Mexico and Arizona.[9] With George Bush looking to shore up Republican support among this traditionally Democratic leaning group, and with newly elected Mexican president Vicente Fox pushing immigration issues to the top of his foreign policy agenda, the stage seemed ready-made for a sea change in national immigration policy.

But the terrorist attacks of September 11, 2001, would provide a different U.S. policy approach to immigration. Security interests, rather than electoral blocs, now colored Washington's perception. Immigration *reform* tumbled from the U.S. foreign policy agenda, much to the consternation of Mexico, only to be replaced by a more straightforward and narrow policy of immigration *restriction*.[10] To underscore the emphasis on security, the Border Patrol was merged with the Customs Service, and both fell under the new Department of Homeland Security. But this renewed emphasis on security linkages should not be construed as a solid shift by immigration into high politics. As noted, the real impact of immigration is felt in local communities, and here immigration concerns continue to be addressed unevenly. Regulations may be instituted to deny services to illegal residents, but crackdowns on the hiring practices of business have yet to transpire, so the lure for migrants remains. Though 2001 seemed to augur change, by 2003 U.S. immigration politics was back to normal—Congress had a number of reform proposals under consideration yet faced a White House with "little to say" on the matter; significant reform of any sort faced bleak prospects.[11] The 2004 elections gave the Bush administration cause to play the immigration card with a new proposal, but that has been soundly criticized even among Republican supporters, and the administration itself has not followed up with supportive efforts.[12]

Why is immigration not able to sustain itself on the high politics plane? One answer is that the legion of interested pressure groups, social activists, and relevant government bureaucracies create so much distinct noise that it is difficult for Washington to sense a comprehensible, immediate tie to national economic and security interests—ties that are imperative if the issue is to make it onto the foreign policy agenda with any consistency (Wiarda 2000). Generally speaking, the issue really sends no clear national signals on costs or benefits—immigration affords both positive and negative externalities, and these are distributed unevenly across states and counties. And the rise of the Latino vote is unlikely to shift the issue decisively onto high politics due to the fluidity of electoral cycles and voting blocs. In the end, immigration falls from high politics because its low politics characteristics are too strong. It may hold stakes for national policy makers when unique linkages to security or national economic interests arise, or as electoral cycles come and go, but over the long run the stakes are more regional or even local and the impact too ambiguous.

Drug Trafficking

Drug trafficking is a quintessential transnational, cross-border problem. While the cultivation and processing of illicit drugs tend to be restricted to one or two countries in Latin America, their transshipment and marketing are anything but restricted. Drugs are packaged and distributed worldwide, then sold on the streets of foreign countries. The cocaine grown and processed in Colombia finds its way to the United States and other nations via Central America and the Caribbean. Drug traffickers move and operate across frontiers via land, river, and air with relative ease and great frequency. In this respect, the problem of narcotics is neither internal nor external; it is both.

Thus, and as with environmental degradation and immigration, drug trafficking generates huge externalities. Traffickers and their drugs are repeatedly seized crossing over into the territories of other states. Drug consumption drives criminal activity, medical bills skyrocket from drug-related hospitalizations, dope peddlers are arrested, and the bill for prison construction and maintenance to cope with the influx of drug criminals gets passed on to the U.S. taxpayer. These costs borne by the United States to Colombian coca and opium cultivation are well known and measurable.

However, they do not always amount to a high politics dilemma, at least for a drug-consuming state like the United States. As menacing as drug cartels may be, they do not in themselves pose a physical threat to the territory of this nation. Drug peddling and consumption are issues of individual—not national—security and insecurity, health and ill health. They are societal afflictions, but ones that trigger the intervention of law enforcement, social workers, and health care officials—not military personnel. Economically, drugs produce black market riches for a few, but by and large neither energize nor sap the U.S. economy. Thus, drug trafficking from Latin America to the United States on its own does not affect in any direct and significant way the key security and economic interests of the United States.

Nonetheless, the United States has enmeshed itself in the internal affairs of Colombia, acting as if its vital interests were at stake. Though initiated via invitation, the U.S. role has so expanded as to infringe on Colombia's policy-making autonomy. Colombia cannot prosecute its war on drug traffickers without involving the United States in the decision-making process.[13] Washington's average annual outlay in military assistance to Colombia has totaled more than a billion dollars, thus shouldering a large part of the financial burden of the operation. Hundreds of its military personnel advise the Colombian armed forces on the use of U.S.-made hardware, and counternarcotics tactics. And an American team has had a hand in drafting the plan to modernize the Colombian armed forces, as well as Plan Colombia itself—that country's strategy to put an end to its decades old civil war.[14]

How are we to explain the anomaly of U.S. intrusion in Colombia over an issue that does not on the face of it present a high politics dilemma for the United States? Periodically, drug consumption has certainly risen to the top of our nation's political agenda, as during the 1980s,[15] but its prominence has since waned and cannot account for the escalation of U.S. involvement in Colombia's civil war during the beginning of the twenty-first century. While U.S. support for counternarcotics efforts in Colombia goes back to the early 1980s, its insertion into that nation's internal wars occurred on a grand scale beginning in 1999, when it became apparent that much more was at stake than the flow of illicit drugs across our borders.

It was in July of that year that President Clinton's drug czar, General Barry R. McCaffrey, sounded the alarm that narco-traffickers were in league with left-wing guerrillas and that together they were creating a security emergency for Colombia—one that could potentially implicate other U.S. allies in the region.[16] It was then that the administration committed itself to financing Plan Colombia to the tune of $1.3 billion. The prospect of the Colombian government being run over by a drug-financed leftist revolutionary group, and the possibility that this could spur like-minded insurgencies elsewhere in Latin America, was an externality that gave pause to U.S. policy makers.[17] With Rio Treaty commitments in mind, the risks to the Colombian state and possibly others became national security concerns for Washington policy makers, who now saw a direct link between drug consumption, drug production, and national security.

The security link was then strengthened after September 11, 2001. The Bush administration quickly placed the FARC (Revolutionary Armed Forces of Colombia) and other radical insurgency groups on its terrorist list. Colombia's problems were now visualized from a global vantage point; its internal conflict was one theater of operation in a broader war against terrorism. The FARC, it claimed, was a terrorist organization possibly in league with Hezbollah and Al Qaeda,[18] whose activities were financed via a protection racket with coca growers and drug distributors. The fight against the narcos *was* the fight against terror; the United States believed it could not hope to stem drug trafficking unless it undercut those who gave it protection and, conversely, could not stem terrorism unless it cut off its financial lifelines.

In June 2002, President Bush met with newly elected Colombian president Alvaro Uribe, and the two leaders formally rid themselves of the separation between counterdrug and counterguerrilla operations—they would henceforth go hand in hand, thus freeing up military aid for the purpose of defeating a so-called terrorist organization. In September of that year, the White House issued its national security strategy report in which it said that the United States was now more menaced by weak states than conquering ones. A state like Colombia that could not control its own territory would more easily fall prey to the designs of terrorist groups, thus endangering it, its neighbors, and ultimately the United States. The report said that if left unchallenged, the "violence of drug cartels *and their accomplices*" could "imperil the health and security of the U.S." [authors' emphasis].[19] Thus, by guilt through association drugs had become a national security issue that warranted U.S. immersion in the internal affairs of a Latin American state.

Colombia's drug-related armed conflict poses problems not only for the United States, but for that Andean nation's neighbors as well. Analysts of the drug wars often subscribe to the "balloon analogy," whereby pressure on the surface in one location creates expansion in another (Millett 2002). The harder the Colombian government and the United States prosecute the war against narco-insurgents, the more likely that drug cultivators will move their operations into other territories. That has occurred in Bolivia, where after years of decline coca cultivation has steadily risen again, from 14,600 hectares in 2000 to 28,450 hectares in 2003 (Center for International Policy 2004). Guerrillas, hoping to find sanctuaries from which to regroup and launch incursions back into Colombia, will also likely flee across borders and be tailed by paramilitary units looking to defeat them. That has occurred along Colombia's eastern edge with Venezuela, creating renewed tensions between those two countries, with accusations that the Hugo Chávez government gave sanctuary and arms to the FARC and allowed its air force to fly into Colombian territory to provide cover for guerrilla raids.[20] Colombia and Venezuela have long viewed each other as potential threats, and geopolitically driven conflicts, especially over the Gulf of Venezuela, have periodically flared up. Colombia's internal drug war has just made matters worse.

By 1999, Ecuador had become a staging ground for the Colombian rebels (Millett 2002). In 2003, the Ecuadorian army commander admitted that his territory was being used by the FARC and that the guerrillas had stolen arms from their military stockpiles and were trafficking them back into Colombia.[21] In short, the spillover from the Colombian civil war has become a security problem for Venezuela and Ecuador involving those nations' armed forces.

Brazil too has felt the heat of the Colombian war. Its $1.2 billion Amazon-based surveillance system (SIVAM), operated by the armed forces, has been configured to detect and apprehend Colombian guerrillas and narco-traffickers who may be using the Amazon's expansive jungle habitat as bases of operations. Brazil has redeployed thousands of troops toward its northern frontiers and in May 2002 conducted the largest military exercise ever held in the Amazon close to the Colombian border.[22] President Lula da Silva has agreed to serve as mediator in future talks between the FARC guerrillas and the Colombian government.[23] So far, nothing has come of the offer, but the diplomatic angle continues to be pursued, as are military and internal security solutions. There has been growing coordination between Brazilian and Andean militaries over the narco-guerrilla problem. In February 2004, Brazil, Colombia, and Peru signed an accord to utilize naval forces to patrol the rivers at the borders between these three countries in order to cut FARC supply lines. The signatories suggested this agreement might be the first step toward the creation of a regional multinational force.[24] These moves indicate that for now the spillover from the Colombian drug war has induced a high politics security concern in neighboring capitals, as it has in Washington. Because of geographical proximity, Venezuela, Ecuador, Peru, and Brazil all feel the adverse impact of Colombia's externality more directly and intensely than does the United States.

Moreover, U.S. involvement in Colombia's internal war may not be self-sustaining in the long term. While Colombia may be one theater of operations in the global war against terror, it is a relatively small one compared to the likes of Iraq, Afghanistan, or the Middle East. The United States will undoubtedly retreat from its Colombian commitments when overwhelmed by ongoing resource, military, and manpower needs in Iraq, and other equally strategic and vital battlegrounds. Also, if the tide turns against the narco-guerrillas and in favor of the government, the United States will be anxious to extricate itself from Colombia. Finally, it must always be remembered that drug is a supply and demand problem. While coca production was increasing during the 1990s, drug use in the United States was actually declining. When it does, then the drug problem becomes a less urgent national priority.

In sum, the drug problem is a low politics issue for the United States that will periodically capture high politics interests. Alone, drug production and consumption will seldom be treated as a threat to U.S. vital interests. National security and economic well-being are not at risk, and the public's attention to this affliction ebbs and flows. It is more likely to be seen as a high politics issue only when: (a) illicit drug use and related crimes escalate; (b) links between drug traffickers, guerrillas, and terrorist groups are credible; (c) the war lingers; and (d) Colombia's conflict triggers serious guerrilla and terrorist activity outside its borders that threaten the political stability and viability of other Latin American states.

Case Comparisons

These three cases all illustrate how low politics issues can generate externalities that occasionally prompt foreign state consideration and intrusion. Environmental degradation, immigration, and drug trafficking are problems that attract some attention from foreign policy makers—patchy as it may be. But none do so consistently and with any ease. Drug trafficking must at one moment be constructed as a problem of domestic crime with international origins, at another as a source of regional instability in areas of concern to the United States, or at yet another as a means of financing for international terrorists. Immigration must make its way onto the foreign policy agenda disguised as an economic, security, or electoral concern. And environmental issues are dependent on unique historical confluences between problems, activists, and practitioners—a nexus that is destined to be transitory.

The related difficulty is that none of these issues pass the tests of national prominence and immediacy with any consistency. Environmental issues fail the immediacy test because the spillover effects take their toll in the distant future and thus are so difficult for national policy makers to seize upon and the public to grasp. Immigration and drug trafficking can generate more immediate externalities, but neither can easily gain national attention. The effects of immigration are more local and regional, and drug use impinges most directly on individuals and neighborhoods.

Sovereignty draws a line between the domestic and the international, and this barrier to outside influence is more formidable in low than in high politics. To recapitulate, foreign states are not sufficiently motivated to intervene and foreign nonstate actors are not suitably strong. Those propositions remain true. But it also follows that sovereignty's strength as a barrier varies depending on the influence of political actors inside the offending state who may have a stake at walling the nation off from intruders. It is the tug-of-war between domestic and international actors that largely determines how thick a line of sovereignty a nation can draw. Here, there is a difference between the environmental issue on the one hand and immigration and drugs on the other, a difference that has ramifications for the high-low politics divide.

When it came to deforestation in Brazil, very powerful domestic, rural interests keep the sovereignty issue alive and keep the government trained on the right of Brazilians to exploit their own natural resources for their own economic gain. These interests have gotten the upper hand over ecological activists with links to the outside. Thus, even when foreign states and IFIs are momentarily aroused to care about environmental ruin, it is exceedingly difficult for them to exert influence on Brazilian internal affairs. They cannot compete effectively against a government that answers to economically powerful nationalistic groups by reasserting its nation's right to control its own jungle habitats.

But sovereignty is a much weaker barrier for U.S. drug or immigration policies. The United States has been able to negotiate away some of Colombia's policy-making autonomy, while Colombian groups opposed to U.S. immersion in the narco-guerrilla wars are substantially weaker than those in support. On immigration, Mexican sovereignty is often irrelevant: the United States can and does make immigration policy unilaterally. Accordingly, the immigration and drug issues can occasionally rise to the level of high politics, when they achieve national prominence at home and breach the targeted state's sovereign barriers to overcome national resistance abroad. By contrast, environmental destruction remains in the realm of low politics even as it occasionally prompts foreign state reaction, because it cannot effectively overcome sovereign resistance.

Though the barrier of sovereignty is sometimes transgressed for immigration and drugs this is not cause to lump these issues in with high politics issues such as economics and security. The value of issue distinctions remains. The critical difference is that immigration and drug problems do not in themselves pose high stakes threats to the United States. They must be linked up with economic or security matters to achieve high politics stature. Those linkages can and have been made but only on occasion, with difficulty, and for short moments in time. Hence, while the immigration and drug issues can dance their way onto the plane of high politics, they manage nothing more than a brief waltz. High politics issues, on the other hand, evoke a more regular concern and an incessant vigilance. There is always the sense that the economic, security, and political stakes are great and that protecting those interests is practically inherent to the conduct of foreign relations.

It is in this sense that some low politics issues prone to externalities come to be treated as if they were high politics affairs, even as they fail to become high politics in nature. True high stakes, high politics issues are those that induce national and immediate costs for foreign states, leading them to hurdle sovereign barriers imposed by an offending state, to become standard items on that foreign country's national agenda. Policy makers are expected to address them, and key institutions are created to organize policy specialists, coordinate responses, and mobilize resources on a regular basis. Hence, the rise of the United States as a superpower with global reach gave impetus to the creation of the National Security Council after World War II. The United States' full insertion into the world economy led to the creation of the Department of Commerce at the turn of the nineteenth century and the Office of U.S. Trade Representative just after mid-century. The formation of the Department of Homeland Security may presage terrorism's move into the high politics realm.

But as noted, issues that do not on their own generate high stakes externalities must depend on linkages, some association with electoral strategies or peculiar circumstances to occasionally gain national prominence. And, ultimately, the absence of a centralized, powerful bureaucratic institution to sustain the nation's attention shortens their appearance in the limelight. Hence, immigration issues are addressed by a multitude of agencies—from the Border Patrol and U.S. Army to local law enforcement, school officials, and social workers. And though drug policy looks to a national drug czar, the military missions of South Com and aid allocations from the State Department wield actual policy control, while state and local officials devise their own policies to deal with the consequences.

These capsules have allowed us to widen the theory's applicability by extending the framework to cover challenging cases. The cases also help us to identify the conditions under which an issue warrants identification with high politics. In each the message is clear—issue orientation, and the dynamics of low and high politics more precisely, has an enduring impact on the respective roles played by external and internal actors.

8. Issues, Political Science, and Policy Making

This book has been about political influence and where it comes from. We have examined the shifting balance between foreign and domestic sources of political change in Latin America, exploring the reasons why external influences seem to dominate more on some occasions and internal influences more on others. Why does the question of external versus internal influence matter? Ultimately, we want to know whether Latin America is losing its autonomy, self-identity, and purpose. Is it becoming more vulnerable, as it falls under the grip of external forces? Is it becoming more like the rest of the world, as it gets sucked into a vortex of uniformity: one culture, one media, one economy, one polity? And is it becoming more subservient to the United States?

In a globalized era with the United States as the world's sole superpower, there are powerful forces at work that threaten to undermine what is different about Latin America as a region and what is unique about the countries that compose it. Latin America is, in a sense, doubly challenged; it is not only subject to the global order pulling at all nations but is situated within the United States' hegemonic sphere of influence. Thus, as an interconnected region, it is awash with influences from abroad: its cinema, technology, goods, and financing are mostly imports. As a region living in the shadow of the Northern giant, it is constantly reminded of its disadvantages and Washington's usual ability to impose its preferences when it so desires. If Latin America is a region that increasingly succumbs to influences transmitted from afar, if it cannot forge its own decisions and products, or define its own strategies and purpose, then it has lost a vital component to its identity. For that reason alone, our devotion to the topic of internal versus external influence is amply justified.

In Latin America, diversity and autonomy do seem to survive—however unevenly and intermittently— even in the midst of great pressures to conform and submit. They survive when the push and pull of domestic politics within such a variegated collection of states proves decisive. Domestic agents, institutions, and events rub up against the global order, shaping how each country chooses to respond or not respond to the world outside. As our study has suggested, foreign influence is sometimes blunted by dint of sovereignty or transformed by domestic agents and institutions. And even in the face of the hegemon's daunting military strength, the domestic, as we have shown, has had its moments.

Of course, there are a few instances when it may be beneficial for Latin America to succumb to outside pressures. When dictators or would-be dictators suspend elections and infringe on other basic democratic rights, when militaries rattle their sabers, or when courts refuse to bring repressors to justice, citizens who find no recourse inside their countries must seek help abroad. Even voluntary submission to multilateral diplomatic pressures, electoral commissions, and international courts or arbitrators does represent some loss of sovereignty for the offending state. And compliance with external rules or norms that other states also adhere to does imply conformance. On occasion, this can be a good thing, and we would not go so far as to claim that political autonomy or uniqueness is an inherently worthy trait if used in defense of unworthy goals.

Whether Latin American states fend off, submit to, or invite in outside influences, we need some systematic means of understanding when and why they do what they do. And that has been the main contribution of this study—to provide a framework comprehensive enough to yield consistent explanations for shifts in the balance of external versus internal influences across a range of subjects. As we have suggested throughout, the strength of actors and institutions to chart their own course from the inside depends on the barrier that sovereignty poses, and the motivations and capabilities of change agents from the outside. Those in turn vary with the issue at hand. Issues are like clustering agents; they gather into their midst an aggregation of actors, interests, assets, and impulses. As the issue shifts so too does the aggregation. These and other features of our framework and findings are summarized in table 8.1.

High politics issues brought together strong and sometimes highly motivated foreign states, MNCs, and IFIs that were driven by the pursuit of security and material interests, utilized hard forms of power, and usually overcame sovereign barriers so as to impact domestic processes. The domestic affairs of others mattered to these actors either because of the threat of externalities or the lure of riches that a given state could generate. External influences normally prevailed

8.1. The Sources and Nature of Influence on Latin America

	Issue Areas				
Variable	Neoliberal Support	Democratic Defense	Democratic Deepening	Human Rights	Security
High or Low Politics	high	from low to high	low	low	high
Usual Source of Influence	external	from internal to external	internal	internal	external
Unusual Source of Influence	external actors must coordinate	n.a.[a]	n.a.[a]	international moments, due to gain in capacity	domestic moments, due to fall in motivation
Sovereignty as Barrier to Intervention	weak	increasingly weak	strong	strong, but less so over time	weak
Key Actors	states, IFIs, MNCs	states, IGOs	NGOs	NGOs, TANs, courts	states
Motivation/ Capacity of Key Foreign Actors	high/shared	higher/higher	high/low	high/low	variable/high

a. Not applicable.

over internal ones. Low politics coalesced less powerful, but highly motivated, norm-driven domestic, nonstate, and multistate actors that resorted to soft power. Sovereignty remained a force to be reckoned with here, and internal influences usually proved decisive.

The value added by our framework is to be able to assess, in a systematic and comprehensive fashion, the conditions under which the foreign or the domestic matters more to political change in Latin America. By knowing the issue at hand and whether it has a high or low profile, we know what interests are up for grabs and what the stakes are for foreign governments. Then we can assess just how attentive or inattentive foreign states are likely to be with respect to the domestic affairs of a Latin American nation. When a powerful polity like the United States turns its full attention to an issue in the Western Hemisphere, it tends to dominate, as do the institutions (such as IFIs) within which it wields clout. If it perceives its vital interests are endangered by events inside a given country, or if it is lured by the prospect of great material gain, it can intervene with relative ease in the internal affairs of others, notwithstanding long-held principles of sovereignty and nonintervention. Similarly, when weaker Latin American states sense their own vital interests hang in the balance, they can, with the aid of IGOs, ban together to thwart developments inside a state that may adversely affect them.

When the stakes are lower for foreign states, their desire to intrude in the affairs of others is attenuated, and their attention is diverted elsewhere, as other actors move front and center. Domestic actors of all kinds become more important in the absence of concerted pressures from abroad, as do nonstate foreign actors. When the players change, so too do the forces that motivate them and the tools of influence at their disposal. Nongovernmental organizations, activists, and networks are more driven by ideals than interests and commonly resort to soft rather than hard forms of persuasion. But in this realm of low politics, sovereignty is a force to be reckoned with, making it more difficult for outsiders to make their voices heard. Even on those occasions when foreign states are persuaded to join a cause spearheaded by NGOs or TANs, they too must overcome sovereign barriers that seem more formidable in the realm of low politics than they do in high politics.

The high-low politics dichotomy gives us some rules for knowing when the balance of influence favors the foreign or the domestic, state or nonstate actors. Then there are the interesting deviations from the rules, made understandable by our framework and illustrated by some of our cases. The domestic had its moments in the realm of high politics when the hegemon was less motivated to exert its power within its security sphere of influence. The United States has never forsaken its goal of keeping the region a secure and tranquil place, free from threats to its borders, investments, allies, and very way of life. But with the Soviet Union collapsed, and most violent, left-wing movements and revolutionary governments a thing of the past in Latin America, the United States could afford to relax its Southern guard, turning its attention to more troubled regions. As it did, Central America could make its voice heard by constructing its own regional security institutions based on its security needs, not the requisites of the Cold War. While the United States may remain hegemonic, it is only motivated to enforce that hegemony episodically—a fact that falls to the advantage of weaker Latin American states.

The international had its moments in the realm of low politics when nonstate actors found the capacity to leverage states into action in defense of their causes. Frustrated by barriers to justice at home, domestic activists sought it abroad with the help of foreign lawyers, judges, and politicians. Foreign governments are not normally motivated to act on behalf of human rights victims elsewhere, but the tireless work of Chilean and European activists and families finally paid off with the arrest of Pinochet and the trials that followed. A window of opportunity opened up that permitted foreign actors to weigh in on a Chilean matter, notwithstanding the indignation that was felt inside Chile and the countless appeals to sovereign rights. In the realm of low politics, sovereignty was and remains a tough barrier to pierce, but for a moment European courts and governments did just that.

We found that motivation and capacity were the keys to understanding when and why moments arose. For domestic moments to occur within the high politics realm of security, the hegemon must temporarily lose the motivation to enforce its will even as it retains the ability to do so. For international moments to occur, it is quite the reverse. Highly motivated but relatively weak nonstate transnational actors must discover a capacity to effect change by forging links with foreign state actors. As moments, neither of these sources of influence endures. The domestic eventually falls back under the grip of a hegemon anxious to reassert itself. And the international cannot sustain its influence in low politics issues, as domestic agents regain the advantage.

Differences emerged *within* the high politics and low politics cases. When it came to security, power was very much concentrated in the hands of the United States. As the hegemon, it and it alone decided when and when not to make its presence known in the region, while hemisphere-wide security institutions were either ineffective or complacent. Because perceived security threats to the United States waxed and waned, so too did Washington's attention, creating the spaces for the domestic moments described above.

By contrast, neoliberal economic reform involves multiple actors with overlapping though distinct agendas. Institutions like the IFIs and private businesses are as important to economic outcomes as are foreign governments like the United States. Should Washington's interest in the economic fortunes of any given Latin American nation wane, there is another foreign actor, be it a multinational corporation or the IMF, to take the lead or to lure the United States back in. For this reason, domestic moments are unlikely, because some significant external agent is always there to fill a power vacuum, to pursue its vital interests, and to prevail. In this respect, foreign influence is more steadfast in the economic than in the security realm.

But while persistent foreign intrusion in the economics of Latin American states forecloses the promise of domestic moments, it does not foreshadow a uniformity of influence or a conformity of response. Depending upon which foreign agent has taken the lead, the international will express its power differently from case to case, raising or lowering the prospects for neoliberal consolidation. Where business is forced to lobby Washington for support of its investments in Brazil, that support will be forthcoming only after crises that sufficiently prompt the hegemon. Chile's road is also potholed, but the vagaries of Washington's political interests, rather than the incidence of crises, drive international support. Argentina exemplifies the bleakest case for successful neoliberal reform, where indifference from the United States and insufficient concern by business leave only the IMF to handle crises.

Within the realm of low politics, differences emerge as well. In human rights foreign influence is transitory, in democratic defense (which is moving from low to high) it is increasingly long-lived, and when it comes to democratic deepening it is absent. Why is this so? In human rights, there is a growing collection of organizations and networks devoted to preventing abuses or punishing perpetrators. They have been able to occasionally leverage the attention and action of foreign states but cannot sustain them. Even Europe's momentary involvement in the highly visible Pinochet case took tremendous prodding by transnational activists. Foreign administrations were not automatically drawn to Chile's human rights problems, and they certainly were not prepared to leverage Chile into improved human rights performance—whether under dictatorship or democracy—using the stick of economic or security assistance suspension. Moreover, there were no strong institutional bridges between Chilean and European courts that would have provided a setting for mutual ties, understandings, and agreements.

By contrast, the self-interest of states within Latin America was implicated when it came to the defense of democratic systems and elections in the Andean region. Beginning in the early 1990s, governments increasingly tied their own political fortunes—indeed survival—to the fate of other governments in the region. A coup in one country could set the stage for coups in their own countries. A stolen election allowed to stand could invite electoral theft to repeat itself. To avert these outcomes, states would find strength through solidarity, using the institutional machinery (OAS, Rio Group) at their disposal to demonstrate mutual resolve, to sign agreements, and thus to lock themselves into compliance with newly shared democratic norms.

Is this simply the difference of proximity? Does the fate of Peruvian democracy have a greater bearing on other Latin American democracies because those states are so geographically close, whereas the more distant Europe cannot possibly be so affected? Perhaps. The goings-on in the Andes are bound to be more contagious for neighboring states than for those overseas. But the case for proximity should not be overstated. The interest demonstrated by other Latin American states in Peru's internal affairs came up against firm limits on questions of democratic deepening. The collective will dissipated once elections were over and the issue shifted to how well Peru would comply with its promises to fortify democratic institutions. OAS members do have some institutional machinery at their disposal to press for democratic deepening; they have chosen not to use it. And unlike human rights, there are fewer external or transnational NGOs or networks devoted to deepening democratic institutions, processes, and commitments. Thus, when states lose their interest as do the IGOs they are associated with, a vacuum is created that can be filled only by domestic actors, if at all.[1]

Parenthetically, it should also be observed that although the United States is geographically closer to Latin America than are the European states, it has not been more involved in its human rights affairs. Proximity did not create any greater sense of urgency in Washington. To the contrary, under Bill Clinton the United States played a very low-key role in the Pinochet affair, and under George W. Bush has shown great reluctance to support any human rights causes in the Western Hemisphere.[2]

The high-low political distinction holds up well as a much better explanation for Latin America's strategic shift in behavior toward threatened democracies. In the past, when democracy was a low politics issue, states would not involve themselves in the internal political struggles of other states of the region. They were generally respectful of the principles of sovereignty and nonintervention and saw nothing to be gained for themselves by intervening. Today, these same states seem less respectful of those same principles and more willing to collectively intervene if need be. Why? Are there countervailing principles at work? Certainly at the end of the twentieth century and beginning of the twenty-first, the democratic ideal is a much vaunted notion and one deemed worth defending. But as appealing a norm as democracy may be in its own right, it is not sufficient to drive states to defend others under siege. At other points in history, democracy has been widely embraced in the Western Hemisphere, but only recently has the region taken such vigorous collective action on its behalf.

Rather, it is the emergence of a critical mass of elected governments, each of whom has associated its vital self-interests with the survival of elected governments next door or nearby. States may embrace democratic virtues wholeheartedly but are moved toward collective intervention only when their own interests are at stake. Once enough states saw it this way, then the votes were there within the OAS to forge historic commitments to collectively defend fellow democracies in trouble. That is the logic of high politics immersion into the domestic affairs of other states, and that is the emerging logic of democratic defense, which is moving from the low to high politics arena.

Then, there are other interesting low politics issues that generate externalities but by themselves do not generate sufficient concern abroad to thrust them into the high politics arena with any regularity. The fallout from Brazilian environmental degradation may in the end prove to be devastating for the region and hemisphere. But in the short to medium term, it is a largely invisible threat that can only sporadically create a sense of urgency in foreign capitals. The unchecked flow of illegal aliens from Mexico and points south across the border is an externality but one with a greater regional than national impact on the United States. Reform of immigration laws occasionally hits Washington's radar screen, only to be obscured from view by more pressing concerns. After September 11, President Bush's preoccupation with homeland security and militarizing the border placed immigration reform in abeyance, dashing the hopes of Mexican president Vicente Fox for an early foreign policy victory. And drug cultivation and trafficking in Colombia spill over the borders, precipitating violence, crime, and health risks elsewhere. Yet in and of itself, drugs pose no clear and present danger to U.S. security or economic well-being. Links between traffickers, guerrillas, and terrorist groups must be both credible and sufficiently threatening to the United States and its Latin American allies—at the same time that drug consumption and drug-related crimes escalate—for the issue to gain more national prominence.

Like human rights, all these external issues do experience their international moments. But the mechanisms by which issues are sometimes transformed into matters of urgency to outsiders set apart human rights and the environment on the one hand from immigration and drugs on the other. Foreign states (and IFIs) respond to environmental crises in Latin America less because they see the harmful spillovers per se and more because of the dedicated work of nonstate actors to focus their concerns and forge the linkages necessary to make a case compelling. As in the example of human rights in Chile, it takes transnational activists to bring a distant ecological problem home to foreign government officials who might otherwise pay no attention. Drugs, drug traffickers, and illegal immigrants, on the other hand, need less introduction; they spill directly into U.S. communities and affect the lives of those inhabitants. The externality is visible, and its impact is often felt immediately. Constituents and domestic interest groups can and do easily bring these matters to the attention of their local, state, and federal representatives. Then the only question is whether national leaders respond to domestic pressures for change as if vital interests were in the balance. They do so only on those occasions when drug or immigration difficulties mesh with key security, economic, or electoral concerns.

Finally, an evaluation and comparison of our cases studies also forces us to refine a point made about the role of institutions. In the realm of low politics, states are more likely submit to an organization's conventions and decisions than they would in high politics. Institutions should thus enjoy greater levels of autonomy. That, it turns out, is a generalization that disguises some important variations. Not all institutions are the same. There is a significant difference between nongovernmental organizations (NGOs) and networks on the one hand, and intergovernmental organizations (IGOs) on the other.

NGOs are not beholden to states, act independently of them, and answer to their own constituents. Human rights groups, along with legal and family associations, helped set the stage for the Pinochet case in defiance of the wishes of the Chilean government. IGOs, by contrast, do answer to their member states and enjoy only limited amounts of autonomy. The OAS could not get beyond its members' reluctance to press for a deepening of Peruvian and Ecuadorian democracies. In principle, that leaves it either to the few resource-poor NGOs committed to democratic deepening, or to domestic state actors themselves to do the job.

Comparative Politics and International Relations

What message does our research convey to the community of scholars? There is a gulf in Latin American studies that separates developmental and foreign policy concentrations. This divorce between the examination of domestic and international politics finds a parallel in the broader fields of comparative politics and international relations (IR) within political science. Scholars began to address the divide over two decades ago, and important bridges have been erected. While we certainly do not advance our study as the last word on a comprehensive, unifying theory of international and comparative politics, we do submit that it holds relevance for such efforts.

Questions about internal and external boundaries and influence inevitably intersect with intellectual debates between comparativists and international relations specialists. For many years, thick walls separated these two fields, owing to differences in basic assumptions about how the political world operates. The international arena is horizontally organized: independent sovereign states are left to fend for themselves in an anarchic world, without the benefit of a higher authority to arbitrate disputes between them. The predominance of the structural realist approach, with its overriding emphasis on capacity, has anchored this perception for IR scholars. By contrast, the domestic arena is vertically ordered, and conflict is limited and adjudicated by a hierarchy of institutions and laws to which all parties are bound. Accordingly, international theorists long presumed that the political logic that drives interstate behavior could not be usefully applied to intrastate behavior, and vice versa.

The walls separating the two fields broke down in the late 1970s with the introduction of the "second image reversed" literature, which understood that just as domestic politics shape foreign policy making, international politics can shape the domestic (Gourevitch 1978; Katzenstein 1978). Soon thereafter, theorists moved from the question of *whether* systemic forces mattered to the conduct of internal politics to the *how*: what were the precise causal mechanisms by which external forces shaped the formation of domestic preferences, the organization of coalitions, or the lines of conflict (Rogowski 1990)?

The problem with this literature is that the international is almost always preeminent. Its position as the principal or original causal agent is unchallenged and unwavering. Domestic political variables are reduced to intervening agents that serve as transmission belts conveying influence from the foreign to the domestic (Keohane and Milner 1996). Others attribute somewhat greater impact to domestic forces, suggesting that states adapt to external changes without succumbing to them (Katzenstein 1978; Stallings 1995). Because domestic configurations are different, so too are the adaptations. But even here the domestic plays a subsidiary role that accounts for the residual variance—what's left over after the more powerful forces from the outside work their will (Moravcsik 1993, 11).

As Andrew Moravcsik has persuasively argued, decisions to begin with the systemic as opposed to the domestic are completely arbitrary. International explanations are not inherently more rational, parsimonious, or powerful than others (Moravcsik 1993, 14). Too often, the choice seems to be a function of the academic division of labor; IR theorists are prone to rely more heavily on systemic explanations because that is their home turf. Moreover, internationally driven explanations are laden with presumptions about domestic preference formation and state vulnerability to systemic forces—presumptions that may not be accurate. There is no reason to assume that state leaders and other significant domestic actors formulate preference or policy based *primarily* on a calculation of internationally derived costs and benefits. To resort to the often cited economic analogy, Latin American states are not exactly akin to small firms in the market place; they are not simply price (decision) takers. If they were, and if they were all equally receptive to the will of foreign forces, we would see an unmistakable policy convergence among states of the region. As the opening paragraphs of our introduction make abundantly clear, that is not the case in Latin America. And even where some conformity has appeared, as in the rise of democracy and neoliberal economics, strong domestic antecedents have set the stage for these developments (Frieden 1991; Diamond, Linz, and Lipset 1995; Weyland 2002). The smaller, weaker states of the South not only behave differently from one another but also often make choices that defy the will of foreign powers.

It is not the *whether* or *how* of international influence but the *when* and *why*. Many IR realists have missed out on this due to their fixation on states, military power, and anarchy. Motivation is reduced to self-interest and survival, and the strong are thought to chart the course of political change. But Latin America's periodic assertion of its autonomy, even as it must survive in a global system bent on conformity and living within the shadow of U.S. hegemony, warrants a more nuanced approach to political change. And of course comparativists who shun outside forces do no better, for globalization and hegemony are realities.

It is our view that the international and the domestic take turns being the principal causal agents behind political change in this region. There are times when the international fades from view entirely and domestic forces dominate domestic decisions. Problems of democratic strengthening or human rights justice open a Pandora's box for outside states. Most foreign leaders have no stomach to take on these problems and only rarely are prepared to exhaust any political capital by leveraging democratic or human rights improvements using economic or military sticks and carrots.

On other occasions, especially economic ones, domestic institutions and agents do intervene between foreign influences and internal results, as the second image reversed literature suggests.[3] But in the realm of security, when the United States is determined to flex its muscles, there is little that Latin American actors can do to intercede between the hegemon and its ambitions. Here the foreign *overwhelms* the domestic, and it makes little sense to think of domestic conveyors or transmission belts. The only way in which we can understand the shifting balance of power between the foreign and the domestic is, as we suggest, to study the flow of influence issue by issue. From that vantage point, the general patterns begin to emerge—patterns missed by approaches that primarily focus on actors and their environment.

But what of diplomacy and bargaining across issues? Scholars have made great strides to connect the international and the domestic through the valuable metaphor of two-level games (Putnam 1988). Here the domestic and the international mesh when diplomats cater to, or play off, the interests of domestic groups as they pursue foreign policy goals. Insofar as international negotiators horse-trade on agenda items, or run roughshod over issue boundaries through issue linkage, our issue-based framework weakens. But issue linkage is much more limited than the metaphor suggests. First, we should note that when issue linkage is advanced as a bargaining method, it is an inherently coercive strategy. It threatens the withdrawal of support in one area if compliance is not forthcoming in another. It is steeped in self-interest and the calculus of costs and benefits. It is, therefore, most effective where hard power holds sway and has less impact on those issues more attuned to soft power. For example, Mark Peceny and William Stanley (2001) depict the successful resolution of civil wars and movement toward democracy in Central America as a soft power process. It occurred as liberal norms and practices—in the form of mediation, observation, verification, and assistance for the development of democratic institutions—were diffused from the international arena. This outcome implies that linkages based on hard power—the withdrawal of economic and military assistance, sanctions, or threats to sever diplomatic ties—may be less potent than we think.

Another restraint on issue linkage is more institutional in nature. As more issues of a disparate nature are raised, so too are the interests associated with them. Different governmental bureaucracies with legitimate claims of expertise jockey for influence, weakening the ability of any one official to retain his effectiveness, or perhaps even his position, as an international negotiator. For example, when Chilean politics crossed paths with U.S. attempts to legitimate an invasion of Iraq with a UN resolution in early 2003, U.S.-Chilean relations grew muddied as economic, security, and diplomatic policy processes intermingled. It became unclear who the lead representative was. The Office of the U.S. Trade Representative, the Department of State, the Pentagon, and the White House all vied for position. Likewise, the linkage of disparate issues attracts more varied interest groups, making it more difficult for the government to sustain a coherent bargaining position.

Issue linkage is most successful when it takes a more narrow form of subissue linkage. When issues fall under the same general concern—be it economics, environmental problems, arms proliferation, human rights, or otherwise—power resources can be more effectively transferred from one subissue to the other, and the diversity of input from government bureaucracies or domestic coalitions narrows. Hence, while tariff reductions among various economic goods can be strategically bundled, moves to make trade promotion contingent on democratization, or to tie foreign aid to certified efforts in the drug war, more often result in diluted standards where the hegemon's self-interest is threatened. Linkage may be little more than fiction in such cases. The NAFTA negotiations illustrated the reality of issue boundaries. Efforts to attach environmental and labor issues to free trade and investment were effectively checked by the subsequent delinking of these issues through the creation of two powerless commissions (Cameron and Tomlin 2000, 186–200).

Outside the literature on negotiation and bargaining, studies of transnational social activism also point to issue linkage. For scholars in this field, linkages emerge through "leverage politics"—when social movements attach their low politics goals to the high politics reality of money and diplomacy wielded by powerful states and certain international organizations (Keck and Sikkink 1998, 23–24). This literature explicitly raises the issue of linkage, but it does so in a way that acknowledges just how difficult a process it is. Transnational networks with impeccable credentials must aggressively lobby diplomats long after the issues are joined. Linking issues is a viable strategy, but the bar for success is high and infrequently hurdled, as the capsule on the Brazilian rain forest makes clear. Activists made the connection between environmental protection and foreign state vigilance. However, it was a connection that outside powers bought into only momentarily. In another situation, the United States tied foreign aid to human rights advances in both Guatemala and Argentina. But only the Argentine military leaders succumbed to pressure, due largely to the protracted efforts of social activists. Tenacious perseverance by organized groups, rather than linkage *per se*, proved to be the critical variable (Martin and Sikkink 1993). It is thus little wonder that leverage politics is but one of many strategies transnational social activists will resort to.

It is clear that the scholarship must still traverse a long distance to unite comparative politics and international relations. Too many IR scholars remain intent on colonizing comparative politics by crediting domestic factors with no more than an intervening role, and an equal number of comparativists either intentionally or unintentionally shunt international politics to the side. An issue-based orientation provides the conceptual tools required to overcome these differences because it remains neutral on the debate over which field reigns supreme. We address the when and why of international versus domestic dominance not as a field restrictive assumption, but as an open matter of inquiry—one that stands at the forefront of our exploration of political change.

Neither field will have the last word on this subject, nor will we. Our more modest goal throughout has been to advance the discussion beyond the confines of one field, and more important, beyond the narrower confines still of any subfield. It was with subfield limitations and barriers in mind that we first tempted fate by undertaking this project. Were there some very general patterns to political influence that had escaped our attention by virtue of our having been cloistered within our respective concentrations? Could we move beyond our subfield interests, assumptions, and limitations by situating these within a larger framework of understanding?

To do so, we have had to pull back from the Latin American trees to see the forest. In an age when political scientists have increasingly chosen the microscope to unveil the motives and strategies of individual actors, we have opted for the telescope to capture the wider gamut of political change agents, organizations, and relations. With the aid of that telescope and from a distance, patterns and clusters come into view that cannot be seen up close. Those patterns and clusters are our clues as to when and why international forces for change overshadow domestic ones, and vise versa. We believe that being able to make that determination across a wide range of issues constitutes an important contribution to the intermestic literature on Latin America.

Policy Implications

Knowing when and why foreign forces matter to the conduct of events in Latin America takes on policy salience as well. As Latin America moves into the twenty-first century, it faces problems of considerable gravity: democracies that are weakly institutionalized, governments that perform poorly or not at all, militaries that are asked to fill functional gaps, crime and insecurity that sweep through once relatively safe and secure communities, courts that fail to bring perpetrators to justice, poverty that reaches up and grabs vast portions of an erstwhile middle class, double-digit unemployment rates, and indigenous populations at the very bottom who will not wait any longer for a slice of the pie. The political life spans of Latin America's leaders have grown progressively shorter as they either cannot or will not remedy these ills; worse still, they are sometimes part of the problem. It is always at times of great frustration and great need when the question is asked: what will the wealthier industrialized countries offer this beleaguered region? And specifically, what will the United States offer?

The answer is not comforting, but it is at least more comprehensible once viewed through the lens of our framework. The United States is not likely to invest any significant resources or effort in a campaign of direct economic or social assistance targeted at in-need populations. This is not a bold prediction of course; the foreign aid spigot was more or less turned off years ago and remains closed. Naturally there have been both ideological and fiscal changes in the United States in recent decades that can account for the diminished importance of foreign aid. But the problem goes beyond the hegemony of fiscal conservatism to one of general hegemonic attention and motivation. U.S. governments—whether Democratic or Republican controlled—have very little interest in any of the aforementioned problems, and less interest still in doing anything about them. Their lack of interest derives from a perception that the burdens of the region's poor, its workers, its unemployed, its peasants, its pensioners, indeed its average citizens, generate no imminent threats to U.S. national interests, and efforts to assist them generate no tangible benefits in return. These are low politics difficulties that do not reach out and grab the attention of powerful executives or lawmakers from the North.

This view is not just a kind of bias toward the impoverished masses. The U.S. government demonstrates an equally indifferent attitude toward the elites. It refuses to commit significant attention, expertise, or sums of money to strengthen and reform Latin America's courts, legislatures, police units, defense ministries, and other institutions of the democratic state. Elites desperately need stronger institutions if they are to govern effectively. But however vital democratic deepening may be to Latin America's future, it just does not appear on Washington's radar screen because it too resides in the realm of low politics, meaning the stakes are appreciably lower for foreign states.

Scholars can wax eloquent about how the afflictions of poverty, unemployment, crime, the environment, institutional decay, and human rights left unattended now will fester and create crises that will *eventually* harm U.S. interests. But the arguments fall on deaf ears to policy makers who view the long term as very long indeed and who are eager to discount the future costs to their current inaction. Unless Latin America's low politics problems can cause considerable and immediate angst at a national level within the United States, they will not become a political agenda item in Washington.

Washington's attention deficit is selective, and issue sensitive. Within the high politics realm of economics, the United States is willing (with some misgivings) to work toward the creation of a free trade zone with its Latin American partners. It is ideologically predisposed to do so, and it envisions a short- to medium-term gain in the form of new, expanded, and unrestricted markets for U.S. exporters and investors. But it is much less willing to associate free trade with low politics reforms within Latin American states that would humanize the workplace, boost wages, or create jobs. In the longer term, assisting Latin American workers and unemployed should, in theory, rebound to the benefit of the United States by bolstering disposable incomes, which in turn would mean greater consumption of very competitive U.S. goods. Even though there is a logical linkage between these sets of issues, it is still perceived as an indirect and less urgent connection and one that Washington policy makers seldom make. They would rather place their bets on a free trade deal alone that quickly solidifies their nation's export earnings and profit remittances.

Similar issue splits are visible elsewhere. The United States wants Latin American armed forces to leap into wars against guerrillas and terrorists but shows little concern that military immersion in these campaigns might have negative consequences for professionalism, democratic society, and civilian control in those countries. It devotes scant resources to help fully professionalize those forces and less still to equip civilians with the tools they need to institutionalize control over their soldiers. It wants its Southern neighbors to fight hard against transnational crime but will not help finance judicial reform that would allow Latin American courts to process their criminal caseloads more efficiently and prosecute more frequently, or help fund police reform to reduce the rampant corruption of those units. The United States visualizes the struggle against left-wing insurgents, terrorists, and their criminal associates as high-stakes contests of high politics that must be won to enhance its own national security and that of its allies in those struggles; it does not visualize improvements in Latin American civil-military relations or judicial and police systems in quite the same way.

In not addressing the latter issues, the United States may be cutting off its nose to spite its face. Without low politics reforms to assist Latin American judges, police, investigators, soldiers, and their civilian managers, those groups will be less equipped to lend a hand in transnational struggles deemed vital by Washington. But so it goes. The hegemon's indifference to these groups and their problems persists, and the balance of influence remains tilted in the direction of domestic politics and away from the foreign. On these issues, Latin America is left to fend for itself, and only time will tell whether its independence proves to be a blessing or a curse.

Notes

Chapter 1: Explaining Political Change in Latin America

1. Some of the more recent attempts to survey political change in Latin America include Smith and Korzeniewicz (1997), Oxhorn and Ducatenzeiler (1998), Buxton and Phillips (1999), Gwynne and Kay (1999), Veltmeyer and Petras (2000), Stark (2001), and Tulchin and Espach (2001).

2. The 1992 debacle in Somalia, for example, provided additional evidence for critics of nation building (Dempsey 2001). The U.S. experience in Iraq may further reinforce this thinking.

3. For the OAS Charter, see that organization's Web site, at http://www.oas.org/juridico/english/charter.html.

4. As Stephen Krasner (1999) has argued, there are two logics in the international system: one of appropriateness and one of consequences. Appropriateness pertains to roles, rules, and norms; consequences pertain to power.

5. The point also being that while intervention is always at odds with invitation, loss of sovereignty is not. States can and do lose some measure of decision-making sovereignty voluntarily or involuntarily, wittingly or unwittingly. Naturally, our book considers instances of intervention, since it falls under the umbrella term of foreign influence.

6. Much has been written on the challenges faced by the state in the face of globalization. See Ohmae (1996), Schwartz (1998), and *Daedalus* (1995). For an alternative view on the enduring economic role of the state, see Gilpin (2000).

7. To illustrate how the perception of appropriateness evolves, Finnemore (2003) documents how the rules of intervention have changed dramatically over the course of history.

Chapter 2: Issues and Political Change

1. Hence, David Barkin reflects on "the millions [of Latin Americans] who are unwilling to accept the inevitability of their absorption into the neoliberal quagmire" in an edited volume that documents successes in alternative forms of development (2001, 184), while Peter Smith persuasively charts how Latin American economic options have slimmed as the "asymmetrical significance" in U.S.-Latin American relations deepens (2000, 319–70).

2. Important studies appeared on parties (Mainwaring and Scully 1995), presidentialism (Mainwaring and Shugart 1997), bureaucracy (Geddes 1996), NGOs (Levy 1996), social movements (Eckstein 2001), business (Bartell and Payne 1995), technocrats (Centeno and Silva 1998), civil-military relations (Pion-Berlin 2001), and other components of democracy.

3. Because ideals like these are tools of convenience rather than principles of unconditional allegiance, the U.S. commitment to those principles waxes and wanes depending upon their utility. Thus, U.S. support for democracies in the region has been and will continue to be variable (Lowenthal 1991b).

4. For example, see Goldstein and Keohane (1993), Keohane (1984), Klotz (1995),

Finnemore (1996), Thomas (2001), and Simmons and Martin (2002). Also, see "Legalization and World Politics" (2000).

5. Katzenstein (1996) made an effort to apply constructivist approaches to national security in an edited volume. While the contributors' efforts are laudable, the self-criticism contained in the review chapter (Kowert and Legro 1996) is indicative of the power still held by approaches to security guided primarily by material interests.

6. There are certainly more instances of linkage between high politics issues themselves. Recently, the United States stalled free trade talks with Chile in retaliation for Chile's refusal to support the U.S.-led invasion of Iraq.

Chapter 3: Neoliberal Reform in Argentina, Brazil, and Chile

1. While dependency approaches erroneously portray the international as a monolithic actor (i.e., the international capitalist structure), second image reversed approaches incorporate the effects of foreign influences only as economic shocks rather than sustained processes. More contemporary policy studies tend to focus on neoliberal initiation and domestic processes and to underplay outside pressures.

2. On a global scale, Griffith-Jones and Stallings (1995) note how international finance appeared differently across regions in the early 1990s. Foreign direct investment dominated transfers to Asia, portfolio investment headed outlays in Latin America, and official transfers led the pack in Africa.

3. "Inestabilidad debilita la posición del Mercosur," El País Digital (Montevideo), March 3, 2002, http://www.diaroelpais.com/.

4. Lorenzo Pérez, Assistant Director, Western Hemisphere Department, International Monetary Fund, interview with Craig Arceneaux, July 8, 2002, Washington, DC.

5. Philip Gerson, Deputy Division Chief, Western Hemisphere Department, International Monetary Fund, interview with Craig Arceneaux, July 8, 2002, Washington, DC.

6. Pérez, interview, July 8, 2002.

7. Both of these changes were mentioned in the interview with Gerson, July 8, 2002. For a statement on IMF adoption of these policies, see "New Conditionality Guidelines Put Country Officials Back in the Driver's Seat," IMF Survey, December 16, 2002, 390–91.

8. Just as important, an 85 percent majority is demanded for the fund's most important decisions, giving the United States alone effective veto powers.

9. Philip Gerson and Lorenzo Pérez, interview with Craig Arceneaux, July 8, 2002, Washington, DC. It is no surprise that the IMF admits such political influence (e.g., the organization's Web site emphatically denotes its status as a member-driven organization)—this deflects policy criticism from the organization and places it squarely on its members.

10. Income paid to the rest of the world before the 1998–1999 crisis was 28 percent of the total. All figures are in 1995 constant dollars (ECLAC 2001).

11. This leverage was expressed not only through default but also insofar as Brazil's intransigence exposed the banks' vulnerabilities in the eyes of credit rating regulators and their shareholders (Lehman 1993, 147–48).

12. Paulo Roberto de Almeida, Minister Counselor, Embassy of Brazil, and Roberto Jaguaribe, Minister Counselor, Deputy Chief of Mission, Embassy of Brazil, interviews with Craig Arceneaux, July 10, 2002, and July 3, 2002, respectively, Washington, DC. More generally, Edwards also argues that the march of neoliberalism in Latin America was a trial-and-error, pragmatic journey.

13. Also see Baer (2001, 199–219); "Definitely Not Going to the IMF, Maybe," Latin American Weekly Report, WR-97-47, November 25, 1997, 554.

14. "Wall Street Heavyweights Speak of Backing Brazil," Wall Street Journal, September 18, 1998, A7; "Big Banks Cool to Major Role in Brazil Bailout," Wall Street Journal, October 13, 1998,

A16; "U.S. Banks Grow Cautious on Scope of Aid to Brazil," *New York Times*, November 7, 1998, C2; "U.S., IMF Prod Big Banks to Aid Brazil," *Wall Street Journal*, March 9, 1999, A17.

15. "Turmoil in Brazil: The U.S. Role," *New York Times*, January 14, 1999, A1.

16. Weisbrot and Baker are not alone in their skepticism. See José Carlos de Faria and Piero Ghezzi, "Brazil Debt Dynamics: Improving, but Still Vulnerable," *Emerging Markets Research*, February 17, 2003 (New York: Deutsche Bank Securities, Inc.); also see Morris Goldstein, "Debt Sustainability, Brazil, and the IMF," *Working Paper 03-1*, February 2003 (Washington, DC: Institute for International Economics). Lula increased the primary surplus target to 4.25 percent, but these authors still perceive this as insufficient.

17. "IMF Loan Counters Strict Bail-Out Policy," *Financial Times*, August 8, 2002, http://web.lexis-nexis.com/universe/.

18. *Address by the President of the Federative Republic of Brazil, Fernando Henrique Cardoso, at the Opening Session of the Third Summit of the Americas*, Quebec City, Canada, April 20, 2001, available at the Web site of the Brazilian Ministry of Foreign Relations, http://www.mre.gov.br.

19. Almeida and Jaguaribe, interviews, July 10, 2002, and July 3, 2002, respectively.

20. For a good overview of Brazilian qualms over U.S. trade practices, see "Brazil's Brush-Off," *National Journal*, April 14, 2001, http://web.lexis-nexis.com/universe/. According to the article Brazilians claim that U.S. trade barriers affect 60 percent of Brazilian goods, including tariffs of 236 percent on cane sugar, 44.7 percent on orange juice, and 19.7 percent on soybeans. Also see "Brazil Warns U.S. It Must Lower Trade Barriers," *Financial Times*, August 6, 2002, http://web.lexis-nexis.com/universe/.

21. These dynamics were spelled out by Almeida, in the July 10, 2002, interview.

22. Ibid.

23. Feinberg (1997) and Wiarda (1995) note that much of the push for free trade in the hemisphere came from Latin American governments. This was no less true for Chile. Roberto E. Matus, Economic Counselor, Embassy of Chile, interview with Craig Arceneaux, July 2, 2002, Washington, DC.

24. Correspondence with John O'Leary, United States Ambassador to Chile, 1998–2001, September 2, 2002.

25. "Fast-track authority" refers to the congressional consent for presidents to negotiate trade barrier reduction agreements, which are then to be put to a simple vote by Congress, with mandatory deadlines, limited debate, and no amendments or deletions. The rationale is that with fast-track authority, the executive can negotiate with greater confidence. The measure has since been renamed "trade promotion authority."

26. "Clinton Asks GOP to Back Free Trade," *New York Times*, November 11, 1994, A8.

27. Correspondence with John O'Leary, November 11, 2002.

28. Information for this and the following paragraph from correspondence with John O'Leary, November 11, 2002.

29. Matus, interview, July 2, 2002.

30. Ibid.

31. "White House Hard Pressed on Americas Trade Bloc," *Financial Times*, March 30, 2001, http://web.lexis-nexis.com/universe/.

32. "Brazil Warns Chile against Reaching FTA with U.S.," *Xinhua News Agency*, December 7, 2000, http://web.lexis-nexis.com/universe/. Both states are members of the Latin American Integration Association, which demands that all states offer most-favored nation status to each other.

33. Correspondence with John O'Leary, September 2, 2002.

34. "Washington's Slow Pace in Trade Talks Annoys the Chileans," *New York Times*, June 25, 2002, A1.

35. Quoted in "Chile—A Giant Step Toward Free Trade in the Americas," *Business Week*, June 16, 2003, 53.

36. "Argentina's Reward for Good Behaviour: No IMF Funds, and Banks Ask for More," *Latin American Weekly Report*, WR-91-11, March 21, 1991, 7.

37. Data are for year 2001 and are drawn from World Bank (2003).

38. Argentina did fall in 2001 due to its economic crisis. In 1999, Brazil, Argentina, and Chile ranked 11th, 26th, and 32nd, respectively (nonetheless, it should be noted that 1999 saw recessions in Brazil and Chile as well). Data collected in 2001 from the Web page of the U.S. Census Bureau, Foreign Trade Division, http://www.census.gov/foreigntrade/balance/index .html.

39. "American Investors in Argentina Mostly Taking Losses in Stride," *New York Times*, December 25, 2001, A17.

40. Such criticisms are well represented in the *Meltzer Report*, commissioned in 2000 under a majority Republican congressional committee and headed by Carnegie Mellon University economist Allan Meltzer. The report is officially titled *International Financial Institutions Reform Report of the International Financial Institution Advisory Commission* (U.S. Congress, March 2000), http://www.house.gov/jec/imf/meltzer.pdf.

41. "Bush's Policy on Argentina Signals Shift in Policy," *New York Times*, January 5, 2002, A3.

42. Growth rates for individual years are 10.6 percent (1991), 9.6 percent (1992), 5.7 percent (1993), and 8 percent (1994). *IMF Financial Statistics Yearbook* (2001).

43. *Statistical Yearbook for Latin America and the Caribbean 2000.*

44. "Resisting the IMF," *Latin American Weekly Report*, WR-94-19, May 26, 1994, 223; "Warning to Cavallo from the IMF: Government Over-Spending, Targets Under Threat," *Latin American Weekly Report*, WR-94-39, October 13, 1994, 464.

45. Also see "Point of View: Legalized Theft," *Forbes*, March 4, 2002, 120; "Deficit Spending Got Argentina into This Mess," *Business Week*, February 11, 2002, 26; "Argentina Should Embrace Free Market, Bush Says," Knight Ridder Tribune News Service, January 16, 2002, http://web.lexis-nexis.com/universe/; "For IMF, Argentina Was an Unsolvable Puzzle," *Washington Post*, January 3, 2002, E1.

46. Data and analysis from Cibils, Weisbrot, and Kar (2002). The authors also downplay the often cited problem of spending in the provinces. With fiscal deficits of just 1.1 percent of GDP in 2000 and topping at 1.9 percent in 2001, the authors add that the borrowing was much more a consequence than cause of the crisis.

47. "Giving Argentina the Cinderella Treatment," *New York Times*, August 11, 2002, A14.

48. "IMF Approves Augmentation of Argentina's Stand-By Credit to US$14 Billion and Completes Second Review," International Monetary Fund, press release no. 01/3, January 12, 2001, http://www.imf.org/external/np/sec/pr/2001/pr0103.htm.

49. Interview reported in "A Fiscal Crisis, Paid in Credibility," *New York Times*, December 25, 2001, A16.

50. In the same article, a report documenting the stringent conditionality of a $1.2 billion IMF package for Argentina described a $15 billion extension to Brazil as a "surprise," which "represents the second time in three years that Brazil has successfully appealed for a multi-year emergency program." Joseph Kahn, "IMF Ready for Brazil and Argentina Rescues," *New York Times*, August 4, 2001, A4.

51. "Estados Unidos volvió a condicionar la ayuda," *La Nación*, July 18, 2002, http://www .lanacion.com/; "Paul O'Neill: Viajaré a la Argentina para ver qué está mal," *La Nación*, July 18, 2002, http://www.lanacion.com/; also see "O'Neill Leaves it to IMF to Plan Argentina's Aid," *Wall Street Journal Europe*, August 8, 2002, A2.

52. It is notable that Mr. Martinez is a Cuban refugee—confirming that for the Bush administration, Florida politics outweigh Argentine politics. "Argentina's Chief Is Sworn In and Comes Out Fighting," *New York Times*, May 26, 2003, A3.

Chapter 4: Democratization in the Andean Region

1. It was not until the late 1980s with the Esquipulas agreement between the Central American states that the connection between regime choice and regional security was officially made.

2. In the late 1970s, the Carter administration had taken a forceful stand specifically on human rights and less on redemocratization. Moreover its policies were implemented bilaterally rather than through the OAS. During that era, the OAS passed some resolutions but never really pressured or punished states for noncompliance with human rights standards or for failure to democratize. See Lars Schoultz (1981, 133).

3. Washington had a selfish interest in signing the document. In the 1930s FDR agreed to abide by the principle of nonintervention in exchange for Latin American cooperation to deter Nazi influence in the Western Hemisphere.

4. Ironically, the early struggle to achieve both human and democratic rights only reinforced the classic opposition to intervention. The earliest construction of a democratic right in international law was that of self-determination, the thrust of which was to defeat colonialism and neocolonialism. To protect a people's right to determine their own political destinies meant to be free from the oppression of tyrannical systems imposed from abroad. There was a stigma attached to intervention that connoted a kind of inappropriate intrusion into the affairs of a sovereign state, whether done unilaterally or collectively (see Reed and Kaysen 1993).

5. Despotic regimes took over postcolonial states, trampling on the political rights and freedoms of their subjects. The rest of the world community began to question whether such regimes should enjoy unfettered protection. Legitimate sovereignty, the argument went, springs from the consent of the governed. But if basic rights of free expression, organization, participation, and representation were being denied, then a regime would have forfeited its claims to exclusive jurisdiction within its territorial borders (see Tesón 1996). New international agreements would emerge that obligated ratifying states to monitor, protect, and enlarge democratic freedoms, while the international community was coming to the view that some forms of multilateral intervention may be justified—even necessary—to restore those freedoms where they had been violated.

6. The charter spelled out in greater detail what constituted democratic rule and stipulated regional responses to and penalties for *alterations of*—not just interruptions of—the constitutional regime (article 19). The charter's new language acknowledged the region's increased awareness that threats to democratic functioning can take various forms, while at the same time reinforcing its conviction that coups would not stand. The charter was invoked for the first time in April 2002 when members of the armed forces temporarily removed Venezuelan president Hugo Chávez from office (see OAS 2001).

7. Democracy's decline is not a statement about the erosion of one particular form of representation. It is common knowledge that some political systems of interest representation are more party centered while others are more clientelistic and that some leaders are more populist in style, preferring to make direct rather than institutional connections with voters. The problem seems to be more pervasive, one that has affected nearly all polities in Latin America.

8. Public support for democracy is down. In Latin America in the year 2000, the percentage of people who believed democracy is preferable to any other kind of government was 56 percent, down from 61 percent in 1996. That compares with 78 percent from Western Europe and 80 percent in the United States. Data are from *Latinobarómetro, Opinión Pública Latinoamericana*, Annual Survey, 1996–2002. See http://www.latinobarometro.org/.

9. See OAS, *Unit for the Promotion of Democracy* Web site, http://www.upd.oas.org/.

10. The budget for the entire organization for 2001 was $1.66 million, which is $83,000 for each of twenty Latin American republics. The limitations of the UPD are summed up by its coordinator in charge of institutional strengthening: "the role of the UPD is conditioned by the limits imposed by member States on its autonomy (it may take action only at the behest and/or

instructions of member states), and by the dearth of human and financial resources at its disposal to carry out its tasks." See Ruben Perina, "The Inter-American Democratic Regime: The Role of the OAS" (unpublished paper, July 2002, 23, obtained from the author).

11. Ibid.

12. An OAS ad hoc reunion of foreign affairs ministers reconvened on December 14, 1992. A resolution sponsored by nine countries said: "The November 22, 1992 elections represented an important phase in the process of re-establishing democratic institutional order. . . . With installation of the constituent assembly, the ad hoc meeting of foreign affairs ministers will come to an end."

13. The OAS ignored Fujimori's disturbing maneuvers in the run-up to the election, including the imposition of a very short time (two weeks) for parties to mount a campaign; the stipulation that those in Congress would be ineligible to run for office for one term; the determination that the assembly would be one chamber and would last for his entire presidential term, till July 28, 1995, instead of disbanding once a constitution was written; and the dismissal of the head of the national elections tribunal and his replacement with a Fujimori loyalist. See McClintock (1993).

14. David Scott Palmer has suggested that the ability of the international community to sanction Peru for antidemocratic practices right after the *autogolpe* was constrained because the Peruvian public attributed so many of the country's ills to the democracy itself and not to the popular Fujimori (1996). That sentiment would change eight years later when the public would hold the president himself accountable.

15. Catherine Conaghan (2001a, 3) has argued that as a result of the reelection project spearheaded by Fujimori, Montesinos, and their allies Peru became more authoritarian and the regime transformed into something more sultanistic than democratic.

16. According to Luigi Einaudi, assistant secretary general of the OAS, Stein operated with a kind of presumed autonomy: that he embodied the will of the OAS, without actually consulting with it at every step. Thus, he probably went further than the members would have preferred or would have endorsed on their own. Interview with David Pion-Berlin, June 25, 2002, Washington, DC.

17. These statements of Eduardo Stein in *A Hazy Transparency: Peru's 2000 Elections*, Films for the Humanities and Sciences, 2002, videocassette.

18. "Peru Voters Give President a Shock," *New York Times*, April 10, 2000, http://web.lexis-nexis.com/universe/.

19. "Peru Election: Cries of Fraud As President Moves Closer to Victory," Associated Press, April 11, 2000, http://web.lexis-nexis.com/universe/.

20. "Triunfo la Voluntad Popular," *La República*, April 10, 2000, http://www.larepublica.com.pe/2000/abril/pdf10/politica.htm.

21. "Peru Election: Cries of Fraud As President Moves Closer to Victory," Associated Press, April 11, 2000, http://web.lexis-nexis.com/universe/.

22. "Fraud Charged in Peruvian Elections," *Washington Post*, April 11, 2000, http://web.lexis-nexis.com/universe/.

23. "Push for Runoff in Peru Seen As Democratic Boost," *Los Angeles Times*, April, 14, 2000, http://web.lexis-nexis.com/universe/.

24. For example, the U.S. State Department commented, "Reliable sampling of actual election returns revealed that no single candidate won an absolute majority and that there will be a runoff." Of course it was legally within the purview of Peru's own ONPE to make that decision, not a foreign power. Reportedly, Secretary of State Madeline Albright herself told Fujimori before half the votes had been counted that her government expected there to be a second round. That was followed up by Thomas Pickering, U.S. Undersecretary of State for Political Affairs, who called Peruvian prime minister Alberto Bustamante on April 12 to say U.S. relations with Peru would be seriously strained if there was no runoff. The Peruvians were taken aback by

these comments, causing Francisco Tudela, Fujimori's vice presidential running mate, to defensively declare, "I have never seen this level of U.S. interference in South America before. They have tried to do it in Central America before, but Peru is different. We are not a banana republic. We Peruvians need to defend our national sovereignty." See "Peru's President, Short of Majority, Now Faces Runoff," *New York Times* April 13, 2000, http://web.lexis-nexis.com/universe/.

25. Ibid.

26. Ibid.

27. "OAS Will Not Endorse Peruvian Elections if Anomalies Persist," EFE News Service, April 15, 2000, http://web.lexis-nexis.com/universe/.

28. "Campaign Flawed but Viable OAS Says," Inter Press News Service Agency, April 4, 2000, http://web.lexis-nexis.com/universe/.

29. "Arrested Arms Trafficker Allegedly Funded Fujimori Re-election Campaign," *World News Connection*, October 2, 2003; McClintock and Vallas (2002, 149).

30. "Laws and Taxes Harm Press Freedoms," Inter Press News Service Agency, May 2, 2000, http://web.lexis-nexis.com/universe/.

31. "International Observers Say They Fear Fujimori May Steal Peru's Election Runoff," *New York Times*, May 15, 2000, http://web.lexis-nexis.com/universe/.

32. "OAS Issues New Fraud Warning in Peru Runoff: Monitoring Mission Halted over Vote-Counting System," *Washington Post*, May 23, 2000, http://web.lexis-nexis.com/universe/.

33. "Peru Elections: OAS Objects to Electoral Body," EFE News Services, May 22, 2000, http://web.lexis-nexis.com/universe/.

34. The Jurado Nacional de Elecciones set the date on April 30, as soon as the ONPE had finally finished its tabulation of the congressional vote. See Conaghan (2001a, 16).

35. "OAS Envoy Leaves Peru, Criticizes Vote," *Washington Post*, May 27, 2000, http://web.lexis-nexis.com/universe/. This decision came a day after news that a journalist had been tortured to reveal sources within intelligence services who gave him videotapes of Vladimir Montesinos meeting with election officials. Apparently, the president of the Jurado Nacional de Elecciones had made various visits to SIN headquarters. See "As Protests Grow Violent, Peru Says Runoff Will Go On," *New York Times*, May 26, 2000, http://web.lexis-nexis.com/universe/; "Crimen Electoral," *Caretas*, edición no 1620, May 26, 2000, http://www.caretas.com.pe.

36. Given the fact that Stein had all but conceded that the next round would be rigged, it seemed reasonable for Toledo to withdraw. But the United States changed its position, criticized Toledo's decision, and was increasingly skeptical about Toledo himself. See McClintock and Vallas (2002, 151).

37. It is interesting to note that a respected poll conducted a week prior to the election had Fujimori leading Toledo by 54 to 46 percent. Conceivably then, the president could have legitimately won a delayed election. "Fujimori Is Victor in Peru's Runoff As Protests Grow," *New York Times*, May 29, 2000, http://web.lexis-nexis.com/universe/. Instead, Fujimori chose to declare the actual runoff election to be legal and legitimate in an interview with CNN on May 29. See Conaghan (2001a, 17–18).

38. OAS, Boletín de Noticias, Departamento de Información Pública, June 1, 2000.

39. As Cynthia McClintock has noted, Resolution 1080 had never been reconfigured to qualify a fraudulent election as a trigger for OAS action. The United States introduced 1080 only as a tactic to ensure that the OAS General Assembly meeting, scheduled for June 4–5, would place the Peruvian elections on its agenda. See McClintock and Vallas (2002, 152).

40. Ibid.

41. U.S. OAS ambassador at the time, Luis Lauredo, claimed that he introduced the 1080 resolution for two reasons. One was to make the point that principles of nonintervention could not justify the view that "anything can happen on the other side of the border" (border being sovereign Peru). The other reason was a strategic maneuver to force the foreign ministers to

discuss the issues at the General Assembly meeting. Telephone interview with David Pion-Berlin, June 19, 2002.

42. OAS, Boletín de Noticias, June 6, 2000, 1. The Canadian-sponsored resolution was written and spearheaded by Peter Boehm, the permanent representative to the OAS at the time. Despite the rather tame nature of this mission, it was a "struggle," as he put it, to get the other members on board. In particular he had to fend off efforts by Mexico to have it made a declaration rather than a resolution, since the former was not binding on members. Peter Boehm, interview with David Pion-Berlin, June 26, 2002, Washington, DC.

43. OAS, Boletín de Noticias, June 6, 2000.

44. Ibid., 3.

45. Ibid.

46. It is a position that the assistant secretary general of the OAS has embraced as well. Said Luigi Einaudi: "It has also underscored that there is no single model of democracy or of anything else. It is precisely because each country is unique that countries must be approached in terms of their uniqueness and their histories. Although the issue may be a thorny one at times, we must respect sovereignty" (Einaudi 2001).

47. Ibid.

48. From that point on, the United States, convinced that Fujimori would serve out his term and that he would remain a valuable ally in the move toward free markets and the fight against narcotics, would take no bilateral actions against Peru for its failure to advance the cause of democratic deepening (McClintock and Vallas 2002, 153).

49. "OAS to Address Fraud Charges in Peruvian Vote," New York Times, June 1, 2000.

50. Mission members were cognizant of the danger of co-optation and tried to be "implicitly critical of the regime." Boehm, interview, June 26, 2002.

51. "OAS Mission Delivers Reform Blueprint," Latin American Weekly Report, WR-00-26, July 4, 2000, 305.

52. "OAS Mission to Peru Says Intelligence Boss Must Go," New York Times, June 30, 2000, http://web.lexis-nexis.com/universe/.

53. OAS, press release, "Proposals Presented by the OAS Mission in Peru," June 2000; OAS, press release, "OAS Mission to Peru Presents First Report to Foreign Ministers," July 21, 2000.

54. OAS, press release, "Proposals Presented by the OAS Mission," June 2000.

55. One would have to go back to the early-twentieth century to find an occasion upon which any Latin American nation had been placed under formal oversight by a foreign actor. Then, it was at the hands of the United States alone, and the objective was to secure debt repayments from the Dominican Republic.

56. "Peru Must Heed OAS," Ottawa Citizen, July 1, 2000, http://web.lexis-nexis.com/universe/.

57. "OAS Head Gaviria Comments on Results of Visit," BBC Summary of World Broadcasts, July 3, 2000.

58. "Lo que se juega la OEA," Caretas, July 6, 2000, http://www.caretas.com.pe. The mission's statement said, "It is imperative that the expression of this commitment be accompanied by a clear timetable for the implementation of reforms so that concrete measurable results can be achieved." But Peru's foreign minister, Fernando de Trazegnies, had a different idea, saying "there is no time limit for the mission's work, and all depends on what they find and what has to be done." See OAS, Boletín de Noticias, June 7, 2000. "We are not going to establish a schedule, never," the foreign minister added. See "Peru's Fujimori Says OAS Mission Can't Question His Re-election," Associated Press, June 6, 2000, http://web.lexisnexis.com/universe/.

59. "Fujimori Backpedaling on Pledge to Repair Peru's Damaged Democracy after Flawed Re-election," Associated Press, July 12, 2000, http://web.lexis-nexis.com/universe/; "Peruvian

Congress and Fujimori Show Limits of Compliance with OAS Plan, *Latin American Weekly Report*, WR-00-27, July 11, 2000, 313.

60. "Vergüenza Nacional y un Farol Presidencial," *Caretas*, edición no. 1637, September 22, 2000, 1–5, http://www.caretas.com.pe; "Peru: Fujimori's Eminence Grise Caught Red-Handed," Inter Press News Service Agency, September 15, 2000, http://web.lexis-nexis .com/universe/.

61. Chronology of Mesa del Diálogo proceedings, provided to author by Peter Boehm.

62. Ibid.

63. "Delay Tactics Test Patience in OAS Dialogue," Inter Press News Service Agency, August 22, 2000, http://web.lexis-nexis.com/universe/.

64. Ibid.

65. Chronology of Mesa del Diálogo proceedings, Boehm.

66. Ruben Perina, Coordinator, Strengthening of Institutions Area, Unit for Promotion of Democracy, interview with David Pion-Berlin, June 24, 2002, Washington, DC.

67. "Indian Protest Prompts Calls to Oust Ecuador's President," *New York Times*, January 22, 2000, A3.

68. Mahuad was transported to an air force base. Once there, military units loyal to the Junta de Salvación made another effort to secure his resignation. But Mahuad refused, saying, "I am not going to facilitate things. I am not going to allow them to leave saying they had achieved an appearance of democratic continuity for this clownish thing" (Lascano Palacios 2001, 61).

69. At a graduation ceremony in December 1999, Colonel Gutiérrez had refused to shake the president's hand. Mahuad expressed to his commanders his concern over Gutiérrez, and yet General Mendoza invited Gutiérrez on January 7 to work at the Joint Command (see Lascano Palacios 2001). Diego Iturralde, Mahuad's advisor on indigenous affairs, told the president that the Indian leader Vargas had told his followers the night before the coup that they could count on the support of the military and therefore could go forward with their plans (Lascano Palacios 2001, 29). Iturralde also revealed that the military had arrived at a park outside the center where the Indians had assembled to prepare their assault, with food to distribute to the protesters. General Mendoza denied any knowledge of these plans (Lascano Palacios 2001, 30). A day earlier, his defense minister and top army commander had told him everything was under control. Thus, the president asked, how could things have materialized like this?

70. Lascano Palacios (2001, 63). Peter Romero, assistant secretary of state for Latin America, told the coup leaders they faced "political and economic isolation" like Cuba's if they did not step down. See "Ecuador Junta Seizes Control, but Steps Aside," *New York Times*, January 23, 2000, 11.

71. "Ecuador's Mahuad Ousted Amid Massive Protests," January 27, 2000, Facts on File News Digest, http://lexisnexis.com/.

72. OAS, Permanent Council, CP/RES 763, January 22, 2000.

73. "Ecuadoran Coup Attempt Draws Widespread Condemnation," Agence France Presse-English, January 22, 2000, http://web.lexis-nexis.com/universe/.

74. Ibid.

75. "Vice President Takes Charge of Ecuador," *USA Today*, January 22, 2000, http://web .lexis-nexis.com/universe/.

76. Ibid.; Lascano Palacios (2001, 61–78).

77. Lifted by the buoyancy of petroleum-driven revenues, the military expanded the state's role in the economy and pursued redistributive social justice measures without choking off growth and without threatening the propertied classes.

78. *Latinobarómetro*, Annual Survey, press report, 1999/2000, 4, 7, http://www .latinobarometro.org/.

79. OAS, Permanent Council, CP/Res 764, "Support for the Constitutional Government of

the Republic of Ecuador," January 26, 2000; "Ecuador Junta Seizes Control, but Steps Aside," *New York Times*, January 23, 2000, http://web.lexis-nexis.com/universe/.

80. "Ecuador Vice President Takes Power after Coup," Reuters, January 22, 2000, http://web.lexis-nexis.com/universe/.

81. Republic of Ecuador, *Constitution of 1998*, articles 167, 168.

82. In interviews with David Pion-Berlin, certain U.S. and Ecuadorian officials later insisted that Mahuad had resigned. But according to other officials, Mahuad never formally tendered his resignation; he simply said he would not stand in the way of Noboa's ascension. Lauredo, telephone interview, June 19, 2002; Ecuador's OAS ambassador Blasco Peñaherrera, interview with David Pion-Berlin, June 26, 2002, Washington, DC.

83. "Ecuador Coup Shifts Control to No. 2 Man," *New York Times*, January 23, 2000, http://web.lexis-nexis.com/universe/.

84. "I Am a President Overthrown by a Military Coup," EFE News Service, January 25, 2000, http://web.lexis-nexis.com/universe/.

85. OAS, "Acta de la Sesión Extraordinaria Celebrada," January 26, 2000, OEA/Ser.G/CP/ACTA 1221/00.

86. Peñaherrera, interview, June 26, 2002.

87. President Abdalá Bucarám's presidency (August 1996–February 1997) was plagued from the start by problems stemming from corruption, economic incompetence, repression, and his own erratic personality. His congressional foes were biting at the bit to remove him. But rather than proceed via the lengthy process of impeachment—requiring that legislators gather sufficient evidence of criminal wrongdoing—they took the constitutionally questionable but expedient move of removing the president on grounds of "mental incompetence." A defiant Bucarám barricaded himself in his office, but the military announced it would no longer recognize him as president, precipitating his resignation shortly thereafter. The military then demanded that Congress work out constitutional succession rules, while the vice president stood in as interim chief of state. See Fitch (1998, 90–91, 152).

Chapter 5: Human Rights and the Chilean Courts

1. Many Chileans had sought exile in Europe and were developing fruitful contacts with European parliamentarians. The Chilean presence helped to keep their patria on the European agenda.

2. Orlando Letelier was the former Chilean ambassador to the United States during the Salvador Allende administration. He was later exiled and murdered in Washington, DC, by agents of the Pinochet regime, on September 21, 1976.

3. "Apelación sentencia definitiva contra Contreras Sepúlveda, Manuel y otros" (1995).

4. Numerous primary and secondary references were consulted regarding the Pinochet case. Among the secondary sources used were Audiencia Nacional (1999); Francisco Coloane (2000); García Arán and López Garrido (2000); Lagos Erazo (1999); Rojas Aravena and Stefoni Espinoza (2001); Wilson (1999); Woodhouse (2000).

5. Like any regime, the human rights one represents a collection of "principles, norms, rules and decision-making procedures around which actors' expectations converge in a given area of IR" (Krasner 1983, 10). The question is whether those expectations translate into collective behavior shaped by the regime itself, or whether those expectations translate only into shared understandings. Is this a regime defined by results or merely by what it stands for? Scholars generally agree that the human rights regime, if there is one, is strong in terms of defining, codifying, and advocating standards of conduct, disseminating information, monitoring behavior, and creating obligations. It is weaker when it comes to concentrating power, coordinating action, and enforcing decisions. David Forsythe (2000, 75) argues this human rights order reveals a "proliferation of weak implementation agencies and a further lack of coordination."

6. For more detailed analyses of the transition, see Drake Jaksic (1991); Loveman (1991); Constable and Valenzuela (1991); Andrade Geywitz (1991).

7. Appellate court judge Carlos Cerda was singled out for punishment for his courageous efforts to keep alive judicial investigations into the disappeared. Interview with David Pion-Berlin, July 1995, Santiago, Chile.

8. República de Chile, Junta de Gobierno (1978).

9. República de Chile (1997, art. 413, 184).

10. Following on the heels of the Senate's impeachment of one Supreme Court justice for having delayed an appeal decision, the new president of the court, Marcos Aburto, stated in 1993 that the amnesty should not thwart investigations. This was the first time a high court official had made such a statement. See Lisa Hilbink (1999, 401).

11. "Chile pide comprensión a España por la amnistía a los asesinos del caso Soria," El País, June 6, 1996, http://web.lexis-nexis.com/universe/; "Slain Diplomat's Daughter Will Seek ICJ Action on Father's Case," Agence France Presse-English, August 25, 1996.

12. "Un Juez Español admite una denuncia por genocidio contra Pinochet," El País, July 31, 1996, http://web.lexis-nexis.com/universe/.

13. These motivations for pursuing the case were corroborated by Joan Garcés in a talk held at California Polytechnic State University, Pomona, and in private conversations with David Pion-Berlin, January 30, 2002, Pomona, CA. Garcés added that he was further motivated to act by changes in the political climate, including the end of the Cold War.

14. Pey, also a Spaniard, had fled his country during the civil war that brought Francisco Franco to power and went to Chile where he became a newspaperman. The paper he owned was confiscated by the military after the coup, and he was placed on a death list and forced to flee to Venezuela. Victor Pey, interview with David Pion-Berlin, October 17, 2001, Santiago, Chile.

15. See articles 101 and 270 of the Spanish Law of Criminal Procedure, cited in Richard Wilson (1999, 934).

16. This occurred in the Netherlands, in November 2000. See Kamminga (2001, app., 971).

17. The Geneva Conventions on War were ratified by Spain on September 5, 1952. The Convention on the Prevention and Punishment of the Crime of Genocide, of December 9, 1948, was signed by Spain on February 8, 1969, and codified into Spanish Criminal Code (article 137) in 1971. Thus, this law was on the Spanish books prior to the actual commission of human rights crimes in Chile.

18. If the defendant cannot be produced by the oral phase of the proceedings, the trial must be suspended. Spanish Penal Code, article 841, cited in Rothenberg (2002, 928).

19. This idea was conveyed to David Pion-Berlin in an interview with Viviana Diaz, head of the Association for Chilean Families of the Disappeared, October 8, 2001, Santiago, Chile.

20. Ibid.

21. The interaction between these groups closely resembles what Margaret Keck and Kathryn Sikkink (1998, 1–38) describe as a transnational advocacy network, or TAN.

22. Diaz, interview, October 8, 2001; Joan Garcés, interview with David Pion-Berlin, January 29, 2002, Pomona, CA.

23. Spanish criminal trial law explicitly says you cannot bring to trial a case in Spain when a trial is already underway in another country where the crime was committed.

24. Diaz, interview, October 8, 2001.

25. So offended was the mainstream Chilean mass media that it refused to cover the trial, leaving it to the small left-wing weekly Punto Final to carry the news. Pey, interview, October 17, 2001.

26. Ibid. Pey knew Aylwin and went to his home before his departure to Europe to urge him to testify. Aylwin declined the request. Also see "Patricio Aylwin rechaza declarar sobre los Españoles desaparecidos en Chile," El País, May 26, 1997, http://web.lexis-nexis.com/universe/.

27. "Estados Unidos ayudará a España en el caso contra la dictadura del general Pinochet," *El País*, June 25, 1997, http://web.lexis-nexis.com/universe/.

28. "El General Chileno Torres Reconoce que se Entrevistó con el Magistrado," *El País Internacional*, 1997, http://web.lexis-nexis.com/universe/.

29. Supreme Court judge Alberto Chaigneau had no doubt that Marín's lawsuit was precipitated by the Spanish court actions and the foreign minister's reaction to them. Interview with David Pion-Berlin, October 17, 2001, Santiago, Chile.

30. Audiencia Nacional (1999).

31. On a vote of three to two, the lord judges said he should not be entitled to immunity that is normally conferred on leaders whose actions were taken in the exercise of official functions because the crimes Pinochet was accused of could never be construed as official acts of government. See *Regina v. Bartle and Commissioner of Police for the Metropolis and Others Ex Parte Pinochet*, November 25, 1998, http://www.parliament.the-stationery-office.co.uk/pa/ld199899/ldjudgmt/ jd990324/pino1.htm.

32. *Regina v. Bartle, Regina v. Evans*, March 24, 1999, http://www.parliament.the-stationery-office.co.uk/pa/ld199899/ldjudgmt/jd990324/pino1.htm.

33. "Britain Decides to Let the Pinochet Extradition Proceed," *New York Times*, April 16, 1999, http://web.lexis-nexis.com/universe/.

34. Ultimately, Pinochet's lawyers would prevail on grounds that he was too frail to survive the ordeal of a lengthy trial. Text of Jack Straw's March 2, 2000, decision not to extradite Senator Pinochet found at La Tercera Web site, "Caso Pinochet," http://www.tercera.cl/casos/pinochet2/documentos/straw.html/.

35. Another forty-six of these prisoners had been murdered and their bodies recovered. See "Caravana de la Muerte procesada por secuestro," *La Tercera* (Santiago), June 9, 1999, CHIP News Service, http://www.chipnews.cl; "Judge Guzmán Clarifies Caravan of Death Ruling," *Santiago Times*, June 11, 1999, CHIP News Service, http://www.chipnews.cl. For a thorough investigation into these occurrences, see Patricio Verdugo (2001).

36. Should the body be found eventually, and it be established that the time of death fell within the amnesty period, then the accused could be set free. If the body were to be found and the execution had occurred after the amnesty period had expired, then the accused could be prosecuted, convicted, and sentenced based on penalties set for homicide. And if the remains were never found, then the accused could be found guilty of aggravated kidnapping and sentenced on that basis. Juan Guzmán, interview with David Pion-Berlin, October 11, 2001, Santiago, Chile. Guzmán's interpretation of the law was not entirely new. Some four years earlier, a Supreme Court judge had rejected an appeal by members of Chile's Carabinero force who had been implicated in the disappearance of two Mapuche youth. The judge ruled that the unsolved disappearance should be treated as an aggravated kidnapping. Supreme Court Judge José Luis Pérez, interview with David Pion-Berlin, October 9, 2001, Santiago, Chile. But Guzmán's decision marked the first time such a legal interpretation had been rendered with respect to the amnesty law and would mark a decisive stage in the progressive weakening of that decree.

37. The criminal chamber comprised Judges Luis Correa Bulo, Enrique Cury, José Luis Pérez, Alberto Chaigneau, and Guillermo Navas. Their ruling ratified the decision made by the appellate court in rejecting writs of habeas corpus presented by the five retired army officers in the Caravan of Death case. See "Court Upholds Caravan of Death Indictments," *Santiago Times*, July 21, 1999, CHIP News Service, http://www.chipnews.cl; "Suprema limitó amnistía de 1978," *La Tercera* (Santiago) July 21, 1999, http://www.tercera.cl.

38. Ibid.

39. "Supreme Court Ruling Pressures Military," *Santiago Times*, July 22, 1999, CHIP News Service, http://www.chipnews.cl.

40. "Supreme Court Has Opened Doorway to Democracy," *Santiago Times*, July 28, 1999, CHIP News Service, http://www.chipnews.cl.

41. " Suprema pondrá a prueba nueva doctrina," *La Tercera* (Santiago), July 22, 1999, http://www.tercera.cl.

42. Not surprisingly, soon after the Supreme Court ruling, Judge Guzmán prepared a list of questions to be delivered to Pinochet in London.

43. "Pinochet Immunity Verdict Made Official," *Santiago Times*, June 6, 2000, CHIP News Service, http://www.chipnews.cl; "Pinochet quedó sin inmunidad," *La Tercera* (Santiago), May 23, 2000, http://www.tercera.cl; *La Tercera en Internet*, El Caso Pinochet Web site, "Texto completo del fallo de la corte de Apelaciones que desafuera a Pinochet," http://www.tercera.cl.

44. General Stark also personally conveyed to Pinochet what had occurred. Pinochet not only failed to take any disciplinary actions but actually promoted the general and others involved in the atrocities, while punishing those who had come forward.

45. "Chile's Top Court Strips Pinochet of Immunity from Trial," *London Times*, August 9, 2000, http://web.lexis-nexis.com/universe/.

46. "Human Rights Roundtable Reaches Accord," *Santiago Times*, June 13, 2000, CHIP News Service, http://www.chipnews.cl.

47. "Pinochet Loses Immunity, but a Trial Is Unlikely," *Los Angeles Times*, August 9, 2000, http://web.lexis-nexis.com/universe/.

48. "Chile Revokes Pinochet's Immunity," *Washington Post*, August 9, 2000, http://web.lexis-nexis.com/universe/.

49. These observations taken from interviews conducted by David Pion-Berlin in 2001 in Santiago, Chile, with the following judges: appellate court—Juan Guzmán, October 11, Sergio Muñoz, October 16, Carlos Cerda, October 17; Supreme Court—José Luis Pérez, October 9, Milton Juica, October 10, Alberto Chaigneau, October 17.

50. Sources: "Ex-Chilean Spy Chief Sentenced to 15 Years in Disappearance," Deutsche Presse-Agentur, April 15, 2003, http://web.lexis-nexis.com/universe/; "Former Chief of Secret Police Is Indicted by Judge in Chile, *New York Times*, May 16, 2003, http://web.lexis-nexis.com/universe/.

51. For interviews, see note 49.

52. Sergio Muñoz, appellate court judge, interview with David Pion-Berlin, October 16, 2001, Santiago, Chile.

53. Guzmán, interview, October 11, 2001.

54. Juan Guzmán made this point. Ibid.

55. See República de Chile (1997, 126–27). The Supreme Court judges' reliance on this basis of law can be found in their *desafuero* decision, in "Desafuero del Senador Augusto Pinochet Ugarte" (2000, 169–86).

56. It is not surprising to see the judges reject the notion that the British verdicts had a legal impact upon them. In Chile there is no common law, meaning judgments do not create obligatory precedents. Each verdict rendered is premised solely on an interpretation of the facts in hand and does not derive from prior decisions or have a necessary bearing on future ones. Certainly, if that is true within Chilean jurisprudence, than it would be more so when assessing the impact of verdicts from abroad. Chaigneau, interview, October 17, 2001.

57. Only Judge José Benquis mentioned the Geneva accords regarding the protection of prisoners in a time of war.

58. By the time Chile turned democratic in 1990, it had already ratified the Geneva War Conventions; The Convention on the Prevention and Punishment of the Crime of Genocide; the International Covenant on Civil and Political Rights; and the Convention against Torture, and other Cruel, Inhuman or Degrading Treatment or Punishment. Chile had signed the Convention on Civil and Political Rights on February 10, 1972, and it became decree law on November 30, 1976. Yet the Supreme Court dismissed the treaty, saying it was inapplicable to crimes committed during the amnesty period, since it was not officially published in the nation's registry of laws (Diario Oficial) until April 29, 1989.

59. Hector Salazar, human rights attorney, interview with David Pion-Berlin, October 12, 2001, Santiago, Chile; Hugo Gutiérrez, human rights attorney, interview with David Pion-Berlin, October 8, 2001, Santiago, Chile; Javier Couso, professor of law, interview with David Pion-Berlin, October 11, 2001, Santiago, Chile.

60. Ironically, it was the Chilean center-left Concertación government of Eduardo Frei and two successive socialist foreign ministers in particular that would come to the aging general's defense. Miguel Insulza and then Juan Gabriel Valdés, both of whom had been members of Allende's Unidad Popular coalition and had suffered persecution at the hands of the dictatorship, argued they were not defending the person so much as the principle of Chilean sovereignty. "El polémico documento del gobierno ante los lores," http://www.tercera.cl/casos/pinochet2defensa_gobierno/index_defensa.html.

61. Ibid.

62. In fact, such a suggestion was, in the Chilean view, inconsistent with international covenants on crimes against humanity that stipulated the accused should first be brought to trial in courts within the territory where the criminal acts were committed. Thus, state sovereignty was absolute; it could not be diminished by the gravity of the crime. See representations made by the Chilean government before the foreign affairs secretary of Great Britain, reprinted in Lagos Erazo (1999, 242–44).

63. Ibid., 266.

64. "President Frei Addresses Nation: Chilean Courts Must Judge Pinochet," British Broadcasting Corporation, March 4, 2000, http://web.lexis-nexis.com/universe/.

65. A Socialist party deputy threatened appellate judges with constitutional charges against them should they fail to deimmunize Pinochet. He was swiftly disciplined by his party. Editorial, La Tercera en internet, April 7, 2000, http://www.tercera.cl.

66. Guzmán, interview, October 11, 2001.

67. Chaigneau, interview, October 17, 2001.

68. Juica, interview, October 10, 2001.

69. "Reformas a la Corte Suprema," La Tercera (Santiago), September 5, 1997, http://www.tercera.cl.

70. On July 2 of that year, Chilean UDI deputy Carlos Bombal launched impeachment proceedings against the then president of the Supreme Court. Bombal alleged that Jordan had protected drug traffickers by manipulating criminal proceedings and had inexplicably paroled a convicted drug dealer, Luis Correa Ramirez, in 1991, after Ramirez had served only one quarter of his sentence. "PS and PPD Proceed with Separate Charges," El Mercurio (Santiago), July 7, 1997, CHIP News Service, http://www.chipnews.cl.

71. "Revolución en la Corte Suprema," La Tercera (Santiago), January 11, 1998, http://www.tercera.cl.

72. Among the skeptics was Francisco Cumplido, Aylwin's justice minister who doubted great changes were in store because, as he said, "these same judges that today arrive at the Supreme Court amnestied many human rights crimes when they were in the Court of Appeals." See "Revolución en la Corte Suprema," La Tercera (Santiago), January 11, 1998, 6.

73. Some of the new arrivals were steadfast in their convictions about defending human rights. But they were a minority of the fourteen justices who would vote in favor of the desafuero. Others who had their doubts as to the wisdom of going after Pinochet had to be won over. The effort to do so was described to me by Judge Alberto Chaigneau as a "very, very hard internal struggle." Chaigneau, interview, October 17, 2001. We can only speculate on the politics of that struggle and specifically what arguments ultimately turned the tide. Did the external events factor in? If they did, by helping to tip the balance, it is logical to presume that their greatest effect would be on the majority of justices who stood somewhere in the middle, neither decidedly in favor of human rights nor against. It seems sensible that they were influenced by the events in Spain and Great Britain, and the international attention devoted to them.

74. "Human Rights Roundtable Reaches Accord," *Santiago Times*, June 13, 2000, CHIP News Service, http://www.chipnews.cl.

75. Eventually, it would agree to a formula that would allow officers to disclose the location of the victims confidentially. While this accord would come under sharp attack and would not in the end produce accurate information on the disappeared, the mere fact that the dialogue and agreement occurred meant that a new page had been turned.

76. Appellate court judge Carlos Cerda, interview, October 17, 2001, Santiago, Chile.

77. Editorial, *La Tercera* (Santiago), April 27, 2000, http://web.lexis-nexis.com/universe/.

78. "Pinochet y la mesa de diálogo," *La Tercera* (Santiago), March 8, 2000, http://web.lexis -nexis.com/universe/.

79. "Pinochet es culpable," LASNET archive, December 3, 1998, http://lanic.utexas .edu/la/region/news/arc/lasnet/1998/0277.html.

80. Centro de Estudios de la Realidad Contemporánea (1999). The poll was taken March 31–April 11, 1999.

81. Ibid. (2000). Polls taken July 21–August 4, and September 25–October 7, 2000.

82. In fact, Pinochet was set to inspect two British frigates with the intention of facilitating their purchase when he was unexpectedly arrested in London (Phythian 2000, 142).

83. "Diplomacy with Spain over Pinochet Case Ruled Out by Chilean Minister," Agence France Presse-English, September 24, 1999, http://web.lexis-nexis.com/universe/.

84. Bartle ruled that the case fulfilled the requirements set forth in the 1990 European Convention on Extradition. "Pinochet Loses Latest Round in Extradition Fight," *London Times*, October 9, 1999, http://web.lexis-nexis.com/universe.

85. "Jack Straw's Full Commons Speech," *Guardian Unlimited*, January 12, 2000, http://web .lexis-nexis.com/universe/.

86. EFE News Service, 2 March, 2000, http://web.lexis-nexis.com/universe/.

87. "Supreme Court Rules Pinochet Unfit for Trial," *El Mostrador*, July 2, 2002, CHIP News Service, http://www.chipnews.cl.

88. But it is not impossible. As of the completion of this book, judicial investigations continue into other human rights crimes allegedly involving Pinochet, including Operation Condor and the murder of former army commander-in-chief General Carlos Prats. See "Chile's Court Strips Pinochet of Immunity," *Santiago Times*, December 3, 2004, http://www.tcgnews .com/santiagotimes.

89. This view expressed by Hector Salazar, a leading human rights attorney in Chile. Interview, October 12, 2001.

Chapter 6: Regional Security in Central America

1. See the special issue of *NACLA Report on the Americas* (2001) devoted to the impact of September 11 on U.S. policy toward Latin America.

2. As noted by Holden: "Arms and training (sent to Central America during the 1950–1990 period) not only kept insurgents and radical reformers from taking power; they also preempted the aid from other powers that might threaten U.S. hegemony. That arms and training also bolstered militarism and dictatorship was assumed to be an unpleasant, but acceptable, consequence" (1993, 297). For the detrimental effects of U.S. influence on the development of surveillance and intelligence systems in Central America, see Holden (1999).

3. With U.S. aid levels in 1997 at just one-third their 1990 level, Latin America experienced the most dramatic reductions of any world region. See Lisa Haugaard (1997, 29).

4. The CIVS included states contributing to the Contadora Process, the secretaries-general of the United Nations and Organization of American States, and the foreign ministers of the CA-4 states and Costa Rica.

5. This decision was not made without controversy. Non–Central American members of the

CIVS contended that they were being denied access; the United States wanted to remove from the process Contadora countries sympathetic to the Sandinistas; and the Central American presidents held a general desire to "central Americanize" the peace process (Gomáriz 1988, 94–99; Moreno 1994, 99–101).

6. This call would be repeated in article 3a of the foundational document of the Sistema de Integración Centroamericana (Tegucigalpa Protocol 1991). On the Tegucigalpa Protocol, see note 15.

7. Nonetheless, it should also be noted that the militaries did not lose the conflicts. This especially distinguishes the El Salvadoran and Guatemalan transitions from most of the South American transitions, where the armed forces tended to withdraw as failures (Solís Rivera and Rojas Aravena 1994, 11).

8. The April 1991 Managua meeting illustrated the intransigence of El Salvador and Guatemala. At this meeting, Costa Rica, Honduras, and Nicaragua turned in sealed listings of armament inventories, to be opened when all members' listings were received. El Salvador and Guatemala balked at the motion, again pointing to their domestic disturbances (Eguizábal 1994, 94).

9. General Benjamín Francisco Godoy, General Director for Plans and Operations, National Defense Staff, Army of Guatemala, interview with Craig Arceneaux, July 9, 2002, Washington, DC. Real progress was made only in the area of arms trafficking. At the December 1992 Panama summit, the presidents signed the "Preliminary Mechanism of Assistance, Cooperation, and Coordination for the Elimination of the Illegal Trafficking of Arms in Central America," a document drafted by the CSC.

10. "Central America Studies New Security Mechanism," Xinhua News Agency, August 9, 1995, http://web.lexis-nexis.com/universe/.

11. "Costa Rica Proposes New Functions for Security Commission," Xinhua News Agency, July 28, 1993, http://web.lexis-nexis.com/universe/; "Falta de consenso amenaza acuerdo regional sobre seguridad," La Nación Digital (San José, Costa Rica), December 10, 1995, http://www.nacion.com/CentroAmerica/Archivo/1995/diciembre/10/cablehon.html#1.

12. Godoy, interview, July 9, 2002.

13. "Pugna por reducción de ejércitos del istmo," La Nación Digital (San José, Costa Rica), December 14, 1995, http://www.nacion.co.cr/ln_ee/1995/diciembre/14/pagina06.html); "Istmo choca por reducción de ejércitos," La Nación Digital (San José, Costa Rica), December 16, 1995, http://www.nacion.co.cr/ln_ee/1995/diciembre/16/pagina04.html.

14. While Costa Rica signed the end document, it did so with reservations. The Commission of Legal Affairs in the Costa Rican Congress reviewed the Framework Treaty on Democratic Security in February 1998, and it voted unanimously to reject ratification due to "the lack of distinction between the roles of the military and civilian security forces" and disagreement with articles that "open some room to the intervention of armed forces in civilian security topics." Ana Matilde Rivera, Political Adviser to the Vice Minister of Foreign Affairs, Costa Rica, personal correspondence with Craig Arceneaux, July 30, 2002.

15. The Tegucigalpa Protocol, signed at the December 1991 Presidential Summit in Tegucigalpa, created SICA to replace the Organization of Central American States. SICA became functional February 1, 1993.

16. Ibid.

17. "Army Alliance Threatens Democracy, Analysts Say," Inter Press News Service Agency, December 2, 1997, http://web.lexis-nexis.com/universe/; "Atiéndame, Señor Presidente," La Nación Digital (San José, Costa Rica), December 5, 1997, http://www.nacion. co.cr/ln_ee/1997/diciembre/05/opinion3.html; "Central American Armies Form New Military Alliance," EcoCentral: Central American Economy and Sustainable Development 2 (December 4, 1997), from the Latin American Database, http://www.ladb.unm.edu/ecocentral; "Poder Civil y Fuerzas Armadas

en CentroAmérica," *Al Día* no. 15 (1998), Instituto Centroaméricana de Estudios Políticos, http://www.quik.guate.com/incep/aldia15.htm.

18. "Jefes militares también estuvieron en Managua," *El Universal* (Caracas), September 4, 1997, http://www.eud.com/.

19. Godoy, interview, July 9, 2002. Note also that Honduras and Nicaragua were represented by their army commanders in chief in the final meetings leading to the creation of CFAC.

20. Each military officer interviewed for this research emphasized this point.

21. Many of these activities were listed on the now defunct CFAC Web site. Also see: "Unidad centroamericana de rescate humanitario," *El Nuevo Diaro* (Managua), May 25, 2000, http://www.elnuevodiario.com.ni; "Centroamérica-ejércitos acuerdan acciones contra vuelos ilícitos y el narcotráfico," EFE News Service, June 23, 2000, http://web.lexis-nexis.com/universe/.

22. Brigadier General Manuel Salvatierra, Air Force of Nicaragua, Defense, Military, Naval and Air Attaché to the United States, interview with Craig Arceneaux, July 12, 2002, Washington, DC.

23. Also see Bull (1994) and "¿Integración o desintegración centroamericana?" (2000), also available at http://www.incep.org/reporte1.html.

24. Salvatierra, interview, July 12, 2002. Effort to establish relations, two years after its creation, is noted in "Fuerzas Armadas de la región reafirman subordinación al poder civil," *La Prensa* (Tegucigalpa), November 26, 1999, http://www.laprensahn.com/caarc/9911/c26005.htm.

25. Godoy, interview, July 9, 2002.

26. Salvatierra, interview, July 12, 2002.

27. Anonymous, interview with Craig Arceneaux.

28. "Guatemala: Militares viajan a Honduras para hacer guerra al dengue," Deutsche Presse-Agentur, July 7, 2002, http://web.lexis-nexis.com/universe/.

29. Rivera, personal correspondence, July 30, 2002.

30. See "Central American Forum on Security: Final Report," July 30–31, 2003 (Guatemala City: Canadian Foundation for the Americas, 2003), http://www.focal.ca/ images/pdf/security_report_e.pdf. Also see Francine Jácome, "El Tratado Marco de Seguridad Democrática en Centroamérica: Revisión y reforma desde la sociedad civil" (Ottawa: International Development Research Centre, 2004, http://web.idrc.ca/uploads/user-/10867912571Conclusiones_ y _ recomendaciones.doc.

31. Colonel Joaquín Galvez, Army of El Salvador, Ministry of Defense Attaché to Organization of American States, interview with Craig Arceneaux, July 12, 2002, Washington, DC.

32. Each Central American military officer interviewed for our project expressed this view.

33. Carlos Cordero, Subdirector for Multilateral Policy, Ministry of Foreign Affairs, Costa Rica, personal correspondence with Craig Arceneaux, August 16, 2002.

34. The Defense Ministerials of the Americas first met in Williamsburg, VA, in 1995, specifically for the purpose of promoting cooperative security measures. It has met since in Argentina (1996), Colombia (1998), Brazil (2000), Chile (2002), and Ecuador (2004).

35. Godoy, interview, July 9, 2002.

36. German Bravo, Ministry of Foreign Affairs, Panama, Minister-Counselor under the Ambassador to the United States (2000–2001), correspondence with Craig Arceneaux, August 7, 2002.

37. "Nicaragua-Honduras Tension Rises Again over Troops on Offshore Cay," *Latin American Regional Reports: Caribbean and Central America* (February 22, 2000): 1; "Tegucigalpa and Managua Agree on Confidence Building," *Latin American Regional Reports: Caribbean and Central America* (March 28, 2000): 2.

38. Framework Treaty on Democratic Security, articles 40–41, http://www.state.gov/t/ac/csbm/rd/4368.htm.

39. "Misión de verificación contribuirá a crear la confianza necesaria entre Honduras y Nicaragua," La Prensa (Tegucigalpa), July 20, 2001, http://www.laprensahn.com/natarc/0107/n20005.htm.

40. "Africa and Latin America: Honduras, Nicaragua Seek Way Back from the Brink," Financial Times, April 4, 2001, http://web.lexis-nexis.com/universe/.

41. "Reunión en alta mar para bajar tensiones," El Nuevo Diario (Managua), May 26, 2000, http://www.elnuevodiario.com.ni; "Honduras-Nicaragua: Observadores de OEA podrían verificar acuerdos exclusión militar," EFE News Service, January 16, 2000, http://web.lexis-nexis.com/universe/. Colonel Alex Crowther, Desk Officer for Central America, Joint Chiefs of Staff, met with the army commanders from each country, and they ensured him that they had met and agreed to view the dispute as a political problem, one for them to stay out of. Interview with Craig Arceneaux, July 3, 2002, Washington, DC. General Benjamín Francisco Godoy, while directing Guatemalan troops in CFAC and noting growing interactions among Nicaraguan and Honduran soldiers, stated, "I think in that moment they realized that it was a political problem at the border." Interview, July 9, 2002.

42. Ibid.

43. Major John Ruedisueli, U.S. Southern Command, Miami, FL, personal correspondence with Craig Arceneaux, January 24, 2003.

44. "Prepared Statement of General James T. Hill, United States Army Commander, United States Southern Command before the Senate Armed Services Committee," Federal News Service, March 14, 2003, http://web.lexis-nexis.com/universe/.

45. "Militares de la región estudian estrategias contra el narcotráfico," La Prensa Digital (Managua), May 29, 2003, http://www-ni.laprensa.com.ni; "Ejércitos centroamericanos afinan estrategias antiterrorismo," Inforpress Centroamericana, 1514, June 6, 2003, http://www.inforpressca.com/inforpress/.

46. The path-dependent approach covers a wide range of social, technological, and biological phenomena outside the traditional realm of political science. For discussions of the approach that recognizes contributions from and applications in economics, sociology, and biology, see Krasner (1988) and Pierson (2000b). Other significant works on the approach include North (1990); Collier and Collier (1991); Stienmo, Thelen, and Longstreth (1992); and Thelen and Steinmo (1999).

47. "Improvements in civilian control over the military" refers to all those measures leading to the point of civilian supremacy. Agüero (1995, 19) defines civilian supremacy as "the ability of a civilian, democratically elected government to conduct general policy without interference from the military, to define the goals and general organization of national defense, to formulate and conduct defense policy, and to monitor the implementation of military policy."

48. Crowther, interview, July 3, 2002. A discussion of U.S. mechanisms to promote civilian supremacy through military relations can be found in Addicott and Roberts (2001). For the importance of a civilian minister of defense, see Fishel (2000).

49. Godoy, interview, July 9, 2002. The second sentiment was expressed under the condition of anonymity.

50. "Ministros de Defensa combatirán terrorismo en América Central," Associated Press, December 14, 2002, http://web.lexis-nexis.com/universe/; in La Prensa Digital (Managua), http://www-ni.laprensa.com.ni, see the following articles: "Militares reactivarán órganos de inteligencia," September 21, 2001; "Militares de la región estudian estrategias contra el narcotráfico," May 29, 2003; "Militares informarán de amenazas a la región," April 30, 2004. Also see "Ejércitos centroamericanos afinan estrategias antiterrorismo," Inforpress Centroamericana, June 6, 2003, http://www.inforpressca.com/inforpress/.

51. Carlos Garcia, Ambassador Alternate and Minister Counselor, Permanent Mission of El

Salvador to the United Nations, interview with Craig Arceneaux, March 15, 2001, New York, NY.

52. We thank David Mares for the view that educational prerequisites can be used by militaries to hinder civilian oversight.

53. Crowther, interview, July 3, 2002.

Chapter 7: Environmental Degradation, Drug Trafficking, and Immigration

1. The 1988 assassination of Chico Mendes, leader of the rubber tappers, heightened international concern even more.

2. Activist organizations and individuals were able to concentrate attention on Brazil, attracting increased activity on the part of European and international NGOs. Environmental groups from the United States and Europe established branch offices in Brazil, while helping to organize a network of Brazilian-based advocacy groups. International financing for many of these groups increased and allowed them to operate more effectively.

3. "Ecology Movement Crumbling Five Years after Mendes Murder," Associated Press, February 28, 1994, http://web.lexis-nexis.com/universe/.

4. "Governments Failing to Act on Rio Pact, Activists Say," Toronto Star, June 2, 1993, http://web.lexis-nexis.com/universe/. As late as 2002, Brazil's environmental minister calculated that the developed countries had followed through on less than 1 percent of the commitments made to improve the environment. "Ministers Urge Compliance with Rio Summit Promises," January 1, 2002, EFE News Service, http://web.lexis-nexis.com/universe/.

5. "Burning of Amazon Picks Up Pace, with Vast Areas Lost," New York Times, September 12, 1996, http://web.lexis-nexis.com/universe/.

6. "Amazon Forest Still Burning Despite Good Intentions," New York Times, August 23, 2002, http://web.lexis-nexis.com/universe/.

7. "Brazil's Government Announces Measures to Slow Amazon Deforestation," Associated Press, July 2, 2003, http://web.lexis-nexis.com/universe/; "Amazon Deforestation Rate Up 40% in Brazil," Los Angeles Times, June 27, 2003, A15.

8. The Bracero program was administered under the War Manpower Commission until 1948, when it was handed over to the Department of Labor.

9. "The Rising Latino Tide," The American Prospect 13 (November 18, 2002): 22–25.

10. The dramatic decline in U.S. media coverage of immigration issues and Mexican relations from 2001 to 2002 illustrates how September 11 intercepted immigration's movement toward high politics. A search of U.S. newspapers from "northeastern regional sources" on the Lexus-Nexus database using the words "Fox," "immigration," and "Mexico" produced 75 hits for the year 2000, 192 for 2001, and 74 for 2002. On the sudden drop-off in U.S. Mexican relations, see Castañeda (2003).

11. "Signs of Movement on Migrants: A Guest-Worker Plan and Other Reforms on Hold Since 9/11 Are Gaining Support Again—But the President Appears Less Interested This Time," Los Angeles Times, September 6, 2003, A1.

12. "Immigration Reform Is off Front Burner: A Bipartisan Senate Panel Says the Bush Administration Is Unwilling to Promote a Guest-Worker Program in an Election Year," Los Angeles Times, March 24, 2004, A14; "Bush's Cynical Immigration Gambit," Business Week, February 9, 2004, 20.

13. If this is an erosion of Colombia's sovereignty, Eduardo Pizano, general secretary to the Colombian president, has argued that his nation's sovereignty was already at risk by virtue of the rebels' control over large swaths of territory. See Pizano (2001).

14. Retired general and former drug czar Barry McCaffrey and former undersecretary of state Tom Pickering were members of a State Department team that worked on Plan Colombia.

15. In 1989, Secretary of State James Baker cited a national survey saying that illicit drug use was the number one problem according to half the respondents. See Baker (1989).

16. The theory that guerrillas were in league with narcos had been bantered about well before the late 1990s but was not officially accepted by U.S. government officials until 1999–2000. See Tickner (2003).

17. As other nations get sucked in, the problem becomes regional, not national, thus making it difficult for the United States to turn its back entirely. Luz Nagle says, "Given the linkage between narcotrafficking and guerrilla insurgency in much of South America, and the ability of narco-guerrillas and drug cartels to utilize long-established pipelines for the shipment of drugs and weapons, it is evident that the U.S. cannot but play an ever increasing role in national security, counternarcotics, and regional development programs in the hemisphere" (2002, 39). Here, Nagle probably overstates the urgency for the United States.

18. The guerrillas and narcos have been known to have ties to Islamic fundamentalist groups like Hezbollah, receiving training from them in exchange for providing passports and other means of entry to the United States (Nagle 2002, 38–39).

19. President George W. Bush, *The National Security Strategy of the United States of America*, September 2002, White House.

20. "Venezuela Aids FARC Rebels," United Press International, September 10, 2003, http://web.lexis-nexis.com/universe/.

21. "Ecuadorian Army Commander Admits Weapons Crossing Border into Colombia," *World News Connection*, September 13, 2003, http://web.lexis-nexis.com/universe/. At the same time, refugees from the Colombian war also migrate across the borders hoping to find safe refuge. Some thirty thousand Colombians entered Ecuador and were living in refugee camp–like conditions (Millett 2002, 16).

22. "Brazil Employs Tools of Spying to Guard Itself," *New York Times*, July 27, 2002, http://web.lexis-nexis.com/universe/; "Military Flexes Muscles in Amazon," *New York Times*, May 29, 2002, http://web.lexis-nexis.com/universe/.

23. "Brazil, Colombia Look for Harmony," United Press International, February 23, 2004, http://web.lexis-nexis.com/universe/.

24. "Anti-Farc Deal Signed with Colmbia and Peru," *Latinnews Daily*, February 12, 2004, http://web.lexis-nexis.com/universe/.

Chapter 8: Issues, Political Science, and Policy Making

1. In the case of democratic deepening, we note a divergence from the low politics patterns shown in table 8.1 Here, the principal foreign actors are regional states that have the capacity to intervene but are poorly motivated to do so. Some NGOs from abroad lend their services to countries that are trying to improve the quality of their democratic institutions and processes (outside the electoral arena). They are few in number, resource poor, and have had a limited impact.

2. The United States has rejected transnational justice, except where it has had an obvious security stake. Thus, Washington has been enormously reluctant to support efforts by either foreign courts or the domestic criminal courts to go after human rights violators from the Western Hemisphere but has offered great support to The Hague war crimes tribunal, which placed Serbian and Croatian defendants on trial. The difference is that Serbia and Croatia are part of Europe, had posed a potential threat to the security of neighboring European states, and had triggered the intervention of NATO forces.

3. It is telling that the second image reversed approach has focused so intently and been at its most persuasive when applied to economic issues, which gives credence to the view that it may be issue-specific.

Works Cited

Acevedo, Domingo E., and Claudio Grossman. 1996. The Organization of American States and the Protection of Democracy. In *Beyond Sovereignty: Collectively Defending Democracy in the Americas*, ed. Tom Farer, 132–49. Baltimore: Johns Hopkins University Press.

Addicott, Jeffrey F., and Guy B. Roberts. 2001. Building Democracies with Southern Command's Legal Engagement Strategy. *Parameters* 31 (1): 72–85.

Agarwal, Jamuna P. 1980. Determinants of Foreign Direct Investment: A Survey. *Weltwirtschaftliches Archive* 116: 739–73.

Agüero, Felipe. 1995. *Soldiers, Civilians, and Democracy: Post-Franco Spain in Comparative Perspective.* Baltimore: Johns Hopkins University Press.

Aguilera Peralta, Gabriel. 1994. Las políticas de defensa en Guatemala. In *De la guerra a la integración: la transición y la seguridad en Centroamérica*, ed. Luis Guillermo Solís Rivera and Francisco Rojas, 98–127. San José, Costa Rica: Fundación Arias/ FLACSO-Chile.

Alba, Francisco. 1989. The Mexican Demographic Situation. In *Mexican and Central American Population and U.S. Immigration Policy*, ed. Frank D. Bean, Jurgen Schmandt, and Sidney Weintraub, 5–32. Austin: Center for Mexican American Studies.

Ames, Barry. *Political Survival: Politicians and Public Policy in Latin America.* Berkeley: University of California Press, 1987.

Amman, Edmund, and Werner Baer. 2003. Anchor's Away: The Costs and Benefits of Brazil's Devaluation. *World Development* 31 (6): 1033–46.

Amnesty International. 1999. *United Kingdom: The Pinochet Case; Universal Jurisdiction and the Absence of Immunity for Crimes against Humanity.* London: Amnesty International, International Secretariat.

Andrade Geywitz, Carlos. 1991. *Reforma de la Constitución Política de la República de Chile.* Santiago: Editorial Jurídica de Chile.

Andreas, Peter. 1999. The Escalation of U.S. Immigration Control in the Post-NAFTA Era. *Political Science Quarterly* 113 (4): 591–614.

Apelación sentencia definitiva contra Contreras Sepúlveda, Manuel y otros, Corte Suprema. 1995. *Revista de Derecho y Jurisprudencia y Gaceta de los Tribunales* 92 (January–April): 70–95.

Armijo, Leslie Elliott, and Philippe Faucher. 2002. We Have a Consensus: Political Support for Market Reforms in Latin America. *Latin American Politics and Society* 44 (2): 1–40.

Audiencia Nacional. 1999. *La Acusación del Juez Baltazar Garzón contra El General Augusto Pinochet.* Juzgado Central de Instrucción, Audiencia Nacional, Madrid. Santiago: Ediciones Chile América.

Axelrod, Robert, and Robert O. Keohane. 1993. Achieving Cooperation under Anarchy: Strategies and Institutions. In *Neorealism and Neoliberalism: The Contemporary Debate*, ed. David Baldwin, 85–115. New York: Columbia University Press.

Baer, Werner. 2001. *The Brazilian Economy: Growth and Development.* Westport, CT: Praeger Publishers.

Baer, Werner, Pedro Elosegui, and Andrés Gallo. 2002. The Achievements and Failures of Argentina's Neo-Liberal Policies. *Oxford Development Studies* 30 (1): 63–85.

Baker, James. 1989. *Democracy, Diplomacy, and the War against Drugs.* Washington, DC: U.S. Department of State, Bureau of Public Affairs.

Barkin, David. 2001. Neoliberalism and Sustainable Popular Development. In *Transcending Neoliberalism: Community-Based Development in Latin America,* ed. Henry Veltmeyer and Anthony O'Malley, 184–204. Bloomfield, CT: Kumarian Press.

Barkin, J. Samuel, and Bruce Cronin. 1994. The State and Nation: Changing Norms and the Rules of Sovereignty in International Relations. *International Organization* 48 (Winter): 107–30.

Barnett, Michael. 1995. The U.N., Regional Organizations, and Peacekeeping. *Review of International Studies* 21 (4): 411–33.

Barrera, Mario. 1979. *Race and Class in the Southwest: A Theory of Racial Inequality.* Notre Dame: University of Notre Dame Press.

Bartell, Ernest, and Leigh A. Payne. 1995. *Business and Democracy in Latin America.* Pittsburgh: University of Pittsburgh Press.

Baum, Lawrence. 2001. *The Supreme Court.* 7th ed. Washington, DC: CQ Press.

Bergsten, C. Fred. 2002. A Competitive Approach to Free Trade. *Financial Times,* December 5.

Bhagwati, Jagdish. 1998. The Capital Myth: The Difference between Trade in Widgets and Dollars. *Foreign Affairs* 77 (3): 7–12.

Bird, Graham. 2001. The Political Economy of the IMF: A Check List of the Issues. Prepared for delivery at a workshop on The Political Economy of the IMF held at the Fletcher School of Law and Diplomacy, Tufts University, April 13.

Bird, Graham, Antonella Mori, and Dane Rowlands. 2000. Do the Multilaterals Catalyse Other Capital Flows? A Case Study Analysis. *Third World Quarterly* 21 (3): 483–503.

Bird, Graham, and Dane Rowlands. 2002. Do IMF Programmes Have a Catalytic Effect on Other International Capital Flows? *Oxford Developmental Studies* 30 (3): 229–49.

Blasier, Cole. 1976. *The Hovering Giant: U.S. Response to Revolutionary Change in Latin America.* Pittsburgh: University of Pittsburgh Press.

Bonilla Martinez, Colonel Jorge Alberto. 2000. La Conferencia de las Fuerzas Armadas Centroamericanas "CFAC": Antecedentes, evolución, proyecciones y medidas para el fortalecimiento de la seguridad y desarrollo regional. Unpublished manuscript, Interamerican Defense College, Fort Lesley J. McNair, Washington, DC, May.

Boutros-Ghali, Boutros. 1992. *An Agenda for Peace, Preventive Diplomacy, Peacemaking and Peace-Keeping.* New York: United Nations. http://www.un.org/Docs/SG/agpeace.html.

Bresser-Pereira, Luiz Carlos. 1996. *Economic Crisis and State Reborn in Brazil: Toward a New Interpretation of Latin America.* Boulder: Lynne Rienner.

Brysk, Alison. 1994. *The Politics of Human Rights in Argentina: Protest, Change, and Democratization.* Palo Alto: Stanford University Press.

Buchanan, Paul G. 1996. U.S. Defense Policy for the Western Hemisphere: New Wine in Old Bottles, Old Wine in New Bottles, or Something Completely Different? *Journal of Interamerican Studies and World Affairs* 38 (1): 1–31.

Bull, Benedicte. 1999. New Regionalism in Central America. *Third World Quarterly* 20 (5): 957–70.

Bulletin of Latin America Research. 2000. Special Issue: Old and New Populism in Latin America 19 (2).

Bulmer-Thomas, Victor. 1996. Strategy and Policy Recommendations for Central American Integration. In *Regional Integration and Economic Reform in Central America,* ed. Jaime Behar, 11–66. Stockholm: Institute of Latin American Studies, Stockholm University.

Bulmer-Thomas, Victor, and James Dunkerly. 1999. Conclusions. In *The United States and Latin*

America: The New Agenda, ed. Victor Bulmer-Thomas and James Dunkerly, 311–26. Cambridge: Harvard University Press.

Burbano de Lara, Felipe. 1998. *Cultura política y democracia en el Ecuador: una aproximación a nuestros vacíos*. Quito: Proyecto CORDES-Gobernabilidad.

Buxton, Julia, and Nicola Phillips, eds. 1999. *Developments in Latin American Political Economy: States, Markets and Actors*. Manchester: Manchester University Press.

Buzan, Barry, Ole Wæver, and Jaap de Wilde. 1998. *Security: A New Framework for Analysis*. Boulder: Rienner.

Cajina, Roberto. 1998. Relaciones civiles-militares en Nicaragua, 1990–98. *Diálogo Centroamericano* 32 (August). http://www.ciponline.org/dialogue/0901dia.htm.

———. 1999. Paradojas de la transición política Nicaragüense: Entre la incompetencia del poder civil y las fortalezas del poderío militar. *Diálogo Centroamericano* 38 (March–April). http://www.ciponline.org/dialogue/0901dia.htm.

Cameron, Maxwell A., and Brian W. Tomlin. 2000. *The Making of NAFTA: How the Deal Was Done*. Ithaca: Cornell University Press.

Cardoso, Eliana. 2000. Brazil's Currency Crisis: The Shift from an Exchange Rate Anchor to a Flexible Regime. In *Exchange Rate Politics in Latin America*, ed. Carol Wise and Riordan Roett, 70–92. Washington, DC: Brookings Institution.

Carothers, Thomas. 1991. *In the Name of Democracy: U.S. Policy toward Latin America in the Reagan Years*. Berkeley: University of California Press.

Carranza, Mario Esteban. 2000. *South American Free Trade Area or Free Trade Area of the Americas? Open Regionalism and the Future of Regional Economic Integration in South America*. Aldershot, UK: Ashgate.

Castañeda, Jorge. 2003. The Forgotten Relationship. *Foreign Affairs* 82 (3): 67–81.

CEDOC. 1999. Reacciones de la cancillería Chilena durante el caso Pinochet. In *Entre la II cumbre y la detención de Pinochet: Chile 1998*, ed. Facultad Latino Americano de Ciencias Sociales, 137–50. Santiago: FLACSO.

Centeno, Miguel A., and Patricio Silva, eds. 1998. *The Politics of Expertise in Latin America*. New York: St. Martin's Press.

Center for International Policy. 2004. Memorandum, U.S. State Department's Data on Drug-Crop Cultivation, March 22, p. 3. http://ciponline.org/colombia/040322coca.pdf.

Centro de Estudios de la Realidad Contemporánea (CERC). 1999, 2000. *Barómetro*. CERC: Santiago.

CFAC (Conferencia de las Fuerzas Armadas Centroamericanas). 2000a. Discurso inaugural por el Presidente del Consejo Superior. In *Memoria de Labores, 98–99*, 7–8. San Salvador: CFAC.

——— (Conferencia de las Fuerzas Armadas Centroamericanas). 2000b. Misión y objetivos de la "CFAC." In *Memoria de Labores, 98–99*, 9. San Salvador: CFAC.

Chudnovsky, Daniel, and Andrés López. 1997. Market or Policy Driven? The Foreign Direct Investment Boom in Argentina. *Oxford Development Studies* 25 (June): 173–88.

Cibils, Alan B., Mark Weisbrot, and Debayani Kar. 2002. *Argentina since Default: The IMF and the Depression*. Washington, DC: Center for Economic and Policy Research. http://www.cepr.net/argentina_since_default.htm#_ftnref33.

Clawson, Robert W., ed. 1986. *East-West Rivalry in the Third World: Security Issues and Regional Perspectives*. Wilmington: Scholarly Resources Inc.

Cleary, Edward L. 1997. *The Struggle for Human Rights in Latin America*. Westport, CT: Praeger Publishers.

Cockroft, James D. 1986. *Outlaws in the Promised Land: Mexican Immigrant Workers and America's Future*. New York: Grove Press.

Collier, David, ed. 1979. *The New Authoritarianism in Latin America*. Princeton: Princeton University Press.

Collier, David, and Steven Levitsky. 1997. Democracy with Adjectives: Conceptual Innovation in Comparative Research. *World Politics* 49: 430–51.

Collier, Ruth, and David Collier. 1991. *Shaping the Political Arena*. Princeton: Princeton University Press.

Conaghan, Catherine. 2001a. Making and Unmaking Authoritarian Peru: Re-election, Resistance, and Regime Transition, *The North-South Agenda*, Paper 47. Miami: University of Miami, North-South Center Press, June.

———. 2001b. Reflections on Peru and on a Region in Crisis. In *The Crisis of Democratic Governance in the Andes*, ed. Cynthia Arnson, 103–8. Washington, DC: Woodrow Wilson Center for Scholars.

Constable, Pamela, and Arturo Valenzuela. 1991. *Chile under Pinochet: A Nation of Enemies*. New York: Norton.

Cooper, Andrew F., and Thomas Legler. 2001. The OAS in Peru—Model for the Future? *Journal of Democracy* 12: 123–36.

Corrales, Javier. 2002. The Politics of Argentina's Meltdown. *World Policy Journal* 29 (3): 29–42.

Correa Sutil, Jorge. 2001. Cenicienta se Queda en la Fiesta: El Poder Judicial Chileno en la Decada de los 90. In *El Modelo Chileno: Democracia y Desarrollo en los noventa*, ed. Paul W. Drake and Iván Jaksic, 281–315. Santiago: LOM Ediciones.

Cottam, Martha L. 1994. *Images and Intervention: U.S. Policies in Latin America*. Pittsburgh: University of Pittsburgh Press.

Daedalus. 1995. Special Issue: Globalization and the Nation-State 124 (2).

Dempsey, Gary T. 2001. Fool's Errands: America's Recent Encounters with Nation Building. *Mediterranean Quarterly* 12 (1): 57–80.

Dent, David, and Paul C. Sondrol. 2000. Government and Politics: General. In *Handbook of Latin American Studies: No. 57*, ed. Lawrence Boudon and Katherine D. McCann, 399–410. Austin: University of Texas Press.

Desafuero del senador Augusto Pinochet Ugarte. 2000. *Revista de Derecho y Jurisprudencia y Gaceta de los Tribunales* 97 (May–August): 157–223.

Desch, Michael C. 1993. *When the Third World Matters: Latin American and United States Grand Strategy*. Baltimore: Johns Hopkins University Press.

———. 1998. Why Latin America May Miss the Cold War. In *International Security and Democracy: Latin America and the Caribbean in the Post-Cold War Era*, ed. Jorge I. Domínguez, 245–65. Pittsburgh: University of Pittsburgh Press.

Diamond, Larry. 1996. Democracy in America: Degree, Illusion, and Directions for Consolidation. In *Beyond Sovereignty: Collectively Defending Democracy in the Americas*, ed. Tom Farer, 52–104. Baltimore: Johns Hopkins University Press.

Diamond, Larry, Jonathan Hartlyn, Juan J. Linz, and Seymour Martin Lipset. 1999. *Democracy in Developing Countries: Latin America*. Boulder: Rienner.

Diamond, Larry, Juan J. Linz, and Seymour Martin Lipset, eds. 1995. *Politics in Developing Countries: Comparing Experience with Democracy*. Boulder: Lynne Rienner.

Dinsmoor, James. 1990. *Brazil: Responses to the Debt Crisis: Impact on Savings, Investment, and Growth*. Washington, DC: Inter-American Development Bank.

Direction of Trade Statistics Yearbook. 2002. Washington, DC: International Monetary Fund.

Domínguez, Jorge I., ed. 1998. *International Security and Democracy: Latin America and the Caribbean in the Post-Cold War Era*. Pittsburgh: University of Pittsburgh Press.

Domínguez, Jorge I., and Rafael Fernández de Castro. 2001. *The United States and Mexico: Between Partnership and Conflict*. New York: Routledge.

Donnelly, Jack. 1986. International Human Rights: A Regime Analysis. *International Organization* 40 (Summer): 599–642.

———. 1989. *Universal Human Rights in Theory and Practice*. Ithaca: Cornell University Press.

Drake, Paul, and Ivan Jaksic, eds. 1991. *The Struggle for Democracy in Chile, 1982–1990*. Lincoln: University of Nebraska Press.

Dunn, Timothy J. 1996. *The Militarization of the U.S.-Mexico Border, 1978–1992: Low-Intensity Conflict Doctrine Comes Home*. Austin: University of Texas Press.

Dunning, John H. 1999. Globalization and the Theory of MNE Activity. In *The Globalization of Multinational Enterprise Activity and Economic Development*, ed. Neil Hood and Stephen Young, 21–45. New York: St. Martin's Press.

Eckstein, Susan. 2001. *Power and Popular Protest: Latin American Social Movements*. Berkeley: University of California Press.

Economic Commission for Latin America and the Caribbean. 2001. *Statistical Yearbook for Latin America and the Caribbean*. Santiago: ECLAC.

Edwards, Sebastian. 1997. *Crisis and Reform in Latin America: From Despair to Hope*. Washington, DC: World Bank.

Eguizábal, Cristina. 1994. El problema de la seguridad en Centroamérica: El caso de El Salvador. In *De la guerra a la integración: la transición y la seguridad en Centroamérica*, ed. Luis Guillermo Solís Rivera and Francisco Rojas, 75–96. San José, Costa Rica: Fundación Arias/FLACSO-Chile.

———. 1999. Regional Arrangements, the United Nations, and Security in Latin America. In *International Security Management and the United Nations*, ed. Muthiah Alagappa and Takashi Inoguchi, 347–68. New York: United Nations Publications.

Einaudi, Luigi. 2001. Reflections on a Regional Crisis. In *The Crisis of Democratic Governance in the Andes*, ed. Cynthia Arnson, 109–13. Washington, DC: Woodrow Wilson Center for Scholars.

Escudé, Carlos, and Andrés Fontana. 1998. Argentina's Security Policies: Their Rationale and Regional Context. In *International Security and Democracy: Latin America and the Caribbean in the Post-Cold War Era*, ed. Jorge I. Domínguez, 51–79. Pittsburgh: University of Pittsburgh Press.

Etchemendy, Sebastian. 2001. Constructing Reform Coalitions: The Politics of Compensations in Argentina's Economic Liberalization. *Latin American Politics and Society* 43 (3): 1–35.

Evans, Tony, and Peter Wilson. 1992. Regime Theory and the English School of International Relations: A Comparison. *Millennium: Journal of International Studies* 21 (3): 329–51.

Facultad Latino Americana de Ciencias Sociales (FLACSO). 2000. Cronología: Caso Pinochet. *Fuerzas Armadas y Sociedad* 15 (January–March): 76.

Farer, Tom, ed. 1996. *Beyond Sovereignty: Collectively Defending Democracy in the Americas*. Baltimore: Johns Hopkins University Press.

Fawcett, Louise, and Andrew Hurrell, eds. 1995. *Regionalism in World Politics: Regional Organization and International Order*. New York: Oxford University Press.

Feinberg, Richard. 1997. *Summitry in the Americas*. Washington, DC: Institute for International Economics.

Feldstein, Martin. 2002. Argentina's Fall. *Foreign Affairs* 81: 8–14.

Fernández, Damián J., and Jacqueline Anne Braveboy-Wagner. 2000. International Relations: The Caribbean and the Guianas. In *Handbook of Latin American Studies: No. 57*, ed. Lawrence Boudon and Katherine D. McCann, 577–86. Austin: University of Texas Press.

Ferreira, Afonso, and Giuseppe Tullio. 2002. The Brazilian Exchange Rate Crisis of January 1999. *Journal of Latin American Studies* 34: 143–64.

Finnemore, Martha. 1996. *National Interests in International Society*. Ithaca: Cornell University Press.

———. 2003. *The Purpose of Intervention: Changing Beliefs about the Use of Force*. Ithaca: Cornell University Press.

Fishel, John T. 2000. The Organizational Component of Civil-Military Relations in Latin America: The Role of the Ministry of Defense. Paper presented at the meetings of the Latin American Studies Association, Miami, March 16–18.

Fitch, J. Samuel. 1993. The Decline of United States Military Influence in Latin America. *Journal of Interamerican Studies and World Affairs* 35 (2): 1–49.

———. 1998. *The Armed Forces and Democracy in Latin America*. Baltimore: Johns Hopkins University Press.

Forsythe, David. 2000. *Human Rights in International Relations*. Cambridge: Cambridge University Press.

Fournier, Dominique. 1999. The Alfonsín Administration and the Promotion of Democratic Values in the Southern Cone and the Andes. *Journal of Latin American Studies* 31 (1): 39–74.

Foxley, Alejandro. 1983. *Latin American Experiments in Neoconservative Economics*. Berkeley: University of California Press.

Francisco Coloane, Juan. 2000. *Britannia y un General*. Santiago: LOM Ediciones.

Frank, Thomas M. 1992. The Emerging Right to Democratic Governance. *American Journal of International Law* 86 (January): 46–91.

Freedman, Lawrence. 1998. International Security: Changing Targets. *Foreign Policy* 110: 48–63.

Frieden, Jeffry. 1991. *Debt, Development and Democracy: Modern Political Economy and Latin America, 1965–1985*. Princeton: Princeton University Press.

García Arán, M., and D. López Garrido, eds. 2000. *Crimen Internacional y Jurisdicción Universal: El Caso Pinochet*. Valencia, Spain: Tirant Lo Blanch.

Geddes, Barbara. 1996. *Politician's Dilemma: Building State Capacity in Latin America*. Berkeley: University of California Press.

George, Alexander. 1979. Case Studies and Theory Development: The Method of Structured, Focused Comparison. In *Diplomacy: New Approaches in History, Theory and Policy*, ed. Paul G. Lauren, 43–68. New York: New York Free Press.

Gilpin, Robert. 1975. *U.S. Power and the Multinational Corporation*. New York: Basic Books.

———. 2000. *The Challenge of Global Capitalism: The World Economy in the 21st Century*. Princeton: Princeton University Press.

Goldstein, Judith, and Robert O. Keohane, eds. 1993. *Ideas and Foreign Policy: Ideas, Institutions, and Political Change*. Ithaca: Cornell University Press.

Goldstein, Judith, et al. 2000. Special Issue: Legalization and World Politics. *International Organization* 54 (Summer).

Gomáriz, Enrique. 1988. *Balance de una esperanza: Esquipulas II, un año después*. San José, Costa Rica: FLACSO.

Gordenker, Leon, and Thomas G. Weiss. 1995. Pluralising Global Governance: Analytical Approaches and Dimensions. *Third World Quarterly* 16 (3): 357–87.

Gould, Erica A. 2003. Money Talks: Supplementary Financiers and International Monetary Fund Conditionality. *International Organization* 57 (Summer): 551–86.

Gourevitch, Peter. 1978. The Second Image Reversed: The International Sources of Domestic Politics. *International Organization* 32 (4): 881–912.

Greider, William. 1997. *One World, Ready or Not: The Manic Logic of Global Capitalism*. New York: Simon and Schuster.

Griffith-Jones, Stephany, and Barbara Stallings. 1995. New Global Financial Trends: Implications for Development. *Journal of Interamerican Studies and World Affairs* 37 (3): 59–98.

Gwartney, James, and Robert Lawson, eds. 2001. *Economic Freedom of the World 2000 Annual Report*. Vancouver, BC: The Fraser Institute. http://www.fraserinstitute.ca/publications/books/econ_free_2000/.

Gwynne, Robert N., and Cristobal Kay, eds. 1999. *Latin America Transformed: Globalization and Modernity*. London: Edward Arnold.

Haggard, Stephan, and Robert R. Kaufman, eds. 1992. *The Politics of Economic Adjustment*. Princeton: Princeton University Press.

Hagopian, Frances. 1998. Democracy and Political Representation in Latin America in the

1990s: Pause, Reorganization or Decline? In *Fault Lines of Democracy in Post-Transition Latin America*, ed. Felipe Agüero and Jeffrey Stark, 99–143. Miami: University of Miami, North-South Center Press.

Hakim, Peter. 2002. Two Ways to Go Global. *Foreign Affairs* 81 (January–February): 148–62.

Hall, Peter A., and Rosemary C. R. Taylor. 1996. Political Science and the Three New Institutionalisms. *Political Studies* 44: 936–57.

Hartlyn, Jonathan, Lars Schoultz, and Augusto Varas, eds. 1992. *The United States and Latin America in the 1990s: Beyond the Cold War*. Chapel Hill: University of North Carolina Press.

Hashmi, Sohail H., ed. 1997. *State Sovereignty: Change and Persistence in International Relations*. University Park: Pennsylvania State University Press.

Haugaard, Lisa. 1997. Development Aid: Some Small Steps Forward. *NACLA Report on the Americas* 31 (2): 29–35.

Healy, Mark Alan, and Ernesto Seman. 2002. The Cost of Orthodoxy. *The American Prospect* 13 (January 1): 34–37.

Hennelly, Michael J. 1993. Central American Security Issues: A U.S. Perspective. Center for Peace and Reconciliation, Working Paper No. 16. San José, Costa Rica: Arias Foundation.

Henrikson, Alan K. 1995. The Growth of Regional Organizations and the Role of the United Nations. In *Regionalism in World Politics: Regional Organization and International Order*, ed. Louise Fawcett and Andrew Hurrell, 122–68. New York: Oxford University Press.

Hettne, Björn, and András Inotai. 1994. *The New Regionalism: Implications for Global Development and International Security*. Helsinki: UNU/WIDER.

Hey, Jeanne A. K. 1997. Three Building Blocks of a Theory of Latin American Foreign Policy. *Third World Quarterly* 18 (4): 631–57.

Hilbink, Lisa. 1999. Legalism Against Democracy: The Political Role of the Judiciary in Chile, 1964–94. Ph.D. diss., University of California, San Diego.

Hirschman, Albert O. 1945. *National Power and the Structure of Foreign Trade*. Berkeley: University of California Press.

Holden, Robert H. 1993. The Real Diplomacy of Violence: United States Military Power in Central America, 1950–1990. *International History Review* 15 (2): 283–322.

———. 1999. Securing Central America against Communism: The United States and the Modernization of Surveillance in the Cold War. *Journal of Interamerican Studies and World Affairs* 41 (1): 1–30.

Horowitz, Irving Louis. 1985. Militarism and Civil-Military Relationships in Latin America: Implications for the Third World. *Research in Political Sociology* 1: 79–99.

Human Rights Watch. 1994. *Unsettled Business: Human Rights in Chile at the Start of the Frei Presidency*, May 6. New York: Human Rights Watch.

———. 1999. *When Tyrants Tremble: The Pinochet Case*, October 11. New York: Human Rights Watch.

Huntington, Samuel P. 1968. *Political Order in Changing Societies*. New Haven: Yale University Press.

Hurrell, Andrew, and Benedict Kingsbury. 1992. *The International Politics of the Environment: Actors, Interests, and Institutions*. New York: Oxford University Press.

Ikenberry, John G. 1998. Institutions, Strategic Restraint, and the Persistence of American Postwar Order. *International Security* 23 (3): 43–78.

———. 2001. *After Victory: Institutions, Strategic Restraint, and the Rebuilding of Order After Major Wars*. Princeton: Princeton University Press.

IMF Financial Statistics Yearbook. 2001. Washington, DC: International Monetary Fund.

¿Integración o desintegración centroamericana? 2000. *Reporte Político: Panorama Centroamericano* 156 (February): 1–5.

International Monetary Fund. 2001. *Direction of Trade*. Washington, DC: International Monetary Fund.

Isaacs, Anita. 1993. *Military Rule and Transition in Ecuador, 1972–92*. Pittsburgh: University of Pittsburgh Press.

Isaacson, Adam. 1998. Seguridad Cooperativa en Centroamérica. *Diálogo Centroamericano* 35 (November). San José, Costa Rica: Centro para la Paz y la Reconciliación de la Fundación Arias para la Paz y el Progreso Humano.

Johnson, Bryan, and Thomas Sheehy. 1997. *Index of Economic Freedom 1997*. Washington, DC: Heritage Foundation.

Johnson, Simon, Daniel Kaufmann, and Pablo Zoido-Lobaton. 1998. Regulatory Discretion and the Unofficial Economy. *American Economic Review* 88 (2): 387–92.

Joseph, James W. 2000. Stasis and Change in the IMF and World Bank: International Context and Institutional Dynamics. *Social Science Journal* 37 (1): 43–66.

Joyner, Christopher C. 1996. Arresting Impunity: The Case for Universal Jurisdiction in Bringing War Criminals to Accountability. *Law and Contemporary Problems* 59: 153–72.

Kamminga, Menno T. 2001. Lessons Learned from the Exercise of Universal Jurisdiction in Respect of Gross Human Rights Offenses. *Human Rights Quarterly* 23: 940–74.

Katzenstein, Peter. 1978. *Between Power and Plenty: Foreign Economic Policies of Advanced Industrialized States*. Madison: University of Wisconsin Press.

———, ed. 1996. *The Culture of National Security*. New York: Columbia University Press.

Kearney, Christine. 2001. The Poverty of Neoliberalism in Brazil: Economic Culture and Policy Choice. Paper presented at the meetings of the Latin American Studies Association, Washington, DC, September 6–8.

Keck, Margaret E. 1995. Social Equity and Environmental Politics in Brazil: Lessons from the Rubber Tappers of Acre. *Comparative Politics* 27 (July): 409–24.

Keck, Margaret E., and Kathryn Sikkink. 1998. *Activists beyond Borders: Advocacy Networks in International Politics*. Ithaca: Cornell University Press.

Kenworthy, Eldon. 1995. *America/Américas: Myth in the Making of U.S. Policy toward Latin America*. University Park: Pennsylvania State University Press.

Keohane, Robert. 1984. *After Hegemony: Cooperation and Discord in the World Political Economy*. Princeton: Princeton University Press.

———. 1993. Institutionalist Theory and the Realist Challenge. In *Neorealism and Neoliberalism*, ed. David Baldwin, 269–300. New York: Columbia University Press.

Keohane, Robert, and Helen Milner, eds. 1996. *Internationalization and Domestic Politics*. New York: Cambridge University Press.

Keohane, Robert, and Joseph Nye. 1977. *Power and Interdependence: World Politics in Transition*. Boston: Little, Brown.

Keohane, Robert, and Joseph S. Nye, Jr. 1998. Power and Interdependence in the Information Age. *Foreign Affairs* 77 (5): 81–94.

Khagram, Sanjeev, James V. Riker, and Kathryn Sikkink. 2002. *Restructuring World Politics: Transnational Social Movements, Networks, and Norms*. Minneapolis: University of Minnesota Press.

Killick, Tony. 1995. *IMF Programmes in Developing Countries: Design and Impact*. London: Routledge.

Kindleberger, Charles. 1969. *American Business Abroad*. New Haven: Yale University Press.

Kingstone, Peter. 1999. *Crafting Coalitions for Reform: Business Preferences, Political Institutions and Neoliberal Reform in Brazil*. University Park: Pennsylvania State University Press.

Klotz, Audie. 1995. *Norms in International Society*. Ithaca: Cornell University Press.

Kokko, Ari. 2002. Globalization and FDI Determinants. Paper presented at the World Bank's Annual Bank Conference on Development Economics—Europe, Oslo, June 24–26.

Kolk, Ans. 1998. From Conflict to Cooperation: International Policies to Protect the Brazilian Amazon. *World Development* 26 (8): 1481–93.

Kowert, Paul, and Jeffrey Legro. 1996. Norms, Identity, and Their Limits: A Theoretical

Reprise. In *The Culture of National Security*, ed. Peter J. Katzenstein, 451–97. New York: Columbia University Press.

Krasner, Stephen. 1978. *Defending the National Interest*. Princeton: Princeton University Press.

———. 1983. Introduction to *International Regimes*, ed. Stephen Krasner. Ithaca: Cornell University Press.

———. 1984. Approaches to the State: Alternative Conceptions and Historical Dynamics. *Comparative Politics* 16 (2): 223–46.

———. 1988. Sovereignty: An Institutional Perspective. *Comparative Political Studies* 21 (1): 66–94.

———. 1999. *Sovereignty: Organized Hypocrisy*. Princeton: Princeton University Press.

La Acusación del Juez Baltasar Garzón Contra el General Pinochet, Juzgado Central de Instrucción, Número cinco, Audiencia Nacional. 1999. Santiago: Ediciones Chile America.

Lagos Erazo, Jaime. 1999. *El "Caso Pinochet" ante las Cortes Británicas*. Santiago: Editorial Júridica de Chile.

Lake, David A., and Patrick M. Morgan. 1997. The New Regionalism in Security Affairs. In *Regional Orders: Building Security in a New World*, ed. David Lake and Patrick M. Morgan, 4–19. University Park: Pennsylvania State University Press.

Lascano Palacios, Mario. 2001. *21 de Enero: la noche de los coroneles: rebelión de los mandos medios*. Quito: Editorial Kess.

Latinobarómetro, Opinión Pública Latinoamericana, Annual Survey, 1996–2002, www.latinobarometro.org.

"Legalization and World Politics." 2000. *International Organization*, special issue 54 (3).

Lehman, Howard P. 1993. Strategic Bargaining in Brazil's Debt Negotiations. *Political Science Quarterly* 108 (1): 133–55.

Levine, Ricardo. 1937. *A History of Argentina*. Chapel Hill: University of North Carolina Press.

Levy, Daniel C. 1996. *Building the Third Sector: Latin America's Private Research Centers and Nonprofit Development*. Pittsburgh: University of Pittsburgh Press.

Loayza, Norman V. 1996. The Economics of the Informal Sector: A Simple Model and Some Empirical Evidence from Latin America. *Carnegie-Rochester Conference Series on Public Policy* 45 (1996): 129–62.

Lopez, Juan J. 1998. Private Investment Response to Neoliberal Reforms in a Delegative Democracy: Reflections on Argentina. *Quarterly Review of Economics and Finance* 38 (3): 441–57.

Loriaux, Michael, et al., eds. 1997. *Capital Ungoverned: Liberalizing Finance in Interventionist States*. Ithaca: Cornell University Press.

Loveman, Brian. 1991. Misión Cumplida?: Civil-Military Relations and the Chilean Political Transition. *Journal of Inter-American Studies and World Affairs* 33: 35–74.

———. 1999. *For la Patria: Politics and the Armed Forces in Latin America*. Wilmington: Scholarly Resources.

Lowenthal, Abraham F. 1987. *Partners in Conflict: The United States and Latin America*. Baltimore: Johns Hopkins University Press.

———, ed. 1991a. *Exporting Democracy: The United States and Latin America, Themes and Issues*. Baltimore: Johns Hopkins University Press.

———. 1991b. The United States and Latin American Democracy: Learning from History. In *Exporting Democracy: Themes and Issues*, ed. Abraham Lowenthal, 261–83. Baltimore: Johns Hopkins University Press.

Lowenthal, Abraham F., and Gregory F. Treverton, eds. 1994. *Latin America in a New World*. Boulder: Westview Press.

Lowi, Theodore J. 1964. American Business, Public Policy, Case Studies and Political Theory. *World Politics* 16: 675–715.

———. 1972. Four Systems of Policy, Politics and Choice. *Public Administration Review* 32: 298–310.

Lutz, Ellen, and Kathryn Sikkink. 2000. International Human Rights Law and Practice in Latin America. *International Organization* 54 (Summer): 633–59.

Mainwaring, Scott, and Timothy R. Scully. 1995. *Building Democratic Institutions: Party Systems in Latin America.* Palo Alto: Stanford University Press.

Mainwaring, Scott, and Matthew Soberg Shugart, eds. 1997. *Presidentialism and Democracy in Latin America.* New York: Cambridge University Press.

Marchesi, Silvia. 2003. Adoption of an IMF Programme and Debt Rescheduling: An Empirical Analysis. *Journal of Development Economics* 70 (2): 403–24.

Mares, David R. 1997. Regional Conflict Management in Latin America: Power Complemented by Diplomacy. In *Regional Orders: Building Security in a New World*, ed. David Lake and Patrick M. Morgan, 195–218. University Park: Pennsylvania State University Press.

Mares, David R., and Francisco Rojas Aravena. 2001. *The United States and Chile: Coming in from the Cold.* New York: Routledge.

Martin, Lisa L., and Kathryn Sikkink. 1993. U.S. Policy and Human Rights in Argentina and Guatemala, 1973–1980. In *Double-Edged Diplomacy: International Bargaining and Domestic Politics*, ed. Peter B. Evans, Harold K. Jacobson, and Robert D. Putnam, 330–62. Berkeley: University of California Press.

Martin, Philip. 1997. Do Mexican Agricultural Policies Stimulate Emigration? In *At the Crossroads: Mexican Migration and U.S. Policy*, ed. Frank D. Bean, Rodolfo O. de la Garza, Bryan R. Roberts, and Sidney Weintraub, 79–116. New York: Rowman and Littlefield.

Martz, John D., and Lars Schoultz, eds. 1980. *Latin America, the United States, and the Inter-American System.* Boulder: Westview Press.

Massey, Douglas S., Jorge Durand, and Nolan J. Malone. 2002. *Beyond Smoke and Mirrors: Mexican Immigration in an Era of Economic Integration.* New York: Russell Sage Foundation.

McClintock, Cynthia. 1993. Peru's Fujimori. *Current History* 92 (March): 112–19.

McClintock, Cynthia, and Fabián Vallas. 2003. *Cooperation at a Cost: The United States and Peru.* New York: Routledge.

Mearsheimer, John J. 2001. *The Tragedy of Great Power Politics.* New York: Norton.

Meltzer, Allan. 2000. *Report of the International Financial Institution Advisory Commission.* Washington, DC: International Financial Institution Advisory Commission.

Meyerson, Harold. 2002. The Rising Latino Tide. *The American Prospect* 13 (November 18): 22–25.

Middlebrook, Kevin J. 1998. *Electoral Observation and Democratic Transitions in Latin America.* La Jolla: Center for U.S.-Mexican Studies.

Millett, Richard L. 2002. *Colombia's Conflicts: The Spillover Effects of a Wider War.* U.S. Army War College, Special Series on Shaping the Regional Security Environment in Latin America. Miami: University of Miami, North-South Center Press.

Molineu, Harold. 1990. *U.S. Policy toward Latin America: From Regionalism to Globalism.* Boulder: Westview Press.

Moravcsik, Andrew. 1993. Integrating International and Domestic Politics: A Theoretical Introduction. In *Double-Edged Diplomacy: Interactive Games in International Affairs*, ed. Peter Evans, Harold Jacobson, and Robert Putnam, 3–42. Berkeley: University of California Press.

———. 2000. The Origins of Human Rights Regimes: Democratic Delegation in Postwar Europe. *International Organization* 54 (Spring): 217–52.

Moreno, Dario. 1994. *The Struggle for Peace in Central America.* Gainesville: University Press of Florida.

Morgenthau, Hans. 1967. *Politics among Nations: The Struggle for Power and Peace.* 4th ed. New York: Knopf.

Morley, Samuel A., Robert Machado, and Stefano Pettinato. 1999. *Indices of Structural Reform in Latin America.* Santiago: Economic Commission on Latin America.

Muñoz, Heraldo. 1994. *OAS's Comparative Advantage*. Washington, DC: Inter-American Dialogue, May.

———. 1998. The Right to Democracy in the Americas. *Journal of Interamerican Studies and World Affairs* 40 (Spring): 1–18.

———. 2001. Goodbye USA? In *Latin America in the New International System*, ed. Joseph S. Tulchin and Ralph A. Espach, 73–90. Boulder: Lynne Rienner.

Mussa, Michael. 2002. *Argentina and the Fund: From Triumph to Tragedy*. Washington, DC: Institute for International Economics.

NACLA Report on the Americas. 2001. 35 (November–December).

Nagle, Luz E. 2002. *Plan Colombia: Reality of the Colombian Crisis and Implications for Hemispheric Security*. U.S. Army War College, Special Series on Shaping the Regional Security Environment in Latin America. Miami: University of Miami, North-South Center Press.

Naím, Moisés. 2000. Fads and Fashion in Economic Reform: Washington Consensus or Washington Confusion? *Third World Quarterly* 21 (3): 505–28.

Nazmi, Nader. 1995. Inflation and Stabilization: Recent Brazilian Experience in Perspective. *Journal of Developing Areas* 29 (4): 491–506.

North, Douglass. 1990. *Institutions, Institutional Change and Economic Performance*. New York: Cambridge University Press.

Nunnenkamp, Peter, and Julius Spatz. 2002. Determinants of FDI in Developing Countries: Has Globalization Changed the Rules of the Game? *Transnational Corporations* 11 (2): 1–34.

Nye, Joseph S. 2002. *The Paradox of American Power: Why the World's Only Superpower Can't Go It Alone*. New York: Oxford University Press.

OAS (Organization of American States). 1991. *Santiago Resolution*, AG/Res 1080, OAS, General Assembly, Proceedings, vol. 1, August 20, 1991.

———. 1992. *Protocol of Washington*, OAS Charter Amendment, OEA/Ser.P AG/Doc. 11, December 14, 1992.

———. 1997. *OAS Charter*, Secretariat for Legal Cooperation and Information. www.oas.org/juridico/english/charter.html.

———. 2000a. Acta de la Sesión Extraordinaria Celebrada, 26 de Enero, OEA/Ser.G/CP/ACTA 1221/00.

———. 2000b. CP/RES 763, Support for the Democratic Government of the Constitutional President of the Republic of Ecuador, Jamil Mahuad, and for the Institution under the Rule of Law, January 22, Permanent Council.

———. 2001. *Inter-American Democratic Charter*. www.oas.org/charter/docs/.

———. 2002. Situation in Venezuela, CP/Res 811 (1315/02), Permanent Council.

———. 2003. Situation in Venezuela, Agreement between the Representatives of the Government of the Bolivarian Republic of Venezuela and the Political and Social Groups Supporting It, and the Coordinadora Democrática and the Political and Civil Society Organizations Supporting It, May 23. http://www.oas.org/OASpage/eng/Venezuela/Agreement.

———. 2004. *Charter of the OAS*. http://www.oas.org/main/main.asp?sLang=E&sLink= ../documents/eng/documents.asp.

O'Donnell, Guillermo. 1994. Delegative Democracy. *Journal of Democracy* 5 (January): 56–69.

O'Donnell, Guillermo, and Philippe C. Schmitter. 1986. *Transitions from Authoritarian Rule: Tentative Conclusions about Uncertain Democracies*. Baltimore: Johns Hopkins University Press.

Ohmae, Kenichi. 1995. *The End of the Nation State: The Rise of Regional Economies*. New York: Free Press.

Oxhorn, Philip D., and Graciela Ducatenzeiler. 1998. *What Kind of Democracy? What Kind of Market? Latin America in the Age of Neoliberalism*. University Park: Pennsylvania State University Press.

Palast, Greg. 2003. Resolved to Ruin: The World Bank/IMF Takeover, in Four Easy Steps. *Harper's Magazine* 306: 48–51.

Palmer, David Scott. 1996. Peru: Collectively Defending Democracy in the Western Hemisphere. In *Beyond Sovereignty: Collectively Defending Democracy in the Americas*, ed. Tom Farer, 257–76. Baltimore: Johns Hopkins University Press.

———. 2000. Democracy and Its Discontents in Fujimori's Peru. *Current History* 99: 60–65.

Pastor, Manuel, and Carol Wise. 1999. Stabilization and Its Discontents: Argentina's Economic Restructuring in the 1990s. *World Development* 27 (3): 477–503.

Pastor, Robert. 2001. *Exiting the Whirlpool: U.S. Foreign Policy toward Latin America and the Caribbean*. Boulder: Westview Press.

Paz Rojas, B., et al. 1998. *Tarda pero llega: Pinochet ante la justicia Española*. Santiago: LOM Ediciones CODEPU.

Peceny, Mark, and William Stanley. 2001. Liberal Social Reconstruction and the Resolution of Civil Wars in Central America. *International Organization* 55 (1): 149–82.

Philpott, Daniel. 1997. Ideas and Evolution of Sovereignty. In *State Sovereignty: Change and Persistence in International Relations*, ed. Sohail H. Hashmi, 15–47. University Park: Pennsylvania State University Press.

———. 2001. Usurping the Sovereignty of Sovereignty? *World Politics* 53 (2): 297–324.

Phythian, Mark. 2000. *The Politics of British Arms Sales since 1964*. Manchester, UK: Manchester University Press.

Pierson, Paul. 2000a. Not Just What, but When: Timing and Sequence in Political Processes. *Studies in American Political Development* 14: 72–92.

———. 2000b. Increasing Returns, Path Dependence, and the Study of Politics. *American Political Science Review* 94 (2): 251–68.

Pion-Berlin, David, ed. 2001. *Civil-Military Relations in Latin America: New Analytical Perpectives*. Chapel Hill: University of North Carolina Press.

Pion-Berlin, David, and Craig Arceneaux. 1998. Tipping the Civil-Military Balance: Institutions and Human Rights Policy in Argentina and Chile. *Comparative Political Studies* 31 (October): 633–61.

———. 2000. Decision-Makers or Decision-Takers? Military Missions and Civilian Control in Democratic South America. *Armed Forces and Society* 26 (3): 413–36.

Pizano, Eduardo. 2001. *Plan Colombia: The View from the Presidential Palace*. U.S. Army War College, Special Series on Implementing Plan Colombia. Miami: University of Miami, North-South Center Press.

Political Risk Services. 1997. *International Country Risk Guide (ICRG)*. East Syracuse, NY: The Political Risk Services Group, Inc.

Portales, Carlos. 1995. In *The Struggle for Democracy in Chile*, ed. Paul Drake and Iván Jaksic, 251–75. Rev. ed. Lincoln: University of Nebraska Press.

Price, Richard. 1998. Reversing the Gun Sights: Transnational Civil Society Targets Land Mines. *International Organization* 52 (3): 613–44.

Przeworski, Adam, and James Raymond Vreeland. 2000. The Effect of IMF Programs on Economic Growth. *Journal of Development Economics* 62 (2): 385–421.

Purcell, Susan Kaufman, and Françoise Simon. 1994. *Europe and Latin America in the World Economy*. Boulder: Rienner.

Putnam, Robert D. 1988. Diplomacy and Domestic Politics: The Logic of Two-Level Games. *International Organization* 42 (Summer): 427–460.

Reed, Laura, and Carl Kaysen. 1993. *Emerging Norms of Justified Intervention*. Cambridge, MA: American Academy of Arts and Sciences.

Remmer, Karen. 1992. The Process of Democratization in Latin America. *Studies in Comparative International Development* 26 (4): 3–29.

———. 1997. Theoretical Decay and Theoretical Development: The Resurgence of Institutional Analysis. *World Politics* 50 (1): 34–61.

————. 1998. The Politics of Neoliberal Economic Reform in South America. *Studies in Comparative International Development* 33 (2): 3–30.

Report of the Chilean National Commission on Truth and Reconciliation. 1993. Vol. 1. Notre Dame: University of Notre Dame Press.

Republic of Ecuador. 1998. *Constitution of 1998*, Political Data Base of the Americas. www.georgetown.edu/pdba/.

República de Chile. 1997. *Código de Procedimiento Penal*, edición oficial. Santiago: Editorial Jurídica de Chile.

————. 2001. *Código Penal, edición oficial*. Santiago: Editorial Jurídica de Chile.

República de Chile, Junta de Gobierno. 1978. Decreto 2191, *Diario Oficial*, April 19, 1978.

Roberts, Bryan R., and Agustin Escobar Latapi. 1997. Mexican Social and Economic Policy and Emigration. In *At the Crossroads: Mexican Migration and U.S. Policy*, ed. Frank D. Bean, Rodolfo O. de la Garza, Bryan R. Roberts, and Sidney Weintraub, 47–78. New York: Rowman and Littlefield.

Rogowski, Ronald. 1990. *Commerce and Coalitions*. Princeton: Princeton University Press.

Rojas Aravena, Francisco. 2001. La Detención de General Pinochet: notas para su interpretación y evaluación del impacto en el sistema político Chileno. In *El Caso Pinochet: Visiones Hemisféricas de su detención en Londres*, ed. Francisco Rojas Aravena and Carolina Stefoni Espinoza, 21–39. Santiago: FLACSO.

Rojas Aravena, Francisco, and Carolina Stefoni Espinoza. 2001. *El "Caso Pinochet": Visiones Hemisféricas de su detención en Londres*. Santiago: Facultad Latinoamericana de Ciencias Sociales.

Rosenbaum, Robert J. 1981. *Mexicano Resistance in the Southwest: "The Sacred Right of Self-Preservation."* Austin: University of Texas Press.

Rosenberg, Robin L. 2001. The OAS and the Summit of the Americas: Coexistence, or Integration of Forces for Multilateralism? *Latin America Politics and Society* 43: 79–101.

Rothenberg, Daniel. 2002. Let Justice Judge: An Interview with Judge Baltasar Garzón and Analysis of His Ideas. *Human Rights Quarterly* 24: 924–73.

Ruggie, John. 1983. International Regimes, Transactions, and Change: Embedded Liberalism in the Postwar Economic Order. In *International Regimes*, ed. Stephen D. Krasner, 195–231. Ithaca: Cornell University Press.

Ruhl, J. Mark. 1996. Redefining Civil-Military Relations in Honduras. *Journal of Interamerican Studies and World Affairs* 38 (1): 33–66.

————. 2000. Honduras: Militarism and Democratization in Troubled Waters. In *Repression, Resistance, and Democratic Transition in Central America*, ed. Thomas W. Walker and Ariel C. Armony, 47–66. Wilmington: Scholarly Resources.

Schamis, Hector E. 1999. Distributional Coalitions and the Politics of Economic Reform in Latin America. *World Politics* 51 (2): 236–68.

Scheman, L. Ronald. 1988. *The Inter-American Dilemma: The Search for Inter-American Cooperation at the Centennial of the Inter-American System*. New York: Praeger.

Schirmer, Jennifer. 2001. The Guatemalan Politico-Military Project: Whose Ship of State? In *Political Armies: Militaries and Nationbuilding in the Age of Democracy*, ed. Kees Kooning and Dirk Kruijt. London: ZED Books.

Schneider, Friedrich, and Bruno Frey. 1985. Economic and Political Determinants of Foreign Direct Investment. *World Development* 13 (2): 161–75.

Schott, Jeffrey. 2001. *Prospects for Free Trade in the Americas*. Washington, DC: Institute for International Economics.

Schoultz, Lars. 1981. *Human Rights and United States Policy toward Latin America*. Princeton: Princeton University Press.

————. 2001. *Beneath the United States: U.S. Policy toward Latin America*. Cambridge: Harvard University Press.

Schoultz, Lars, William C. Smith, and Augusto Varas, eds. 1994. *Security, Democracy, and Development in U.S. Latin American Relations*. Miami: University of Miami, North-South Center Press.

Schwartz, Herman M. 1998. *States versus Markets: History, Geography, and the Development of the International Political Economy*. New York: St. Martin's Press.

Sewell, William H. 1996. Three Temporalities: Toward an Eventful Sociology. In *The Historic Turn in the Human Sciences*, ed. Terrance J. McDonald, 245–80. Ann Arbor: University of Michigan.

Shifter, Michael. 2002. A Shaken Agenda: Bush and Latin America. *Current History* 101 (652): 51–57.

Sikkink, Kathryn. 1993. Human Rights, Principled Issue-Networks, and Sovereignty in Latin America. *International Organization* 47 (3): 411–41.

Simmons, Beth, and Lisa Martin. 2002. International Organisations and Institutions. In *Handbook of International Relations*, ed. Walter Carlsnaes, Thomas Risse, and Beth Simmons, 192–211. London: Sage Publications.

Skocpol, Theda, and Margaret Summers. 1980. The Use of Comparative History in Macrosocial Inquiry. *Comparative Studies in Sociology and History* 22 (September): 174–97.

———. 2002. Restructuring World Politics: The Limits and Asymmetries of Soft Power. In *Restructuring World Politics: Transnational Social Movements, Networks, and Norms*, ed. Sanjeev Khagram, James V. Riker, and Kathryn Sikkink, 301–17. Minneapolis: University of Minnesota Press.

Smith, Peter H. 2000. *Talons of the Eagle: Dynamics of U.S.-Latin American Relations*. New York: Oxford University Press.

Smith, William C., and Roberto Patricio Korzeniewicz, eds. 1997. *Politics, Social Change, and Economic Restructuring in Latin America*. Miami: University of Miami, North-South Center Press.

Soares de Lima, Maria Regina. 1999. Brazil's Alternative Vision. In *The Americas in Transition: The Contours of Regionalism*, ed. Gordon Mace and Louis Bélanger, 133–52. Boulder: Rienner.

Sola, Lourdes. 1988. Heterodox Shock in Brazil: Técnicos, Politicians, and Democracy. *Journal of Latin American Studies* 23 (1): 163–95.

Solís Rivera, Luis Guillermo, and Francisco Rojas Aravena. 1994. De la guerra a la integración: la transición y la seguridad en Centroamérica. In *De la guerra a la integración: la transición y la seguridad en Centroamérica*, ed. Luis Guillermo Solís Rivera and Francisco Rojas Aravena, 9–35. San José, Costa Rica: Fundación Arias/ FLACSO-Chile.

Sørensen, Georg. 1999. Sovereignty: Change and Continuity in a Fundamental Institution. *Political Studies* 47 (3): 590–604.

Spiro, Peter J. 1995. New Global Communities: Nongovernmental Organizations in International Decision-Making Institutions. *The Washington Quarterly* 18 (1): 45–56.

Stallings, Barbara, ed. 1995. *Global Change, Regional Response: The New International Context of Development*. New York: Cambridge University Press.

Stark, Jeffrey, ed. 2001. *The Challenge of Change in Latin America and the Caribbean*. Miami: University of Miami, North-South Center Press.

Starr, Pamela K. 1997. Government Coalitions and the Viability of Currency Boards: Argentina under the Cavallo Plan. *Journal of Interamerican Studies and World Affairs* 39 (2): 85–133.

———. 2000. International Financial Institutions in Latin America: Adjusting to the Internationalization of Financial Markets. In *The Future of Inter-American Relations*, ed. Jorge I. Dominguez, 131–52. New York: Routledge.

Statistical Yearbook for Latin America and the Caribbean 2000. 2000. New York: United Nations Publication.

Stein, Arthur. 1993. *Why Nations Cooperate: Circumstance and Choice in International Relations*. Ithaca: Cornell University Press.

Stein, Arthur, and Steven E. Lobell. 1997. Geostructuralism and International Politics: The End of the Cold War and the Regionalization of International Security. In *Regional Orders: Building Security in a New World*, ed. David Lake and Patrick M. Morgan, 101–22. University Park: Pennsylvania State University Press.

Steinmo, Sven, Kathleen Thelen, and Frank Longstreth. 1992. *Structuring Politics: Historical Institutionalism in Comparative Analysis*. New York: Cambridge University Press.

Stiglitz, Joseph E. 2002. *Globalization and Its Discontents*. New York: Norton.

Stinchcombe, Arthur L. 1968. *Constructing Social Theories*. New York: Harcourt, Brace & World.

Strange, Susan. 1996. *The Retreat of the State: The Diffusion of Power in the World Economy*. Cambridge: Cambridge University Press.

Taylor, Paul. 1999. The United Nations in the 1990s: Proactive Cosmopolitanism and the Issue of Sovereignty. *Political Studies* 47 (3): 538–65.

Tegucigalpa Protocol to the Charter of the Organization of American States. 1991. Secretaría General de Sistema de Integración Centroamericano, http://www.sgsica.org/tratados -convenios/docpdf/pro-02-13121991.pdf.

Tesón, Fernando R. 1996. Changing Perceptions of Domestic Jurisdiction and Intervention. In *Beyond Sovereignty: Collectively Defending Democracy in the Americas*, ed. Tom Farer, 29–51. Baltimore: Johns Hopkins University Press.

Tetlock, Philip, and Aaron Belkin, eds. 1996. *Counterfactual Thought Experiments in World Politics: Logical, Methodological, and Psychological Perspectives*. Princeton: Princeton University Press.

Thacker, Strom C. 1999. The High Politics of IMF Lending. *World Politics* 52 (1): 38–75.

Thelen, Kathleen, and Sven Steinmo. 1992. Historical Institutionalism in Comparative Politics. In *Structuring Politics: Historical Institutionalism in Comparative Analysis*, ed. Sven Steinmo, Kathleen Thelen, and Frank Longstreth, 1–31. New York: Cambridge University Press.

———. 1999. Historical Institutionalism and Comparative Politics. *Annual Review of Political Science* 2: 369–404.

Thomas, Daniel C. 2001. *The Helsinki Effect: International Norms, Human Rights, and the Demise of Communism*. Princeton: Princeton University Press.

———. 2002. Human Rights in U.S. Foreign Policy. In *Restructuring World Politics: Transnational Social Movements, Networks, and Norms*, ed. Sanjeev Khagram, James V. Riker, and Kathryn Sikkink, 71–95. Minneapolis: University of Minnesota Press.

Thucydides. 1951. *Complete Writings: The Peloponnesian War*. Translated by Richard Crawley. New York: Modern Library.

Tickner, Arlene B. 2003. Colombia and the United States: From Counternarcotics to Counterterrorism. *Current History* 102 (February): 77–85.

Transparency International. 1997. *Transparency International Publishes 1997 Corruption Perception Index*. http://www.transparency.de/press/1997.31.7.cpi.html, October 29.

———. 2001. Press Release: New Index Highlights Worldwide Corruption Crisis, Says Transparency International, http://www.transparency.org/cpi/2001/cpi2001. html.

Tulchin, Joseph, and Ralph H. Espach, eds. 2001. *Latin America in the New International System*. Boulder: Rienner.

Unidad para la Promoción de la Democracia. 2001. *Observaciones Electorales en Peru, 9 de Abril 2000*. Washington, DC: Secretaria General, Organización de los Estados Americanos.

Unit for the Promotion of Democracy. 2004. Electoral Missions, http://www.upd.ogs.org.

United Nations. 1997. *International Instruments of the United Nations*, Convention on the Prevention and Punishment of Crimes against Internationally Protected Persons, Including Diplomatic Agents, December 14, 1973. New York: United Nations Publications.

———. 2004. *United Nations Charter*. http://www.un.org/aboutun/charter/.

U.S. Department of Defense. 1995. Closing Statement: U.S. Secretary of Defense William J. Perry. *Defense Ministerial of the Americas*, July 24–26, 1995. Washington, DC: Department of Defense, http://www.summit-americas.org/williamsburg2.htm.

U.S. Department of State. 1992. Dispatch Supplement, Rio Declaration on Environment and Development, principle 2, volume 3, no. 4, July: 17.

Valenzuela, J. Samuel, and Arturo Valenzuela. 1978. Modernization and Dependency: Alternative Perspectives in the Study of Latin American Development. Comparative Politics 10 (4): 535–57.

Veltmeyer, Henry, and James Petras. 2000. The Dynamics of Social Change in Latin America. New York: St. Martin's Press.

Verbitsky, Horacio. 1996. The Flight: Confessions of an Argentine Dirty Warrior. New York: The New Press.

Verdugo, Patricio. 2001. Chile, Pinochet, and the Caravan of Death. Translated by Marcelo Montecino. Miami: University of Miami, North-South Center Press.

Vial, Joaquín. 2002. Foreign Investment in the Andean Countries. Center for International Development at Harvard University, working paper no. 85 (January). http://www2.cid.harvard.edu/cidwp/085.pdf.

von Doellinger, Carlos. 1995. Brazil's Rollercoaster Response to the Debt Crisis. In Government Responses to the Latin American Debt Problem, ed. Robert Grosse, 39–56. Miami: University of Miami, North-South Center Press.

Vreeland, James Raymond. 1999. The IMF: Lender of Last Resort or Scapegoat? Paper presented at the Midwest Political Science Association Annual Meeting, Chicago, IL, April 15–17.

———. 2003. The IMF and Economic Development. New York: Cambridge University Press.

Wade, Robert. 1996. Globalization and Its Limits: Reports of the Death of the National Economy Are Greatly Exaggerated. In National Diversity and Global Capitalism, ed. Suzanne Berger and Ronald Dore, 60–88. Ithaca: Cornell University Press.

Wæver, Ole. 1995. Securitization and Desecuritization. In On Security, ed. Ronnie D. Lipchutz, 46–86. New York: Columbia University Press.

Waltz, Kenneth. 1979. Theory of International Politics. New York: McGraw-Hill.

Weisbrot, Mark, and Dean Baker. 2002. Paying the Bills in Brazil: Does the IMF's Math Add Up? Center for Economic and Policy Research Briefing Paper. Washington, DC: Center for Economic and Policy Research.

Weiss, Linda. 1998. The Myth of the Powerless State. Ithaca: Cornell University Press.

Weyland, Kurt. 1993. The Rise and Fall of President Collor and Its Impact on Brazilian Democracy. Journal of Interamerican Studies and World Affairs 35 (1): 1–37.

———. 1996. Neopopulism and Neoliberalism in Latin America: Unexpected Affinities. Studies in Comparative International Development 31: 3–31.

———. 2002. The Politics of Market Reform in Fragile Democracies: Argentina, Brazil, Peru, and Venezuela. Princeton: Princeton University Press.

Wiarda, Howard J. 1995. After Miami: The Summit, the Peso Crisis, and the Future of U.S.-Latin American Relations. Journal of Interamerican Studies and World Affairs 37 (Spring): 43–68.

———. 1997. Consensus Found, Consensus Lost: Disjunctures in U.S. Policy toward Latin America at the Turn of the Century. Journal of Interamerican Studies and World Affairs 39 (1): 13–32.

———. 2000. Beyond the Pale: The Bureaucratic Politics of United States Policy in Mexico. World Affairs 162 (4): 174–90.

Williams, Michael, and Keith Krause. 1996. Broadening the Agenda of Security Studies: Politics and Methods. International Studies Quarterly 40 (2): 229–54.

Williamson, John. 1990. What Washington Means by Policy Reform. In Latin American Adjustment: How Much Has Happened? ed. John Williamson, 7–20. Washington, DC: Institute for International Economics.

———. 2002. Is Brazil Next? International Economics Policy Briefs, No. PB 02-7. Washington, DC: Institute for International Economics.

Wilson, Richard. 1999. Prosecuting Pinochet: International Crimes in Spanish Domestic Law. *Human Rights Quarterly* 21: 927–79.

World Bank. 2002. *World Development Indicators.* Washington, DC: World Bank.

———. 2003. *World Development Indicators Database.* Washington, DC: World Bank.

Woodhouse, Diana. 2000. *The Pinochet Case: A Legal and Constitutional Analysis.* Oxford: Hart Publishing.

Woods, Ngaire. 2001. Making the IMF and the World Bank More Accountable. *International Affairs* 77 (1): 83–100.

Wucker, Michelle. 2002. Searching for Argentina's Silver Lining. *World Policy Journal* 19 (4): 49–58.

Wyatt-Walter, Andrew. 1996. Regionalism, Globalization, and World Economic Order. In *Regionalism in World Politics: Regional Organization and World Order,* ed. Louise L'Estrange Fawcett and Andrew Hurrell, 74–121. New York: Oxford University Press.

Zeledón Torres, Fernando. 1998. Security, Agenda, and Military Balance in Central America: Limits to Democratic Consolidation in the 1990s. In *International Security and Democracy: Latin America and the Caribbean in the Post-Cold War Era,* ed. Jorge I. Domínguez, 222–41. Pittsburgh: University of Pittsburgh Press.

Index

Alvear, Mariá Soledad, 135, 144
amnesty law, 129–30, 139–40, 144, 147, 234n36; interpretations of, 129
Argentina, 1, 3–4, 58, 62, 89, 134, 136, 152; Convertibility Plan, 79–80, 82; currency crisis in, 79–83; as a gamble for the IMF, 47, 78–79; government expenditures in, 80–81; human rights in, 134, 218; market draw, lack of, 46, 47, 75–77, 81, 83, 84; military government in, 76, 136; neoliberal reform and, 4, 18, 46, 54–57, 61, 75–83, 210; political utility, lack of, 46–47, 47–48, 75–77, 81, 83, 84; relations with Brazil, 77, 83
Asian currency crisis, 65, 66, 78, 81
Association of Families of the Chilean Detained and Disappeared, 133, 140
Axworthy, Loyd, 109, 110, 111, 112, 115
Aylwin, Patricio, 128, 129, 134, 147, 148, 149
Aznar, José María, 151, 175

Belize, 172, 174
Blair, Tony, 151, 153
Boehm, Peter, 111, 112
Brazil, 58, 152, 200–201; Cruzado Plan, 63; currency crisis in, 65–67, 81, 82; Itamaraty (Ministry of Foreign Relations), 68–69; market draw of, 1, 18, 46, 47, 56, 61–62, 63–64, 66, 70, 73, 76, 84; as Mercosur leader, 62; military government in, 63, 136; neoliberal reform and, 29, 40, 46, 54–57, 61–69, 75, 81, 83, 210; political utility of, 62; Real Plan, 65; relations with the United States, 13, 46, 47, 57, 62–63, 65, 66–69, 73, 74. See also under environmental degradation
bureaucratic authoritarianism, 24
Bush administration (George H. W.), 164

Bush administration (George W.): democratic protection and, 35; drug trafficking and, 199; human rights support and, 211; immigration and, 196, 197, 212; neoliberal reform and, 82, 83, 226n52

CA-4. See Central America
capabilities, 11, 27. See also under issues
Cardoso, Fernando Henrique, 65, 67–68
catalysts. See under political change
caudillismo, 28
Central America, 1, 2, 16, 40, 198, 208; Esquipulas II agreement, 160, 162, 163–65, 227n1; Framework Treaty on Democratic Security, 163, 167–68, 172, 173, 175, 238n14; peace processes in, 160, 162–68, 178, 216; post–Cold War era and, 158–62; regional integration in, 164, 167–68, 169, 170–71, 174, 175, 186
Central American Security Commission (CSC), 156, 157–58, 185–86; accomplishments, 157, 170, 173; genesis of, 163–68; organization of, 167–68, 174; relationship with CFAC, 168, 169, 172–75, 185
Chavez, Hugo, 200, 227n6
Chile, 1, 5, 13, 25, 40, 58, 61, 87, 89, 124–55, 175, 213; amnesty law of (see amnesty law); appellate court of, 138, 140–41, 155, 233n7, 234n37, 236n72; Bilateral Council for Trade and Investment, 70–71; Caravan of Death case, 138–39, 141; democratic transition of, 146; DINA, 125, 130, 140; the disappeared of, 150; Europe's impact on (see Europe); executive-judicial relations in, 143–45, 154; FTA (Free Trade Agreement) with the United States, 4–5, 72–75; high courts of, 130, 135, 138, 144–45, 148–49, 154–55; human rights activists